Charlotte Moon Clark

Baby Rue

Her Adventures and Misadventures, her Friends and her Enemies

Charlotte Moon Clark

Baby Rue
Her Adventures and Misadventures, her Friends and her Enemies

ISBN/EAN: 9783337176358

Printed in Europe, USA, Canada, Australia, Japan

Cover: Foto ©ninafisch / pixelio.de

More available books at **www.hansebooks.com**

George M. Lefferts

NO NAME SERIES.

BABY RUE.

NO NAME SERIES.

"Is the Gentleman Anonymous? Is he a great Unknown?"
                                        Daniel Deronda.

BABY RUE.

[*HER ADVENTURES AND MISADVENTURES, HER FRIENDS AND HER ENEMIES.*]

BOSTON:
ROBERTS BROTHERS.
1881.

Copyright, 1881,
BY ROBERTS BROTHERS.

CONTENTS.

PART I.
CAMP AND GARRISON 11

PART II.
MOUNT HOPE 61

PART III.
BOUIE'S HILL 73

PART IV.
BABY RUE 107

PART V.
THE PURSUIT 133

PART VI.
THE CONFLICT 188

PART VII.
COACOOCHEE 241

THE blessed damozel leaned out
   From the gold bar of Heaven;
Her eyes were deeper than the depth
   Of waters stilled at even;
She had three lilies in her hand,
   And the stars in her hair were seven.

   .   .   .   .   .

And still she bowed herself, and stooped
   Out of the circling charm,
Until her bosom must have made
   The bar she leaned on warm,
And the lilies lay as if asleep
   Along her bended arm.

   .   .   .   .   .

          And now
She spoke through the still weather,
Her voice was like the voice the stars
   Had when they sang together.

                    DANTE GABRIEL ROSSETTI.

PART I.

CAMP AND GARRISON.

STILL when she slept, he kept both watch and ward;
And, when she wakt, he wayted diligent,
With humble service to her will prepared;
From her fayre eyes he took commandement,
And ever by her lookes conceived her intent.

SPENSER.

BABY RUE.

PART I.

CAMP AND GARRISON.

CHAPTER I.

> So I'll not seek nor sue her,
> But I'll leave my glory to woo her,
> And I'll stand like a child beside,
> And from behind the purple pride
> I'll lift my eyes unto her,
> And I shall not be denied.
>   SIDNEY DOBELL.

"IT is hard to leave without seeing her, without a word of farewell. Yet it is the right and honorable thing for me to do."

The words were uttered unconsciously, as the speaker turned into Pennsylvania Avenue.

"Hillo, Leszinksky, in travelling rig? Where the devil are you going, this night of all others? I had heard of your return from Albemarle this afternoon, and was sure I should meet you at the Corcorans' at Miss Cartaret's birthday ball."

"No, I cannot go. I was on my way to look you up. I leave to-night for the West. I have dispatches from the Secretary for Newport and St. Louis."

"Oh, then I suppose you have made your adieux to 'rare, fair, queenly Margaret.'"

"No, I have not seen her for the last two weeks. Part of the time, as you know, I was in Albemarle. You did not know, however, that it was a farewell visit. I am transferred to the dragoons. I join in St. Louis, and we shall leave immediately for service on the frontier."

"You? Why, I thought you were a fixture in Washington. A cousin of the Secretary, and ordered to the plains? Damn it![1] What good are relations? If the War Department serve you such sauce, what the h—l will they do with a poor devil like me?"

"You are a lucky youngster, Carson, and so will fare better than you deserve. My going will make a vacancy that may sweep you with the tide to fortune."

"Sweep me down a gutter into the Potomac more likely! I only wanted to stay in Washington if you were here. It was a touch-and-go that brought me through the West Point squeeze last year, after you left. Your sermons and sister Mary's praying were the spurs that carried me up the home-stretch. And now, when I have a shoulder-strap, if I'm not with you to learn to crow your fashion, the devil will be sure to find me a special tutor."

"If you would like to go with me out on the plains, youngster, mend your manners and your speech, and I will try my interest with the Secretary. If you are not in a hurry for the ball, come with me now. I am to stop at his house on my way to the station."

On under the lamps walked the young comrades. Stanislaus Leszinksky, then just twenty-two years old, but aged before his time by the burden of care he had taken in his boyhood from the frail, thin hands of his mother, and later from his grandfather, Judge Mason, who bent under the weight of sorrows and debts, — debts the payment of which seemed hopeless after the flight of a dishonest agent, who not only took with him all the money in his hands, but had induced Judge Mason to sign acceptances, which had left the trustful gentleman so embarrassed that even the home place must go, where he had been born, and where his daughter had lived with him during her short girlhood and early, crushed womanhood. Stanislaus Leszinksky was at that

---

[1] In 1842 the army had not adopted its present refined and pious method of conversation. I much fear me that, in those old days, it swore as terribly as did the army in Flanders. — EDITOR.

time in the second year of his stay at West Point. The boy's first impulse had been to resign and seek some new and more rapid way of advance to fortune. But a Washington banker, who was the heaviest creditor as well as the personal friend of Judge Mason, dissuaded him. Large-hearted and generous, with a quick, clear insight into the characters and capabilities of men, Mr. Corcoran advised his young friend to stay in the army, where all his natural likings and tastes held him, and to accept from the banker, as a loan, enough to clear the name and the home of his grandfather; and in the years to come to liberate himself from this engagement by strict and close economy. Mr. Corcoran knew the character of Stanislaus Leszinksky; knew the resolution, the honesty, the fidelity that must now be tried by the constant burning of petty things: but he was sure the gold was pure and the fire refining.

The boy accepted more willingly because he remembered another source of assistance which Mr. Corcoran had forgotten, a gift sent by a royal relative, through General Lafayette, to the Virginian Leszinksky,[1] at the time of the marquis's last visit to America, — a miniature portrait of King Stanislaus, set in superb brilliants, which his father had given to his mother as a wedding gift, and which she had kept through many needs for her boy.

During Stanislaus Leszinksky's short leave of absence at that time, he had done much to lighten the weight of his grandfather's anxiety, and to establish himself in the respect and regard of all his grandfather's creditors. The diamonds had been unset and disposed of, and the miniature itself was left with the banker to be kept, if Stanislaus Leszinksky should die suddenly, in lieu of a small balance still owing.

So the brilliants that were worth a knight's ransom did knightly service: they saved the pledged honor of a Virginian gentleman, and bought from that terrible task-master, Debt, the freedom of the last of the Masons of Mount Hope.

[1] See Appendix.

From that time until he graduated the young cadet had to learn the hardest of all lessons to the young, — not only a resolute refusal of self, but something more difficult, the resolute refusal of a self represented by others. The liberal hand was empty, — so empty that the generous heart often ached sorely from its inability to give. Added to this, the boy was proud and reticent: so, like many another noble soul, he was misjudged and undervalued. Youth is a stern lawgiver, rarely excusing and never extenuating; it takes into account only facts that are patent to sight: causes are too remote for its surface philosophy. Every old officer who remembers West Point will remember how irksome was any little economy he was compelled to practise there, and how impossible it would have seemed to him then, to live on the actually necessary. This Stanislaus Leszinksky did; consequently, those of his companions who knew him slightly judged slightingly.

The professors knew better, but their attentions and well-intended comments on Leszinksky's prudence were, to the unthinking young prodigals whom want had not disciplined, additional proofs of the parsimonious meanness with which they had credited him.

Only a pure heart — only a calm, brave, patient soul — could have lived through this false estimate, and gathered no bitterness. It seems like telling the story of our hero in one sentence to say he lived it down, and perfected and completed his own character in the living. We lay stress upon *completed*. Character is more frequently perfected than completed; perfection may be reached through the wearing martyrdom of care and suffering, but the broad whole of a complete character keeps the wholesome sweetness of childhood's trust and faith, the enthusiastic hope and ambition of youth, the broader beliefs and charities of mature knowledge, shrined on the innermost altar, where Wisdom waits for Experience to light the torches.

No comrade had been more true to Stanislaus Leszinksky during the days of his patient endurance than bluff, blustering, bullet-headed William Carson. The

boy was a year younger in grade. He had come from a
plain Western family; but the men of his race had been
fighting pioneers, and, though unlettered and rude in
manner, had the innate pluck and manliness which make
a gallant yeoman the fit friend and trusty comrade of
the chivalric and high-born gentleman.

In his first hazing difficulties at "the Point," Carson
fought his tormentors like a young Turk. True to the
inherited instinct of the old Indian fighter, that even
then waked in him, he disdained complaint or outcry
when overpowered. His hearty cuffs and heavy kicks
had changed the fun of his tormentors to cruel earnest.
Humanity had succumbed to the animal nature; the
pained brutes rushed upon a prey now helpless, and
avenged the victors upon the vanquished.

Leszinksky, coming in, tried reason; but when reason
could not get a hearing, he tried, with better effect,
hard knocks. Carson had both pluck and endurance.
The first brought him to his knees beside his rescuer,
the second helped him fight there. It was two against
twenty, and one of them nearly down; but of the two, one
defended his insulted young manhood, whilst the other
bravely championed the right. So the two triumphed; or,
to speak more truly, they gave their opponents time and
opportunity to *rehumanize*. The brute half in humanity
stopped in its blind cruelty, the manly half began to
reason. Carson, with twice his pluck and four times his
strength, never could have morally so affected them. But
the physical courage of his ally had better backing than
mere endurance. The battle flash in the clear gray eyes
had in it a lightning of scorn that pierced into and
through the souls of his antagonists. The shame in
their souls fought for him. As the brute nature was
cowed and silenced, humanity asserted itself; a few
dropped out of the *mêlée* and waited; the others fought
less heartily. One awakened sinner cried, "Shame!"
The consciences of others assented; all but two fell
back. That was all they would do; that was *their* compromise with conscience.

But that was enough. Ajax on his knees butted one

with that bullet-head of his until he had a stomach full of arguments for peace; whilst the young demigod who fought on the side of Ajax against oppression knocked down the other. Then human nature showed still another of its kaleidoscopic turns. The vanquished twenty cheered the two victors, and, assisting Ajax to rise, found him with a badly sprained ankle. Never was cub more spoilt than that one was in the curing; but the spoiling was wholesome. It was the "little go" which passed him "Gentleman."

So under the lamps walked these two friends, — strangely assorted, it is true, contrasting in all qualities except manliness: *that* was their plane of equality. The fraternity was now a thing of habit; an affection grown so strong that it needed no expression in words; stronger from the difference in their natures. Unlike the attractive difference which in lover and loved charms through its supplemental quality, this was an entire difference — almost an antagonism — of character, harmonized through an affection which on one side was blind devotion, and on the other a clear-sighted overlooking of faults that hid virtues.

The Secretary promised that Carson should soon join his friend. At the station they parted; a pressure of the hand, and then a last word from Leszinksky. "Carson, I think you know how much I care for Miss Cartaret. You do not know that two weeks ago her guardian, Judge Cartaret, refused me permission to address her, — hinted that her fortune attracted. As he is a gentleman, I presume he told her both request and refusal; since then I am silenced if she is silent. So I asked to be exchanged. I cannot stay in Washington. You see now why I go."

"Yes. God bless you! Good-by. I will follow you as soon as they let me."

"Good-by. Tell her I have gone."

"Yes."

And then, as his friend whirled out of sight in the dark night, the faithful fellow turned with a sad heart to the ball, which was now only a painful thing, for he too loved Margaret Cartaret. But not an instant did he hesitate. His own love must be put away: his friend's cause, his friend's trust, were everything. Later in the night he led Margaret into the conservatory.

"You are sad, Mr. Carson."

"Yes, Miss Cartaret; for my friend Leszinksky has to-night left for frontier service."

"Left?" And the stately head bent, and the hand on his arm trembled.

"Did you know that your guardian had refused him permission to address you?"

"Certainly not. I did not know he had asked it."

"I am very glad *you* did not send him to his death."

"I? — send him to his death!" And the fair face grew pale and the trembling increased.

"It would be that if you refused him. I know Leszinksky well. He loves you as few men could love, — deeply, tenderly, — and with him love lives forever. He may live away from you, silenced by your guardian's taunt, but he will never forget you, Miss Cartaret; and that love being hopeless would send him careless of life into every battle."

"My guardian's taunt?" and the blue eyes blazed at Carson.

"Yes; that being penniless he sought your fortune. But do you know how and why he is penniless, Miss Cartaret?"

"No; tell me."

"To save his grandfather's name from a shade of dishonor; to save the home where his mother was born. Ask Mr. Corcoran. He will tell you the story. And this is the man your guardian suspects, — dishonors with his suspicion."

"I am not responsible for my guardian. Will you apologize to your friend for me? Say if I had known this he should not have left without seeing me — if — if my invitation would have brought him."

. . . .

2

Off in the rapidly growing distance the lover was saying to his heart: "If I could only have said farewell — could only have asked her to wait for what the years might bring! But now she must hear of me through deeds. God give me the chance, I pray! Let glory woo her for me."

CHAPTER II.

> The green on the trees looks far greener than ever,
> And the linnets are singing, "True lovers don't sever."
> Thomas Davis.

EARLY in the spring of 1842 Margaret Cartaret, having left "The Cedars," below Richmond, three days before with only her maid as travelling companion, reached Lynchburg, where she was to join Major Anderson and his daughter on their way to Memphis. Two weeks earlier, on her coming of age, she had written Stanislaus Leszinksky that she was willing to accept his fortune if he declined hers, adding, "You will find me in Memphis by the first of May, at the house of my father's old friend, Major Nathaniel Anderson. If you cannot have leave to come to Memphis, I am sure my friends will accompany me to Fort Smith."

It was in the time of the old stage-coaches, when the small discomforts of travel only gave additional zest to the charm of mountain and valley. At three o'clock in the morning after Miss Cartaret's arrival in Lynchburg, our party took the places Major Anderson had secured for them, amidst the confusion attendant on such an early start.

The lanterns were burning brightly, the horses stamping with impatience, — for at that day the horses of the "Mountain Line," as it was called, were nearly all thoroughbred; dogs were yelping; negroes calling and laughing in the delight of parting gratuities; whilst, above all, the throned coachman in a triumph of skill held the lines in one hand, and in the other the musical horn that woke the early echoes, telling sleepy burghers of his departure. When the lights faded he placed his tin treasure in a rough leathern case, until a ten miles run brought them near the post stables. Then again the mellow notes woke the country, and the sleepy passengers stretched themselves in the glow of the newly risen sun.

Post-boys and manager were alert at every stable, and in five minutes with a fresh team the heavy coach was winding up the rocky steeps, or rushing in a rattling gallop into the mists of the valleys.

Twenty miles to breakfast was the usual run; and steaming coffee, hot waffles, and juicy venison had a relish unknown to the modern victims of railway travel.

A few days' rest at the White and Blue Sulphur Springs, a short stay at the Falls of the Kanawha, another at the foot of the Sweet Spring Mountain, which rocky road had shaken Major Anderson's gout into a fit of live fury, brought our travellers to the Ohio River at Guyandotte.

Until their arrival at the Hawk's Nest the major's patience had been sorely tried by his forced attendance, in their mountain climbs, upon his daughter and Miss Cartaret. They needs *must* walk when the slow-going coach crept up the mountain heights. They were aided and abetted by hints from the driver of cross paths and short cuts. The mountain laurel and honeysuckles were in their early flower, and there were armsful of trailing vines and masses of bloom to carry, until their collected treasures made a veritable lady's bower of the lumbering coach.

At the Hawk's Nest a pitying Providence sent the major help.

As our party descended from the coach, which waited while they walked up the wood path that led to this most picturesque of mountain views, they saw immediately before them on the roadside one of those crazy vehicles kept as hackney carriages in the mountain towns. This particular one had lived through decades. In its better days it had been the pride and glory of some old country family. Hung high over dingy yellow wheels, with its silk-lined Morocco curtains in fringed tatters, the door open, and a succession of rusty steps unfolded, it told a tale of change and fallen fortune. The horses were sorry jades; and the driver, with his scant locks of white wool, fitly matched the antiquated equipage He was busy cutting withes of saplings and twisting them into a rope to tie up a broken spring. As Miss Cartaret passed him, touched by his look of patient endeavor as he whittled away with an old broken knife, she took her own from her pocket and gave him.

"Thankee, marm"; and he doffed his torn hat and bowed low before her. "I's desprit obleeged. I's most dazed wid dese breaks. We's done broke down fo' times comin' from Mount Hope. De folks I brung ar' up dar at de Ness, an' I's tryin' to patch her once mo' so she'll hold out to de tavern down dar at de foot ob de mountain whar dey's gwine to take de stage."

"Very well, keep the knife; it may help you home."

"Lord bless you, mistis! You don't mean to guv it to me?"

"Yes, keep it, and my maid will give you a snack: that's hungry work for an old man."

"De Lord lub you, mistis — an' he do; but I ain't no kashun for vittles. De white folks dat's wid me is got plenty, an' dey's mighty good 'bout dat, but you see I's done broke all de knife de gemmun had. Dis one *is* a beauty for sho! 'Pears like I never will want to stop thankin' yer."

"Oh, you are welcome. I hope it will bring you luck."

"Dunno 'bout dat. Cum to dat I mus' guv you sumfin fur it — jis fur luck, you know. Mus' do it, mum."

She stopped, amused, whilst he searched his pockets, drawing out a motley collection of fragments.

"Heah, marm; heah is de very gif I orter to guv you, mistis. It is a habit my young marster cut las' time he was home. It's mighty pretty fur a cherry-stone."

"Thank you; it is beautifully cut. Good-by."

Having relieved a superstition and lifted a sense of obligation, Margaret Cartaret hastened to join the party who waited. Their path ended in a clearing on one side of the mountain summit, where a bold cliff jutted out until it hung over the river which wound around the base of the mountain, like a silver thread hundreds of feet below. In the opposite mountain, facing the cliffs, were clefts in the chain, now opening into valleys, then narrowing into ravines, through which two other streams came to join the one beneath.

On the edge of the overhanging rock called the "Hawk's Nest" grew a scrub-pine, and as the party gained the clearing, Margaret Cartaret, who was in advance, caught by the weird attraction of the dizzy height, fascinated by the subtle charm that waits the unwary upon the threshold of the Infinite, walked to the very edge, catching unconsciously at the frail support of the waving boughs of the little pine, as she bent over to look down. As the party came into the clearing they saw her danger.

Miss Anderson was about to cry out, when a hand was gently placed over her mouth, and a voice said in a low, warning tone:—

"Hush! One cry, and you send her to a horrible death."

Leaving her trembling with the repression of feeling, the stranger was almost instantly behind Miss Cartaret. Catching her firmly in his arms he drew her out of danger; and then only did she realize her near risk of destruction.

From that moment, Major Anderson's troubles grew lighter. William Carson, who, with his sister Mary, was the temporary owner of the antique vehicle which had brought them thus far on their way West, after a week's visit at Judge Mason's, gladly took on his sturdy shoulders the load of care that was inflaming the major's gout and embittering a naturally sweet temper.

Uncle Abram turned back without having to go to "de foot ob de mountain." Seeing Miss Cartaret pale and trembling, the grateful old man asked Carson the cause. Hearing of her risk on the Hawk's Nest,—

"It's de Lord save her. I knowed she was one o' his pet chillun. I seed it in her face when she guv me dis knife, an' sho nuf dat haht dat Marse Stan cut has brought her luck a'ready; dat's why you was privleeged to cotch her from 'struction. An' now mebby she's yo' fortshun, Mr. Carson."

"No, Uncle Abram; I can tell you something better. She is your Master Stan's sweetheart, and she is on her way to Memphis to marry him. Major Anderson has just told me."

"Bless de Lord, dat I guv her dat haht! It save her fur Marse Stan sho. Won't you please tole him 'bout it, sir?"

Carson promised, and the old man busied himself changing the luggage to the stage, and arranging for his return alone. When the coach, with its two new passengers settled into place, was about to start, he came to the window where Margaret's pale face was resting against a cushion.

"I *mus'* say good-by, my young mistis. Mr. Carson's done tole me 'bout you an' Marse Stan. You did n't know I b'longed to de family when I guv you dat haht of Marse Stan's. You see it was de Lord's doin's, fur you's one o' his angels dat he sen's sometimes when dey's wanted bad, and he knows, mistis, how de family has suffered sorely since ole marster was bankrupped, an' you'll let us die easy, us ole uns, fur you'll bring Marse Stan home to us to de New Geruzlum. I'll tell ole marster. I knows it, fur I sees it in yo' sweet face, mistis. Good-by."

CHAPTER III.

> Up on the hill and down in the dale
> And along the tree-tops over the vale,
>   Shining over and over, —
> Low in the grass and high on the bough,
>   Shining over and over.
> O world, have you ever a lover?
>
> . . . . . .
>
> And the hillside beats with my beating heart,
>   And the apple-tree blushes all over,
> And the May-bough touched me and made me start,
>   And the wind breathes warm, like a lover.
>   SIDNEY DOBELL.

FROM Guyandotte to Cincinnati the trip was slow. The Ohio River was at the low stage of water that usually precedes the June rise. The little steamer was heavily loaded, and had to unship and reship part of her freight in crossing the sand-bars, for the yellow ridges were uncovered by the washing of the waves as the wheezing little " stern-wheeler" swept down the narrow channel.

Major Anderson's gout kept him in his state-room, the only change possible being to an easy-chair on the guards near his door. He had on the trip renewed a lang-syne acquaintance with a Kentucky gentleman, an excellent cribbage player; and so in many closely-contested games he was sometimes able for hours to forget his twinges of pain. His daughter and Miss Cartaret were thus left to the companionship and care of the Carsons.

During these long detentions on the sand-bars the obliging captain of the steamer would send them ashore in the yawl. Landing at the nearest farmhouse, when no village was in sight, Carson would hire any conveyance to be had, and drive down the river road through long stretches of emerald-tinted meadows and blossoming orchards that covered the slope from the thickly-wooded chain of hills to the river-side.

To the three girls these rides, with their homely incidents, made the happiest of holidays. There were farm-house snacks; breakdowns that left them afoot upon the road; impromptu luncheons on grassy knolls; climbs up the hillside to see if the laggard steamer was coming through the curves of the beautiful river; then, as the wavy columns of smoke told of its liberation, rushes downward, scrambles through hazel bushes, cross-cuts to catch in running the early blossoms of May-apple and daffodil; cool, shady walks in lonely paths through the tender green overhanging boughs of swamp-willows, with hands laden with buds and trailing vines; ventures on the slippery sands to points where the yawl could land; trembling balancings on the broad blade of a stout oar that bridged the shoal-water line.

For William Carson, the purveyor of these pleasures, this holiday work was a tough trial of honesty. Never in all his after life — in wild Indian fights and desperate frontier shifts, or, later, when facing the veterans of Lee as their solid ranks pressed on to victory, or stubbornly resisting the deadly charge of the Stonewall Brigade — was Carson's courage more severely tested than in this constant attendance upon the woman soon to be his friend's wife, whom he was forcing himself to regard as a sister. The man's honesty was so true, his friendship so loyal, that in the holding himself to account he was a far more rigid moralist than a man of more refined sensibility, more subtile sensitiveness, could have been. There was for him no tampering with temptation, no self-excuses for concealed love. The strength and ruggedness of his character forced its very tendernesses to tear up by the root all that could offend his consciousness of right. It hardly needs the telling to know he reached the aim he had set himself, and framed in his thought, as one with his friend, the woman he had loved.

Their stops in the mountains and their long detentions on the sand-bars so delayed our party that they arrived in Cincinnati a week after they were due in Memphis. As the steamer rounded to at the landing in the early May morning, a pattering shower, that dimpled the river under broken rifts of yellow light, sent the girls down from their point of vantage on the hurricane-deck to the shelter of the guards just as they touched gratings with a newly-arrived steamer from Louisville. In the crowd of passengers that looked at them from the guards of the down-river boat Margaret Cartaret recognized Stanislaus Leszinksky. A happy light came into her clear eyes, — a deeper color to the bronzed face of the young soldier. In an instant he cleared the railing and was by her side. Mary Carson, seeing Miss Anderson's half-shocked, half-frightened expression, explained hastily, "It's Lieutenant Leszinksky. Come." And the lovers were left to the first telling of that old, old story whose past is coeval with the world, whose present is the sunshine of earth's heritage, whose future will last through the ages until Love and his brother Death clasp hands to lead the last human soul through the portals of the infinite.

. . . .

In the glory of the brightest of May mornings, Stanislaus Leszinksky and Margaret Cartaret were married. Never had there been seen in that little chapel at Newport a fairer bride or a quieter wedding. Major Anderson, his daughter, and Mary Carson, Carson and two army officers on duty at Cincinnati, were all the witnesses. The bride's guardian and nearest relative, Judge Cartaret, — a cousin of her father, — had made Leszinksky's resignation from the army and establishment at "The Cedars," in Virginia, a condition of his consent to the marriage; for, although legally of age, Margaret had no control of her estate until she should be twenty-seven, unless she married with Judge Cartaret's consent. She unhesitatingly refused to make this request of her lover. With the intuitive, sympathetic knowledge born of love, she realized what would be to him the humiliation of accepting from her guardian, who had thought her fortune an attraction, the custodianship of that fortune. She also knew Leszinksky's devotion to his profession and what it would cost him to sacrifice, even for her, the only path in life he thought worth following, — the path whose modest pleasures were simple wayside flowers, blossoming in the light of days filled with duties, and whose crown of living would be to carry, unstained in danger and trial, the honor of the name that had come to him through a line of heroes.

So the little chapel in Newport was the point of exodus from which another pair, recreated in oneness, were to lead their descendants through time and change to the perfectness of the Beyond.

CHAPTER IV.

> And all fancies yearn to cover
> The hard earth on which she passes
> With the thymy scented grasses.
>
> And all hearts do pray, "God love her!"
> ELIZABETH BARRETT BROWNING.

FROM Cincinnati to Cairo the party of travellers continued together. At Cairo they separated, the Andersons going to Memphis, while Carson accompanied his sister to their Western home, before joining the 1st Dragoons at Jefferson Barracks, to which place the Leszinkskys journeyed alone. From there Leszinksky was ordered to Leavenworth, with a detachment detailed as escort to emigrant parties crossing the plains.

Headquarters were at Leavenworth, and soon their little home had all the comforts then possible in a frontier station. Many an adornment, before unknown there, proved Stanislaus Leszinksky's care and thoughtfulness for his young wife. The rough walls of her little sitting-room were covered with beautifully-preserved ferns, and garlanded with autumn leaves; from the many-branched horns of elk and deer hung rustic baskets of bark, filled with trailing vines and delicate prairie flowers; here and there a superb butterfly or rare bird proved the taste of the collector and the skill of the taxidermist. The black bear, the grizzly, the white wolf, and the panther furnished rugs, which covered the rough oak floor.

Everything that mountain and forest and plain could furnish had been sought to decorate Margaret's bower. The soldier on the scout was also a lover on a foray, seeking every treasure that Nature hides in wild-wood and dell, — starry-eyed flowers that looked up from the gold-broidered carpet of emerald-green in some narrow stretch of river meadow; delicate harebells from the rocky heights; the blue larkspur and bright-scarlet gillia of mountain passes; modest daisies, hidden beneath the flaunting splendor of sunflower and golden-rod; wild, climbing roses of the ravines; swamp honeysuckle and tiny violets that covered the gnarled, up-springing roots of sentinel oaks, dwarfed by the never-ceasing battle on the forest's edge with raging storms and fierce winds from the plains.

At first the soldiers watched curiously the ways of the silent young officer, as he lifted tenderly from their hidden nooks blossom and flower, or caught in the meshes of his butterfly-net some glittering marvel of rich color. Soon the watching grew sympathetic. There is always infection in companionship with a lover of Nature: first, the curious, half-felt eagerness of pursuit; then the triumph and physical delight of success: through these, more slowly, comes to the inner consciousness an almost indefinable sense of the beautiful, widening and strengthening with use, until the great heart of the All-Mother sends a new thrill into the pulses, a new meaning into all things. So she teaches us that —

> "To know
> That which before us lies in daily life,
> Is the prime wisdom."

Whenever it was possible, Margaret Leszinksky accompanied her husband. The heiress of "The Cedars," the belle of Washington, the beauty of Richmond was soon a hardy and fearless frontierswoman. Come of a race of fox-hunting, hard-riding Virginia planters, the transition was not unnatural.

The accomplished and graceful horsewoman seemed the fit and proper central figure of a cavalry squadron. Splendid health, and the perfect fearlessness which scarcely realized danger until it is past, made the longest and most venturesome expedition not only possible but pleasant to her. To no young subaltern, in all the freshness of a shoulder-strap, was the call "to boot and saddle" more welcome.

Always ready for the start, finding in every discomfort or mischance of the rude encampment some cause for merry laughter; never failing in sweet and womanly sympathy for the suffering of any ill or wounded trooper; always recognizing with a bright smile or clear, low-spoken thanks the homeliest wayside courtesy; with the tact which discerns when speech would be less welcome, less difficult of response, than a glance or smile of acceptance, — Margaret was the idol of the regiment. From the old officer, whose gray mustache and thread-bare uniform were more carefully brushed because of her presence; to the youngest subaltern, whose gaudiest trappings were recklessly exposed to sun and rain when she was of the party; to the roughest soldier, who had been driven to the shelter of the national flag by some outbreak against the law or his neighbor, — all were her worshippers.

Had Mrs. Leszinksky been less a lady, the charm had been less: its completeness was in the perfect grace and womanly sweetness of the thoroughbred gentlewoman. The refining effect of her presence was always perceptible. The officers were more considerate and patient; the men, not only respectful and obedient, but attentive and alert. The entire War Department could not have perfected the discipline as did her presence in camp. The Board of Missions could never have brought about such devout ways. The hardest-swearing adjutant in the army rose at daybreak, when they must march on Sunday, to read the morning service, because it was her wish. Officers and men came together, — the more unlettered in church service in the background, looking with mixed feelings of awe and envy at the lucky "scholards," who stood forward to join in the responses.

The October after Margaret joined (everything in the regiment now dated from that epoch), on their return from escorting a party of Oregon emigrants to the Rocky Mountains, when near Fort Laramie, she was ill, for the first time in her life. The decimation of a company could not have so clouded every face. After two days' rest they started for Laramie, with the beloved invalid on a bed of buffalo-robes, in an ambulance. The sandy shore of the South Platte made a heavy but smooth road. The united strength of as many men as could crowd around the wheels lifted and pushed whenever the road roughened. In two days, they made the forty miles to the post. Then the surgeon declared a longer trip impossible for her: she must winter in Laramie.

The commanding officer of the expedition instantly decided that, for "the needs of the government, and the better protection of the trading-post," a detachment must be stationed there. Leszinksky was left in command; also the surgeon was left for "the good of the service, as there might be wounded to attend," — although the tribes were then peaceful, and they had not found a "hostile" on the plains.

The morning the now low-spirited command left for Leavenworth, they filed by Leszinksky's quarters. Out on the rude porch of the Western cabin sat Margaret, pale, but trying to smile a hopeful farewell. For the first mile or two of the march, caps were drawn low over shaded eyes; officers and men seemed struck with an infectious influenza, until the swearing adjutant turned on the troopers, and rolled out such a volley of weighty oaths, between such suspicious falling inflections, that a ripple of half-hysterical laughter ran along the column, as they closed up, and took on the ordinary manner of godless cavalrymen, — leaving their religion with their saint at Laramie.

It was a happy, quiet, domestic winter for the Leszinkskys. The little cabin of three rooms was decorated with every possible frontier ornamentation. Not a trader or trapper but brought his offering; and after the first few weeks, the little porch constantly echoed the soft patter of beaded moccasins. Indian mothers came with ailing children, and Margaret and her *aide*, the doctor, nursed and fed and physicked them in concert; so in the fulness of her life the influence of this woman went out to the needy. In the crowning glory of her womanhood, approaching maternity, the character of Margaret took on its finishing charm, — the motherhood that gathers and shelters God's afflicted little ones.

There was less whiskey sold at the post that winter than usual, and the profit of the traders fell off; but no one grumbled. The influence which radiated from that log hut in the wilderness led men to think of treasure in heaven. When the springtime came, and a baby was born, rough men stood about with full eyes; and Leszinksky's hand was clasped in close grasps, as husky voices wished mother and child well. For the one day of her agony, the mother's life was in danger. Shops were closed; traders, trappers in from the mountains, Indian women with pappooses on their backs, sat about, on and near the little porch, expectant and sorrowful, in the sunlight of the bright Easter morning, to wait for news; and when the hope of life came, and the wail of a little child was heard, walked away silent and thankful. Men, who for years had forgotten God, and what he had set them here to do, thought of their mothers, and of the great mystery of travail in childbirth.

The little wooden chapel of the Jesuit Mission had strange visitors that day: wild-looking men, clad in skins, came to listen once more to the half-forgotten strains that told of the passion and the glory, the cruel death and triumphant resurrection, of the Child born eighteen hundred years ago in Judæa.

CHAPTER V.

> Oh, he indeed is happy, who still feels,
> And cherishes within himself, the hope
> To lift himself above a sea of errors!
>
> GOETHE.

THE first of December, in '43, found the Leszinskys established in the officers' quarters at Fort Gibson.

The day had been calm and cold and still, and in the fading twilight the stars twinkled and silvered in the frosty air. By the window sat Margaret, waiting, with her baby in her arms. Through the open door of the dining-room the light shone from the lamp on the tea-table, which also waited. Back and forward passed a handsome, stalwart young negro man, arranging the details of the service, changing and replacing article after article noisily, as if to attract attention, with an occasional look at the waiting figure by the window. All to no purpose; for his mistress seemed unconscious of sight or sound within doors. Even the baby had fallen into the same mood, and with solemn eyes peered into the gloaming. A piece of light-wood thrust into the bright coals, and the rattle of a falling shovel, broke the spell. The baby turned to coo her delight at the red flame as a firm, quick step sounded on the stoop. Another moment and the door opened as Margaret reached it, and wife and child were in the arms of Stanislaus Leszinksky. Then the much-tried servant came forward.

"Howd'y', Marse Stan?" and the black hand met the white one in a friendly clasp.

"I's mighty glad you's heah, sir. Miss Margret was gettin' oneasy, an' little Miss Rue looked like she knowed it."

"How did you know I was 'oneasy,' Oscar?"

"Lord, mum, you never looked round when I rattled things. I made a heap o' noise — sounded like I broke most everything on the table."

Leszinksky smiled at his wife, and loosened the clutch of baby fingers from his mustache as he asked: "Were you anxious, Margaret?"

"Yes. You said you would be here to-day, and"—

"I have spoiled you by my punctuality. I always arrive before you have had time to wait. I should have done so to-day but for an unexpected meeting with Carson at the upper ford. They have had a hard time of it on the march from Bent's, and I stayed to help him over with his wagons and sick people."

"I am so glad. Is he not coming to us?"

"Yes; he has gone to headquarters to report, but he will be here to supper in a few minutes. I hope you have enough for two hungry men, Oscar?"

"Thar's prairie chicken an' briled ham, an' two kinds o' bread, an' waffles."

"That is enough; the ham and waffles alone would do for a soldier just from the plains."

"How far did you go, Stan?"

"Out to Castalar's ranch; we stayed there night before last. I was so near I had to go and thank them for their kindness to you and the little one. And now the debt is increased. Madame has sent you a fresh cow. We brought the calf in the ambulance, so had no difficulty."

"That is a welcome gift, — more precious to baby than silver or gold. But here comes our guest."

Together husband and wife hastened to greet Carson in the hall-way, as Oscar opened the outer door.

Margaret and Carson had never met since the week after her marriage. The slight but stately girl had now the noble proportions and full roundness of mature womanhood. For one beat Carson's pulse gave a great throb of half pain, half delight, and then stilled with a strange, new feeling in his heart, as Margaret gently placed her child in his arms, saying: "Stan and I wish you to be her godfather. We have waited for your return. You were a brother to him in the old West Point days. You are a brother to me: that night at the Corcorans', when you told me what gave me to your comrade, made me your sister."

She stopped a moment, then, seeing that the servant was gone, and Leszinksky standing silent, with his face turned from the firelight, she continued: "If she should lose us, we give this child to your care; you will be her guardian. Neither of us has any near relatives. She would be entirely dependent on your protection, — a helpless little woman with none but you. My brother, you have but one fault, but one weakness. Will you give it up for the sake of a little child whose vows to God you must make?"

"Yes!" with a half-choking sob in his voice. Evidently trying to master himself, he added brokenly: "I know perfectly what you mean. I disgraced myself on the boat from Cincinnati to Cairo. I was drunk."

"Oh, but it was after Stan was with me. When I was dependent on your care —"

"Certainly, I was not blackguard enough to drink then, or to come near you ladies when I was drinking; but I was sure you could not fail to know. But I promise you now, holding in my arms this baby, who will always be more precious to me than anything on earth except your respect, your trust, that I will never so disgrace myself again."

As Carson stooped to kiss the child, she looked up at him with that wonderful, far-away look of baby eyes which seems entangled with lost memories.

Leszinksky threw his arm over his friend's shoulder, saying: "Thank God! Carson, I am selfishly glad. Now I can meet the chances of a soldier's life without fear. Wife and child will be safe in your care, if the odds go against me."

"I think you can trust me, Stan. I was true to you when it was harder than this. I loved Miss Cartaret from the first moment I ever saw her, and Margaret

Leszinksky, or any one she cared for, could have my life for the asking. Now you know it all."

He placed the child in Margaret's arms, and faced Leszinksky. For an instant the two young men regarded each other steadily, then Leszinksky extended both hands, which Carson grasped and wrung hard. Margaret had gone out of the room.

"I was stupidly blind, Carson. I did not know."

"I did not intend you should. I knew it was hopeless, even had she never known you."

"I do not know why you should think so. You are the manliest fellow I ever knew. Any woman might treasure, might be proud of your affection."

"Hush, Stan! You always saw the best side of me. There is another for the blackguards I find in the devil's thoroughfares."

. . . .

Christmas came, and baby Rucheil was made a Christian. The first woman-child born to the Leszinkskys since Marie of France bore the name of the Mahometan wife of old King Stanislaus, — the name inscribed in the wedding ring worn by every bride who had come into the line since the time of Janet Macdonald. It was of Margaret's choosing.

"The child," she said, "is all Leszinksky, and Rucheil was the name of the woman whose marriage united the three dynasties of the 'lilies of Kabilovitsch.' The name itself is an inheritance, and the first daughter of the house should bear it."

So the Jewish Angel of the Air and the Winds was the tutelary saint of the little maiden born on the plains.

The pale, delicate, worn wife of Paul Castalar, the *ranchero*, proved the true catholicity sometimes found in the Roman Church by acceding to Margaret's request to be the child's godmother. Carson, we know, was her godfather.

A pagan ancestress, a Jewish name, a Catholic godmother, held at the font in the arms of a hard-swearing, young cavalryman, — what will become of her? Ah!

she is a "Sunday's child," christened on Christmas. Will not the special blessing of the old proverb follow her?

The spotless bud of an Easter morning, consecrated on the day of the Nativity, through change and suffering, through the martyrdom of affections and hopes and ambitions, though broken from the parent stem and soiled with sin, the blessed dew of a fructifying repentance shall fall upon the bleeding flower, until the uplifted chalice of the lily holds its purified sweetness in the soft dawn of the Sun of Righteousness.

CHAPTER VI.

*Now will I show myself to have
More of the serpent than the dove.*
                                MARLOWE.

THAT winter the regiment had a new experience, — a fierce outbreak of temper on the part of its saint.

Leszinksky had gone with the colonel to settle some dispute between two friendly Indian tribes.

Captain Hartley, left in command of the garrison, was disliked by the officers and detested by the men. A coxcomb and a martinet, selfish, cold, and haughty, reasons for dislike were as plenty as blackberries.

Because of this unpopularity Leszinksky had been kind and polite, Margaret impressively hospitable. At Leavenworth the high-spirited young subalterns, who could not well brook his insolent assumption, would turn away from the house if they saw him there, or if there when he came would leave on some subtle pretext that deceived no one. Carson, who now met him for the first time, instinctively hated the man. Whether it was the side of his character that led him to " the devil's thoroughfares " that judged Hartley is a question for the psychologist. At any rate, he judged more correctly than Leszinksky. Margaret's judgment was valueless in the case; for we who know her know she would overrule any estimate which declared against the friendless. So it happened that the man in the garrison the least fit for the companionship of a pure woman was a constant visitor to the Leszinkskys.

Only one member of the family stood proof against

any approach to friendliness. Baby Rue sturdily set herself against Hartley. No blandishment, no bribe, could win her, although her nurse, Margaret's pretty quadroon maid, never wearied in effort to soften her obstinate antagonism.

Carson was boyish enough in his dislike to encourage the child's resistance to the captain's touch, her rejection of his offerings. When Margaret remonstrated, he was prudently silent. To Leszinksky he said: "Children, dogs, and roughs are the best judges of character. I am glad Rue backs my opinion with her dislike. Her mother never will see the bad in any one, — she is too thoroughly good to find it; but Rue is an outcrop of the old Leszinksky shoot. She knows a blackguard, and, thank God, she scorns him. If she did n't, with that devil's temper and obstinate will of her's, — if she grew friendly with Hartley, — I should be in fear and dread of her future. *She* is not the sort that can touch pitch and not be defiled. Young as she is, you can only rule her through love. Damn it, why do you wish her to like a cold-blooded scoundrel?"

"Carson, you are excited, and are letting your prejudice warp your better nature. You know nothing against Hartley, except the general dislike to his manner."

"His manner is the best of him, cool and cynically insolent as it is. The man has n't a noble or generous impulse in his composition. He is only honest in the law's sense. I would trust him with my pocket-book, if he knew I had counted the contents; but I would n't trust the heart of a woman or the honor of a man in his long, slim, white hands. He's a low brute. I could tell you, but you would only think it a prejudiced suspicion —"

Margaret's coming hushed the discussion, and Leszinksky left for the Indian country without learning more from Carson. That was early in February.

Three days after Leszinksky's departure a soldier came to Carson's quarters at daybreak to say Mrs. Leszinksky wished him to come to her as soon as possible. In ten minutes more Carson was in the little sitting-room, where he found only Baby Rue, sitting in Oscar's lap, with the half-frightened look that a baby's face sometimes wears in presence of a grief it cannot understand. She was rubbing her little rose-leaf of a hand over the black cheeks, down which great tears were rolling. Carson had knocked impatiently, and then entered unnoticed.

"What is the matter, Oscar?" and the stout soldier's voice trembled.

"It's — it's Cap'in Hartley, an' because he's a white man an' I's a black one I can't kill him in a far' fight."

Carson's heart stood still as he caught at a chair and gasped, "Your mistress, — where —"

"She's out yonder in the cabin wid Lucy an' — an' *his* chile."

"What child?"

"His'n! That's why Lucy married me las' fall. I was a fool not to suspec' somethin' when she change her mind, after tellin' me so long she never was agoin' to marry anybody. Lord! Lord! Marse Carson, when I seed that chile this mornin', an' Miss Marg'ret a-cryin' over it, I wanted to kill Lucy an' it an' *him*. I'd a-done some desprit harm I know, fur I pushed Miss Marg'ret away, an' hurt her when I cotched her arm; but she would n't let go o' me. She jis cotch the chile in her bres' an' held it, an' stood between me an' Lucy an' kep' sayin', 'Oscar! Oscar!'"

"You did n't strike your mistress?"

"No, Marse Carson, I could n't a-done that never, — not even then, — an' she so good an' pitiful; but I must a-hurt her arm when I tried to take the chile; an' now I's mos' glad I did: for if I had n't a-hurted her, I'd a-killed somebody sho, — that brung me out o' the fit like; an' she said, so steady an' sorrowful that I could n't help but mind her, 'Rue is crying; go keep her until I come.' An' poor little Miss Rue was cryin' hard until she see me so struck an' poorly, an' she jis stop fur pity o' me." And the poor fellow hid his grief-stained face in the child's frock.

Carson looked at the baby, who put out her hands to him, her lip trembling with its pretty quiver of hurt feeling. He bent over Oscar, saying, "Give Rue to me; she is frightened."

As he took the child, Oscar stood up and crossed his arms over his breast, evidently trying hard to repress the gasping sobs that would come.

"How do you know it was Hartley?"

"Thar was Mrs. O'Dowd, an' old Betty the cook, with her all night. Miss Marg'ret sot up, an' I was in heah with Miss Rue while her mother stayed out in the cabin. The doctor had been heah, an' said Lucy was doin' well, an' he 'd come agin early in the mornin'. Miss Rue had waked an' cried, an' her mother had come to her. I was makin' up the fire in the dinin'-room, fur it was near mornin', an' the doctor would be back to breakfas'. When the ole woman came to Miss Marg'ret's room, I wanted to heah 'bout Lucy; so I kep' still, an' I heerd her tell Miss Marg'ret, ' De chile is born, an' it's a white chile.' I dunno what come over me till Miss Marg'ret said, ' Lucy is nearly white.' She laid Miss Rue in the cradle an' went out to the cabin. I was in a maze like when I follered her. I stopped a minute by the kitchen-door, an' the women was talkin' together. One o' them said, ' It's Captain Hartley's chile'; an' I went on quick to the cabin. I heerd Miss Marg'ret say, ' Lucy, I can forgive you; but Oscar ' — an' they seed me, an' Lucy screamed, an' Miss Marg'ret jis turn white; but she stood before them two. I tole you 'bout all the res'. But, Marse Carson, somehow I know I'll kill that man yet."

The door opened and Margaret came in. She spoke first to Oscar, —

"Stay here."

Then taking her child from Carson, —

"I sent for you to ask you to go with Oscar to Van Buren, and send him from there to Memphis. He must leave here at once. Stan will be gone three weeks, and I dare not let him stay."

The negro broke in excitedly: "'Fore God, Miss

Marg'ret, I won't do any one heah any harm! Not Lucy, or even that chile. Don't sell me, mistis!"

"I never thought of it, Oscar. Do you think your Marse Stan *could* sell his foster-mother's child?"

"But I hurt *you*, Miss Marg'ret. 'T will be mighty hard fur Marse Stan to get over that."

"He will know, as I do, that you never intended harm to me. But you must go to Memphis, Oscar, for your own sake, for my sake. I should be constantly anxious if you were here. You would not give me trouble if you could help it; but I cannot be sure of your patience."

"No, Miss Marg'ret, you can't. If I see that man, I's feared I'll kill him."

The light of hate in the bloodshot eyes gave emphasis to the fear. Carson said only, —

"I will be ready to go in an hour. Oscar, will you promise to go with me quietly? I do not want to tell any one or take any one with me."

"Yes, sir; I'll promise to be ready an' wait fur you quietly, an' I'll go peaceably, 'cept the Lord puts him in my hands. If he comes out 'fore we gets off, an' I see him, I ain't ans'erable. I'll kill him or he'll kill me."

Margaret, putting down the child, followed Carson to the outer door, asking, "Can you take him alone? Had you not better have a guard? He has the strength of two ordinary men, and to-night he is mad with the sting of his injury."

Carson looked into the flaming blue eyes, and felt his nerves tingle and his pulses thrill: "I do not need a guard for Oscar more than for myself. If I meet that scoundrel I think Oscar's chance at him will be small. He has outraged Leszinksky's trust and your hospitality. He shall settle the account."

The angry flash was now at Carson. "My husband can care for his cause and mine. I sent for a friend to aid me in a difficulty. I did not think you rated me so lightly that you would add fresh fuel to garrison-gossip."

"I beg your pardon. You are right. You are always right. I will not take a guard, but I will take Oscar to Van Buren, and there shall be no trouble about it. I shall be here with an extra horse for him in half an hour."

And before she could speak he was gone. In the little sitting-room she found Oscar walking back and forward with Rue in his arms.

"Is she not asleep?"

"Yes, 'um; but I's goin' away from her, an' I'll miss her sore. I's loved her an' carried her 'bout, an' thought how my chile would play with her an' grow up with her — like Marse Stan an' me. An' now I's got nothin' but her, an' I's got to leave her. An' to-night she was sorry for me, Miss Marg'ret. Miss Marg'ret, when a man makes a heaven like this was, a hell, ought n't he to be killed?"

"God will judge him."

"But then God's so slow 'bout it. O Miss Rue, little Miss Rue, don't forget poor Oscar!"

He knelt down at her mother's feet and gave up the baby.

"Don't cry, Miss Marg'ret. I'll go now all right. I's goin' to tell Lucy good-by. I won't hurt her — nor *it:* I promise you. You kin trus' me, mistis. You do, — don't you?"

"Yes, Oscar. Come back at once. Get the things you will want and come here."

In a short time he returned. Then came Carson, refusing to wait for breakfast: they could get it at a farm ten miles down the river. And in the rosy light coming through the window Margaret looked in the face of the first grief that had touched her hearthstone.

The blow had struck her pride and her affection. The young wife had a shrinking sense of being soiled with the shame that had befallen her household. Besides this, she loved Lucy. The memory of their first meeting melted her to pity. Only a week from the day her own mother was buried, sitting beside her father in the cemetery of Hollywood, silent through sympathy with the strong man broken by grief, she was roused from the dead ache of her own sorrow by the plaintive wail of a child standing alone in the tangled undergrowth of a remote and neglected corner of the grounds. She put her hand in her father's, saying, "Papa, over there is a little girl all alone. She is crying so! We must go to her."

Near the child they found a woman lying on the sward, her head resting on a newly-made grave. When questioned by Colonel Cartaret the child only moaned, "Mammy, mammy!"

He raised the woman's head and found her quite dead, the soft brown cheek and tangled curling hair lying in a little pool of blood. The dark stains on the pale ashen lips told the story of the broken heart and spent life.

That night Colonel Cartaret learned the history of the dead mother. The next morning he bought the child from the creditors of the estate of Larry Hoyt, the gambler. The woman had been his slave, the child was his daughter. A rough, a gambler, a murderer, shot down on the street by the brother of the man he had killed, society gained by his death. Society gained; but the poor woman to whom he seemed a god in his kindly, rugged strength and grand perfectness of towering height and muscle, lost everything. He had bought her from a man he had seen whipping her brutally. He had held his fiery temper under control until the bargain was made and the bill of sale, which it took his last dollar to pay, was receipted. Then he thrashed her late owner to a jelly. From that moment she never had cause to shed a tear, until the death which demanded so many that they came in the swift rush of the scarlet tide on which her soul floated away in search of the lost.

Old Betty, coming in to ask for orders, changed the current of Margaret's thought, which had strayed into the past. Oscar's departure made the little, every-day things of life more difficult, and Margaret (remember she was only a woman: the regiment, not the church, had canonized her) added these petty irritations to her account with Hartley. The household affairs arranged, directions given as to Lucy's comfort, she added positive orders to old Betty to be silent about the child and Oscar's departure. She also demanded from Mary O'Dowd a promise of discretion in speech. Then the doctor came, but he was Margaret's ancient ally and could be trusted.

Four days later Carson returned. He had seen Oscar leave on the steamer for Memphis. Again Margaret asked his absence. Would he please go to Leszinksky and tell him all, and, if it was not too much out of the way, would he go to Castalar's and ask Madame and Stephanie to come and stay — at least until Stan's return?

Carson was rather vexed at all these trivial errands, when he would so much rather have stayed at the garrison and found some pretext to have it out with Hartley. His grumbling was to himself; his ready acquiescence only was visible. He asked, through his captain, leave of absence, which Hartley was only too glad to give him; for somehow he mixed Carson, in his thought, with the late repulse he had met with at Margaret's door. In place of the smiling and polite Oscar, old Betty had answered his knock. To his inquiry for her mistress, she answered civilly, but with just a shade of defiant asperity in her manner: —

"Miss Marg'ret is not berry well, and can't see no company jis yet."

Carson disposed of, Margaret was ready for her next move. She sent for the chaplain and Captain Moore. Now, the chaplain was very well if these troubled waters were to be stilled, but "fighting Ben Moore" seemed the last man alive to choose for peacemaker, with such a beautiful opportunity to take on his broad shoulders some one's quarrel.

The guests were shown into the dining-room, where they found the doctor. Old Betty was on guard in the sitting-room, to keep out chance callers. Margaret did not put in an appearance until her ally had opened the council and stated the case. After a time she entered, looking very quiet and stately; but there was a red flush in her cheeks, a steely gleam in the blue eyes, an electric quiver in the voice, that half frightened the parson, though it pleased Captain Ben hugely.

"Gentlemen, I wish to have this — this difficult matter settled, as far as it ever can be, before my husband returns. The principal offender is his superior officer; the woman" — here her voice quivered and broke for an instant — "the woman belongs to me. So it will be better to settle this vexing question in his absence."

"But, my dear," broke in good old Mr. Page, "do you not think it would be better — more proper, more delicate — to leave such a — such a scandal as still as possible? I am sure your husband would think it best. He would see at once how disagreeable, how unpleasant, it would be to make any disturbance about what *certainly* is a very improper affair."

"Can *you*, Mr. Page, — a good man like you, a husband, a father, — call this stain of a woman's soul, the grief and pain of her husband, only an 'improper affair'? Why, you gave them the sacrament of marriage!"

"That's all very true, very right, from your standpoint; but you must see, my dear Mrs. Leszinksky, that circumstances modify guilt. With negroes it does not do to expect too high a standard of morals, too —"

"From your standpoint, Mr. Page, has God given one gospel to the white man and another to the negro? How dare you urge his commandments upon them if all sanctity is taken away from their relations in life?"

"I do not think, my dear madam, you exactly understand. I am very pained at this — at this sinful affair; but I do not think your husband would like you to do anything that would bring upon *you* the censure of the censorious or the ridicule of the light-minded."

"If, as a minister of God, that is your judgment,

Mr. Page, then I must appeal to another standard. Captain Moore, I ask you, as a gentleman and a soldier, what you think would be my husband's feeling and expression?"

"I think Leszinksky will feel like holding Hartley to account for betraying his hospitality, and insulting his family with his low intrigue. I think Mr. Page is right about the moral accountability of niggers; but Hartley has certainly failed in respect to you, — he has acted in an ungentlemanly and unofficer-like manner. It will afford me much pleasure to tell him just what I think of his conduct. I will take it as a great favor — a most flattering proof of your confidence in my discretion — if you will permit me, in Leszinksky's absence, to settle this matter with Hartley."

"That is just what I am about to do."

"Thank you, my dear Mrs. Leszinksky. I will go at once." And the bold dragoon started up in a perfect flutter of delight.

"No; not just yet, Captain. I have not given you instructions."

"Instructions? I do not need any. Why, my dear madam, it is the simplest thing in the world. I will just give him the facts — and my opinion. Of course I shall put that rather stronger than I can word it to a lady. After, I will leave him to take the initiative in — in the settlement."

"You mistake, Captain Moore. I do not wish you to have a duel with Captain Hartley: that would touch my husband's honor. It is because I think this man unworthy to cross swords with a gentleman that I wish you to act prudently in the matter before my husband's return. I trust you to be discreet and wise. I wish to give Captain Hartley no opportunity to defend his conduct. I will accept your intervention if you give me your word of honor to do and say only what I could do or say were it possible for me to speak to the — to Captain Hartley."

"My dear madam, the conditions are rather hard. I would much prefer going to him prepared to act as occasion might demand; but if you make me your ambassador, and require me to keep within the strict line of instructions, I promise you I will not dot an *i* or cross a *t* without your permission."

"Thanks. I wish you to deliver this note to Captain Hartley, and bring me an answer. If he asks any question, makes any comment, you will then say to him that you have promised to enter into no discussion, — to do nothing but give the note and bring the answer. Now please read the note aloud."

He read: —

"Captain Hartley, — You have a little daughter at my quarters, the responsibility of whose bringing up — knowing her parentage — I do not choose to take. She is too young to separate from her mother, even were I regardless of the tie of mother and child. The child is yours, the mother *was* mine. I will sell her to you at any price you may name. You are from a free State, and can find a home there for your child (who would else be a slave) and its mother. The bill of sale includes mother and child, that there may be no difficulty in their manumission.

"Margaret Leszinksky."

The three gentlemen regarded each other when the reading was finished. Then Mr. Page cleared his throat nervously, and began: —

"My dear Mrs. Leszinksky, you are too young, too inexperienced, to see what a scandal this will cause if Captain Hartley accepts; and if he refuses it would be no better. As a Christian — you have not thought of it from a religious standpoint. Why, you actually separate the woman from her husband to sell her to — to her partner in sin."

"Damn him! Only a piece of goods he has damaged," muttered Captain Ben, in an aside to the doctor.

The doctor hushed him with a gesture that caused him to turn. Our sweet saint was trying hard to master her temper; but the old Adam had got the better of the new dispensation. When she did reply to Mr. Page the voice was low and clear, but the face was the face of an avenging angel.

"I think, Mr. Page, you and our Judge up there"— and the slender white hand was raised as if in invocation — "would differ as to who is her husband. In His eyes it is not the honest black man, whose affection was made a cloak to hide her seducer. The man who tempted and betrayed Lucy persuaded her into this wrong she has done Oscar. He trusted to Oscar's loving patience, and, like you, thought a false morality, a cowardly regard for conventionalities, would keep us silent. Now that I have been forced to send away Oscar, who is honest and true and loyal, shall this man's child and mistress find shelter here?"

"No, certainly not: but it would cause less talk — it would be better to send her to New Orleans and sell her there."

Then the storm burst. "The Cartarets never were negro traders, neither are the Leszinkskys. My father bought the girl to give her the shelter of his home. She was brought up with me. I despair of making you understand me, gentlemen, if you cannot see the fitness, the absolute necessity, of this offer to the father of Lucy's child."

She turned to leave the room when Captain Ben exclaimed, "Please stay, Mrs. Leszinksky! The church and the army differ in judgment. The church is conservative, and fears scandal; the army is radical, and would stamp it out. Now, you and the doctor — for I see he is your ally — have found a more Christian course than the church, a more courageous way than that of the code, — a way of settlement that is neither cowardly nor brutal. I am not generally a man of peace; but I am a convert to your idea. I will take your note and bring the answer at once."

And the clinking of the dragoon's spurs was lost in the distance.

Mary O'Dowd came to the door for Margaret. In a

twenty-minutes' discussion the doctor convinced fearful but good little Mr. Page that Margaret's cutting of the Gordian knot was just what the parson had always intended to advise, only in the saint's excited condition he had not been able to make his meaning clear.

Captain Moore's embassy was less embarrassing and more immediately successful than he had anticipated. Captain Hartley could guess from the stiff, constrained manner of the ordinarily frank, gay soldier the judgment of the regiment. Brave old Ben's face was a barometer. Hartley read the signs, the bad-weather gauge was past, they pointed to a cyclone.

Though stung by the cool contempt of Margaret's note, Hartley gladly accepted the least troublesome way out of what he felt was a dangerous as well as a contemptible position. Mary O'Dowd *had* leaked. The very night before Captain Moore's visit Hartley's Leporello spent a bottle of bad whiskey on Mike O'Dowd in the detective service. Through two intense Irish imaginations the story had gained size and color. Oscar's outbreak was magnified into a murderous assault upon Lucy, her child, and his mistress; wounds and bruises to her defenders, Mrs. O'Dowd and old Betty; and a desperate fight with Carson. To that was added a lugubrious picture of Oscar's departure for the traders' block in New Orleans, fitted with handcuffs of the valorous Mike's clasping.

The only question Captain Hartley hazarded to Mrs. Leszinksky's ambassador was as to the money value of " the lot ". offered him. Mindful of his *i*-and-*t* promise, Captain Ben's reply was a masterpiece.

"I have no authority to discuss terms. I am not prepared to make suggestions. I am only the bearer of Mrs. Leszinksky's *cartel*. I don't know the price of niggers. I never looked in the girl's mouth; and the young one, I take it, has no teeth."

Hartley laughed. At which Captain Ben turned red as a turkey-cock, puckered his bland face in an effort to frown, with his right hand pulled at his heavy drooping mustache, whilst the left sought his sword-hilt. Hartley's laugh was hastily choked. Asking Captain Moore to wait a few minutes, he said he would return with the money and settle this at once.

He returned with a roll of bank-notes, wrote a line or two, and gave roll and billet to Moore, who received them without a word, gave a stiff salute, and was soon in Margaret's council-chamber, where the doctor and the parson waited. Mr. Page had made his peace with Margaret. At her request, he counted the money. It was two thousand dollars.

"It is the full value," observed the doctor. Mr. Page held it toward Margaret.

"No; I could never even touch that money. I wish you to keep it and invest it for Lucy. She will need it. Now, sir, it is your duty to see to it that this man sends her North and makes some provision for the child."

The doctor suggested, "You have not read his note."

It was: —

"MRS. LESZINKSKY:

"MADAM, — I retain the receipted bill of sale, and send you two thousand dollars. I have no words in which to offer you excuse or apology. I can only obey your intimated wish: I will manumit Lucy as soon as she is able to go North. Respectfully,

"W. HARTLEY."

Mr. Page rubbed his hands, and said, in a feeble, palliative tone: "I think he wants to repair his offence, — to do what is right."

To which the doctor responded: "It was his best way out of it. He is selfish enough to see what is good for him."

Margaret was silent, which argued badly for her temper. A woman is only silent at white heat.

Somehow the story got wind. (Possibly Mr. Page told his wife?) The garrison gossips waited anxiously for new developments. There was a constant flutter of femininities in Mrs. Leszinksky's little cottage, though no one exactly dared question *her*. Every one was in awe of the saint in her anger; and all knew she had shown temper. (Mr. Page *must* have told his wife.) There were lounging masculine groups constantly about the parade-ground in front of Margaret's door. Mike O'Dowd wore an air of mystery and importance, and would come at all hours to the kitchen-gate, calling in a tragic whisper to Mary, as if there were a corpse in the house.

There is no use to try to stifle or conceal the truth: our saint was in a rage, — a rage which all these prickles made explosive. She would have kept her anger hidden in her own house but for these prying, persistent, kindly-enough-meaning intruders. So one evening she appeared on parade-ground at the hour of drill.

Hartley was stupid enough to misunderstand her appearance. He walked up to the group of ladies, and commenced a half-spoken "Mrs. Leszink — " when she turned on him, with eyes flashing and cheeks aflame. A moment's hesitation, and the hastily-closed hand unclasped. She could not give the lie to all the traditions of those stately Virginian ladies whose blood was in her veins; but she would not recognize as an acquaintance a man for whom she had no feeling but contempt. So, looking at him steadily until his eyes dropped before the clear, pure light of hers, she turned without a word, and left him. Captain Ben and every young subaltern uncovered as she passed. Not one did she fail to recognize: she intended to make the difference seen and felt. They would have cheered her if they had dared. Hartley's brow darkened: the evil in the man was forever set against the saint who had scorned him before men's eyes.

Before Leszinksky returned, Lucy and her child were gone. Captain Hartley had given Mike O'Dowd a furlough. Margaret's bitterness (for the saint's anger had not altogether subsided), was somewhat sweetened by the thought that the poor girl would have the kindly care of the O'Dowds to Cincinnati. Mr. Page had arranged, with a friend who lived there, half-yearly payments of the interest of the purchase-money. As the receipts must come back, Lucy would not altogether drift into the unknown.

CHAPTER VII.

The prince of darkness is a gentleman.
MARLOWE.

HARTLEY'S manner was so changed for the better, he was so guardedly courteous in his general demeanor, so modestly generous in the arrangements made, through Mr. Page and the doctor, for Lucy's journey, that he began to win partisans in the garrison. Women, who had hitherto hidden their jealousy of our saint, now " let slip the dogs of war." All admitted that " the painful *fact* had been a *glaring indiscretion*" (the expression and the emphasis were the parson's), but Hartley's after conduct, his defenders [!] claimed, was unexceptionable. Moreover, in a gossip-loving little garrison, Margaret's silence and reserve offended. Little by little, envy and jealousy found tongue. At length one feminine critic hazarded the remark that Mrs. Leszinksky had been " negligent in the supervision of her household, and then unjust in her anger."

The blank look of astonishment in the face of Captain Ben, who was one of her auditors, caused a hastily added, " But she is *so* young and has been *so* spoiled, we all excuse her."

Then the bold dragoon found words: " Very good of you all, I am sure, to excuse *her* for Hartley's misconduct. By Jove, I begin to believe the more thorough a blackguard a man is, the more sure is he of defence from the sex he insults ! A year ago that fellow had n't a friend in the regiment, whilst now, since he has betrayed the hospitality of the house that was opened to him because of his friendlessness, you women take him up and make of him a sort of pattern sample of suffering virtue."

Before the smoke of his hand-grenade had blown away, Captain Ben retired in good order, disregarding the scattering shot fired in his rear.

Notwithstanding the feminine verdict which " recommended to mercy," the officers of the garrison in a courteously cool way sent Hartley to Coventry. The jovial Florida veteran and the beardless graduate of West Point stiffened into a rigid politeness which was not unbent in his presence.

I do not wish the reader to understand that the 1st Regiment of dragoons were unswerving and incorruptible moralists. I regret, as a truthful historian, to be forced to say they fell very far short of such perfection. But they were gentlemen in the main. Graft a gentleman into the army, and to the fearless honesty of the soldier is added a finer quality, — a chivalric clairvoyance, quick and true in its recognition of right, its reverence for purity. It was this that had shrined Margaret in the heart of the regiment, and made devout worshippers of these cavalrymen of facile manners and (I am sorry to record it) loose virtue.

In meeting the difficulties of his position Hartley proved superior to the estimate heretofore made of his ability. With wonderful adroitness he had turned the move of his antagonist to his own advantage. His instant acceptance of Margaret's offer; his ready acquiescence in every proposal made by Mr. Page; the respectful attention given to every suggestion of the doctor; the tact and foresight with which all arrangements were made for the quiet and unobserved departure of the O'Dowd travelling party, — won open compliment from Mr. Page, reluctant approval from the doctor, and fierce oaths from Captain Ben, whose antagonism was growing more and more pronounced as Hartley untangled the meshes of the net into which he had fallen.

Many who had hitherto hesitatingly excused, now openly defended Hartley. Others were willing to ignore the offence in consideration of the changed manner of the man. The doctor, certainly the shrewdest analyst who observed him, regarded curiously, and with no slight admiration, the ease with which Hartley turned every incident to his advantage in his battle with opinion, until he finally plucked " the flower safety from the nettle danger."

Late in the evening after Leszinksky's arrival, Margaret sat in the little sitting-room alone with Baby Rue. Madame Castalar and her daughter had been sent for, and had returned to the ranch two days before. Captain Ben and Mr. Page had both been sometime with her husband in his smoking-den across the hall; now they too were gone, and the doctor alone was there. She was anxious and nervous. She had tried in all ways to tell the story of the last few weeks to her husband, without exciting him to anger. She had done what she could in his absence. It was something, in her excited state, to remember his solemn smile of approval as he read the copy she had kept for him of her letter to Hartley. But she had been interrupted before she could win from him his determination as to his own course of action. It was late : she wished the doctor would go, but there came a knock at the door. She heard her husband answer it. Shiveringly she recognized Hartley's voice. How slowly the minutes dragged! She bent over her baby's cradle and thought of her own orphanage. She had unbounded trust in her husband, but he was a soldier, and in those days men stood face to face in deadly encounter with far less cause than Hartley had given.

Then, for the first time in all those trying weeks, her courage failed, — failed as her anger burnt out, and the Christian remembered she had not forgiven the sinner who had injured her. Prostrate beside her child's cradle, she prayed for forgiveness, for the life of her husband, and also that he might do no murder,— that her pride of heart might not be visited on him. Who dare say the Great White Throne is not reached by such prayers?

To Margaret an answer came. Her husband's arms were around her. From his lips came the prayer of all prayers, and the words, "Forgive us our trespasses as we forgive those who trespass against us," told her that her fear was needless.

Of his interview with Hartley, Leszinksky told no one. The doctor also was silent, but Hartley, meeting Captain Ben with Mr. Page next day, said: —

"Moore, I know you think me a scoundrel: for the past your judgment is correct, but do not judge me now for the future. The truest gentleman of you all is Leszinksky: I saw *him* last night, and old King Stanislaus himself could not have forgiven me more royally."

PART II.

MOUNT HOPE.

No cord or cable can draw so forcibly, or bind so fast, as love can do with only a single thread.
Lord Bacon.

PART II.

MOUNT HOPE.

CHAPTER VIII.

Who ever loved that loved not at first sight?
MARLOWE.

MARCH was going out like a lamb. The air was soft and warm as it swept up the valley from the south, laden with the faint, sweet odours of the early spring; the sky overhead a tender blue, flecked with tiny, white cloudlets. At the horizon's verge it banked in misty, gray rifts, that were lost in the deeper shades of the pine-clad peaks and broken chain of the Blue Ridge. From cleft and ravine, from jutting spur and mountain-top, little rivulets came dancing into the valley, — threads of silver on the mountain-side, burnished steel in the meadows, with the dark-blue sheen of a Damascus blade as they gurgled over rocky beds in the forest, at last all their wild beauty and glad life lost in the rolling, yellow waters of the Hardware, that wound in serpentine coils through the county of Albemarle to its confluence with the James. The valley is some thirty miles in extent, with a northern and western boundary of mountains, while to the south and east stretch the long, rising swells which finally grow sharp and well-defined in the hills on the southern bank of the James that mark the beginning of the Piedmont range.

On a knoll which from its solitary situation seemed a lost spur of the mountains stood an old-fashioned frame house, with a wide hall that divided, and verandas that surrounded it. Everything in its appearance told of decay and changed fortune. On one side the roof of the veranda had fallen, hastened to its doom by the clinging weight of a tangled Virginia creeper, that now shrouded with glossy leaves and tender green shoots the ruin it had wrought. The blurred gray and blue color that had succeeded the worn and weather-stained white paint deepened the artistic effect. The house fronted south, where the ascent was easy and gradual, through an avenue of old Lombardy poplars, their topmost branches palsied and dying. On the north side the knoll was broken to a sharp, bold cliff, and against its base the Hardware chafed and fretted when a spring freshet gave it strength for attack. From the top of this cliff to the north veranda, there had once been a succession of wide terraces; but these were now broken and irregular, overgrown with myrtle and periwinkle that had crowded out the less hardy plants, though here and there the blue eyes of violets gleamed from their hiding-places as the wind played through the leaves.

The view from the terraces was one of the most restful and beautiful in that restful and beautiful county of Albemarle. It overlooked the rich valley of the northern bank of the Hardware with its carpet-like furrows, where later the waving corn and broad-leaved tobacco would ripen in the sun. Beyond this were sloping hillsides, where woodland, orchard, and clearing revealed some modest home; or else steeple-like chimneys, stately trees, far-stretching grain-fields told the presence of some old manor-house. Back of all curved that cloud-touched ridge of wonderful, deep-sea blue.

On the west side, half-hidden by the gnarled boughs of an old orchard, was the kitchen. Lower down the hillside were three or four dilapidated negro cabins, where the "truck-patches" already planted showed some signs of life. Still lower, at the very base of the hill, near the river, were the "folks' quarters," now only a deserted village. It was evident, from all signs, that the Masons of Mount Hope were so nearly obliterated that they would be swept away in the surging rise of another generation.

On the south porch, seated in an old splint-bottomed easy-chair, was the last of a line of Virginian gentlemen whose progenitor had fought with Prince Rupert. A stately negress stood near, arranging on a little table her master's noon-day meal. The white cloth and beautiful old china, the appetizing odour of the chicken broth, the golden butter and clear honey, the snowy bread and rich milk, would have charmed an epicure; but nothwithstanding the kindly yet respectful insistance of his attendant, Judge Mason ate but little, turning from time to time an expectant look down the avenue.

"Sara, it is time that Abram was back with the mail."

"I dunno, marster. Brown Bess can't travel like she used to; an' if de stage ain't come by Dr. Carter's yet, Daddy'll wait. He knows you mus' have a letter to-day."

"I have not many days to wait in, Sara; but I know Stan too well to doubt they will come. If he cannot get leave to come himself, he will send his wife and child, that I may bless them, and tell Mary I have seen them."

"Lord! marster, you'll get well now. You's a heap sight better since de weather's turn. Dese wahm days jis puts new life in us all. An' if Miss Marg'ret an' de baby stay all summer, Marse Stan mus' come fur 'em; an' mebby den dey'll stay fur good."

"No, Stan cannot resign. I would not ask it; I do not wish it. But God knows how my heart yearns to see my Mary's boy before I go to her!"

The rapid patter of bare feet was heard on the west veranda, and a young negro boy came flying around the corner, fairly shrieking: "Oscar's a comin' froo de near way wid Marse Stan's little pickaninny! He brung her straight frum de stage by de near path. Doctor Carter's sendin' Marse Stan an' young mistis in his buggy an' grandaddy's wid dem. Heah he is! Heah's Oscar now!"

Before they had roused from the stupor produced by this announcement, Oscar was on the veranda, with Baby Rue in his arms. He wrung his mother's hand hastily, who broke from his grasp to extend both hands for the child.

"God bless her, — Marse Stan's baby! Give her to me, Oscar."

"No! Old marster first"; and he held her toward the old man.

"Heah she is, sir, — Marse Stan's chile. An' her mother's as good — as good as Miss Mary was. They started jis as soon as they heard you was poorly, sir; an' they ain't stopped day nor night till we's heah."

"Baby darling! My Mary's little granddaughter! Blessed be God, that he has let me live to look on your face!" and the venerable old man took the young child in his arms.

She first looked wonderingly at him, then smilingly at Oscar, after which, with a little, tired sigh (for she was worn with the long, rapid walk through the fields), she laid her head on her grandsire's shoulder, and slept.

When the others arrived the long, scant, white locks rested softly on the deep gold rings that crowned the baby head.

. . . .

Here, O reader, is the proper time and place to introduce to you more particularly our heroine, — the child whose changing fortunes you and I shall follow together; the woman, yet in embryo, whose personality is so strongly marked that her intimate acquaintances have already learned its characteristics. We have heard Carson define her. We know how persistent Captain Hartley found her dislike. Oscar has felt the sweetness of her sympathy, and in his grateful fervor has devoted his life to her service. Her father, with what justice the future will prove, calls her the "young voyvode." Whilst our saint sometimes looks with a sort of pitiful awe into the gray depths of the clear eyes which flash and lighten with a weird consciousness of something we are too far off to fathom. Is it the Past, crying its memories to the soul that is escaping from a riven shell, or the gathering of lost elements that have at length developed new power to force themselves into visible form and shape?

All about the child have already learned that neither force nor restraint will tame her. To pain she is resistant, not submissive, with a queer, baby stoicism that makes outcry rare. Obeying with perfect docility a request, she is imperturbably obstinate to a command; taking with absolute insistance from a hand she dislikes the least of her possessions, she is recklessly prodigal of gifts to one she loves. A wonderful instance of heredity, this child, whose triune nature has come to her through the ages from the Lechzynczski-Kabilovitsch, intensified by change and reaction from change. She has not a feature, not a trace, of the mother who bore her. How could she? Margaret's utter abnegation of self made of her the susceptible and impressionable mould that nursed to life this reincarnation of the race from which her king had sprung.

From the moment of her arrival at Mount Hope there was the closest friendship, the most perfect understanding, between Baby Rue and her great-grandfather. The imperious child ruled the gentle old man with a royal kindliness. He was her playmate, her slave; but he had full payment for service. Bountifully she gave him an overflowing measure of affection. Her father, heretofore chief favorite, was second to his grandsire. The extremes of four generations and opposite temperaments had touched, and flashed into instant recognition and affection through that magical magnetism which, for want of truer definition, we call the instinct of blood. For the old man this baby had blotted out two generations, and seemed his very own, the child of his loins.

In the second week of her stay he made his will, and named her heiress of Mount Hope. He had the less scruple in so doing, as her mother's large estate, in a dozen subdivisions, would make any other children that might come far richer than his heiress. But, barren and in half-ruin as the place was, it was the manor-house of the Masons, and so a fit gift for his darling. He half-apologized to his grandson for his choice of legatee ; but " King Stan," in his grand manner, thanked Judge Mason for the love that singled out as his heiress the first daughter of the Leszinskys.

In her last week, April took payment from March for the days she had lent. A fierce wind blew from the northeast, driving in gusty swells a beating, cold rain. The Hardware was up and over its banks. Mount Hope had its most sombre and gloomy look. The windows rattled ; and the rising and falling tones of the storm had for accompaniment the sound of the swollen waters that surged and whirled around the rocks at the base of the cliff.

In a lofty chamber that had once been the drawing-room, the last of the Masons of Mount Hope lay dying. During the warm days Judge Mason had rallied, but with the first breath of the storm a change had come ; and now the Leszinskys knew that before another day the blessed rest of death would settle on the eyes that had wept and watched and waited so long. The angel of deliverance was at the door.

About four in the afternoon the clouds lifted in the west, and a rich yellow light flooded the room. The rain and the rush of waters were still heard, but over the western horizon the bow of promise spanned the blue arch. The warmth, the light, roused the dying. He looked for an instant at the faces that surrounded him, and then said in a low but distinct voice : —

"And the bow shall be in the cloud ; and I will look upon it, that I may remember the everlasting covenant between God and every living creature of all flesh that is upon the earth." Then the tired hands folded in blessing upon the baby's head, the tired eyelids closed ; and with a low, faint sigh a soul passed into the presence of the Great Teacher, to give an account of the lessons learned in the flesh.

CHAPTER IX.

> But on and up, where Nature's heart
> Beats strong amid the hills.
>
> MILNES.

THE departure of the Leszinkskys from Mount Hope was hurried by the sudden illness of Baby Rue. Moaningly she would put out her hands to be taken from room to room, evidently in search of her lost playmate. Oscar's most subtle wiles to attract her out into the grounds were unavailing. A peculiar, pretty way she had of asking, with a wave of her open hand, and a pathetic quiver of the lip, always brought the faithful fellow back to their ever-failing quest. A letter from Carson decided the immediate return of the Leszinkskys to the garrison. (Leszinksky had thought of leaving Margaret and Baby Rue at the White Sulphur Springs.) The last page of his epistle was: —

"Hartley has resigned, and has gone to New York, where he has inherited the savings of a miserly uncle, who was in the American Fur Company. Chance always favors a scoundrel. *He* a millionaire, whilst honest fellows like you and me live on the pitiful pay this grateful country allows the poor devils who get hashed on the frontiers that peltries may be accumulated!

"I see but one good in Hartley's windfall, — you can bring Oscar back with you. He, too, poor fellow, must bear the chafing of a fretful sore that the *gentleman* may have his pleasure. I am more orthodox than I used to be in the West Point days when sister Mary grieved over my heresies. I believe now in a hell, and a hot one; for there are villains loose here who are fit for no other finish,— they were predestined from all eternity to be damned! I'm going to squeeze through Saint Peter's gate, if it rubs off all my pet sins, for the pleasure of seeing them ordered the other road.

"However, since Judge Cartaret's recent marriage with Hartley's sister, Mrs. Leszinksky may not like even truths said of her new connections,— though I fancy she will not be anxious to include Hartley in the relationship.

"But I have something better than all this to tell you: Castalar was in last week, and he has traded his warehouse at Van Buren for Bouie's pretty little place on the hills. There were logs already hewn for a new addition to the house, and the day after the purchase Castalar had a 'raising.' The new house is well built, and is now three rooms deep each side of a wide hall, with outside kitchen and cabins in good order. The situation is as healthful as it is pretty. Now for the conclusion of my story: Castalar wishes you to live there. He will make a lease for as long as you like, the only condition being that when Madame Castalar or her daughter needs change they may come to you. Stephanie is very delicate, and the doctor advises her to stay here during the spring and fall, to avoid the river malaria at the ranch. I knew Mrs. Leszinksky would be glad to have them, so I promised that you would accept.

"All 'Ours' are helping to get things in order. Castalar begs you to come 'home' soon. By the first of May all will be ready. Some of us will meet you at Van Buren with the ambulance and baggage-wagon."

Preparations already begun at Mount Hope for the break-up, were now more hurried. An offer for the place, on a ten years' lease, for a boarding-school, was accepted. The few servants left were given their choice of being hired at Mount Hope or going with the Leszinkskys. Uncle Abram, the patriarch of the tribe, had packed his belongings for the trip to the Indian Territory some days before this announcement. When the calm and stately Sara suggested that he had better await "Marse Stan's" decision, he said: —

"My ole 'oman went to de New Geruzlum las' fall; an' now ole marster's done follered her, I ain't no kashun to stay at Mount Hope. Whar Marse Stan goes I goes; whar Miss Marg'ret lives I wants to live. Why, don't yer see her a-wearin' dat haht I guv her, dat Marse Stan cut, sot in pure gole? Ef I was sure an' sartin dat de Injins would take my ole skullp, like Oscar says dey do take 'em, I'd go all de same. I can't risk dem young folks to take keer ob demselves no longer; an' Oscar ain't got no prudent sort o' sense. Now, Sara, *you* mout be some use. You's a-gwine, ain't yer?"

"Yes; if Marse Stan'll take me an' my boys."

"In course, he'll take you all. What else is he gwine ter do? You didn't think he'd sell any ob de Mason folks, did yer?"

"Ole marster's debts ain't all paid yet. Mebby he'll have to sell some on us."

"No, he won't have to do no sich thing, an' Miss Marg'ret so rich!"

"Yes; but, Daddy, I heerd ole marster say Miss Marg'ret guv up all to marry Marse Stan. Leastwise, she can't get nuthin' fur a long time. Her chillun'll be rich sometime."

"Den, why didn't ole marster leave Mount Hope to Marse Stan, an' not to dat little pickaninny?"

"Mebby 'twas because ole marster knowed dat Marse Stan would sell de place sooner 'n sell any on us. I's mightily 'fraid some on us mus' go to pay de debts."

"We ain't a-gwine to be sold to pay no debts," said Sara's youngest son, looking with a sharp twinkle of his beady, bright eyes at his mother.

"How you know so much? Whar you git so smart?"

"I wuz in de sittin'-room las' night playin' wid de baby, an' I heerd Miss Marg'ret an' Marse Stan fix up all 'bout us all."

"How *dar'* you listen at de white folks, yer lim'? Ef you heerd so much, I s'pose you kin tell what dey is gwine ter do?"

"Dey 's gwine to rent dé place to de Miss Minors fur a skool, an' hire dem Uncle Abe, cos he kin stay heah an' go like he does now mos' ebery night to Doctor Carter's to see Aunt Sukey an' de chillun. Miss Marg'ret say dat would pay de intruss, an' arter a while, when she got her money, she would pay de res' of it fur little Miss Rue."

"I knowed 't was de Lord send her when I guv her her dat haht!" exclaimed Uncle Abram. "I knowed she was de angel ob deliberance to dis bankrupped place. I 's more sot den eber on gwine to de New Geruzlum straight from whar she 's a-livin'. I 'll want to tell ole marster jis whar dey is."

A few days later the choice was offered Uncle Abram and Sara that Solomon (the young scamp was not badly named) had foretold. Abram the second stayed in the land of his wife; whilst the patriarch, his daughter Sara, Oscar, and the younger boys followed the fortunes of their "Marse Stan."

PART III.

BOUIE'S HILL.

The web of our life is of a mingled yarn, good and ill together.
SHAKSPERE.

PART III.

BOUIE'S HILL.

CHAPTER X.

"Then he will talk — good gods! how he will talk!"
NATHANIEL LEE.

AT Bouie's Hill, two miles from Fort Gibson, on a hot, cloudless day in June, sat Uncle Abram, on a mossy bank at the foot of the hill, looking with justifiable pride at the work he had that morning completed. It was a handsome new gate, opening into the hillside orchard where the road wound back and forth in its gradual ascent to the house, — a gate easily opened by the driver of any conveyance without descending from his seat. The weights and pulleys worked perfectly, as Solomon, who had just brought his grandfather's dinner, proved by repeated trials. The old gate had been a sore grievance to Uncle Abram ever since his arrival at Bouie's Hill. Brown Bess had been left in Virginia to end her days in the home paddock; so the mount of the patriarch was a fractious mule, — a mule capable of a resistance to persuasion equalled only by its disregard of blows.

Mules and negroes, in their perfect adaptability to one another, do somehow arrive at an understanding by which they measure the necessary duration of their contests. They learn to gauge perfectly the length of time a well-bred mule demands before consenting to do the will of an irate African. But *this* mule and Uncle Abram were either too new to each other or else ill-matched in the ordinary mule-and-negro requirements.

Under no stress of compulsion would this hybrid come near the gate without backing at every effort to open it made by the luckless rider. In these daily contests Uncle Abram had never been conqueror. To escape the humiliation of repeated defeat, he had now made a gate the successful working of which was to bring him triumph. Solomon skilfully won permission for each new trial of the *chef d'œuvre* by compliments to his grandfather's skill and defiance of his adversary.

"Hi! but it work s'purb. Dat mule can't holp hisself now; he jis 'bleeged to cum froo widouten a fuss. Golly! ain't he gwine to be mighty mad? Hit's de very fines' gate I ever seed. Why, de white folkses won't know de place w'en dey cum back. Dere ain't nuffin like it out here in Rackinsaw. Hit's mos' like ole-Firginny."

"Yer done pull at dat gate long nuff, Solomon. Go right straight to de house an' holp Mead get things ready befo' de folks cum."

Solomon, looking around for an excuse to linger where he was, caught sight of two horsemen coming up the ravine through which the creek wound its sinuous course to the river, and answered: "Laws! gran'daddy, dere cum Marse Stan now, an' one dem hossifers frum de fote wid him. I better show him how to open dis gate 'fore I go."

"Your Marse Stan done open gates like dat befo' you was bawn. Dey'll want some dinner. He's been two weeks now out in de Injin country, an' I spec he's mos' starved. You jis' run, yer lim', an' tole Mead to hurry all he can 'bout dar dinner."

The reluctant Solomon turned slowly, casting from time to time longing looks of curiosity at the party now within the gate, then, thinking the next best thing he could do was telling the news, he hurried on to Mead.

"Howd'y', Uncle Abram? Why, this looks like the old days at Mount Hope," said Leszinksky, as he caught the ring, made of an old horse-shoe, that opened the gate. "I am glad you can show Captain Moore some of our Virginia inventions."

He then shook hands heartily, as he came through the gate, with the old man, who stood, hat in hand, by the roadside.

"It's a first-class job," said Captain Moore, with his kindliest smile.

"Thank you, sah. I reckon you's from Firginny yo'self, sah."

"No, I have not the honor to belong to the Old Dominion."

"I'm sorry fur it, sah. I'd a thought you was frum dar. We's ob de Mason fam'ly, sah, — de Masons ob Mount Hope."

And the old man straightened himself with an air of dignified consciousness of greatness that wonderfully pleased the fancy of the frank, gay soldier.

"Yes, I know, 'King Stan' is half a Mason."

"Yes, sah; an' de very bestest half. I don't mean no 'fence to de Desinkskys, Marse Stan; but you see, sah," — to Captain Moore, — "he's de very moral ob my Miss Mary. Now, sah, it am a strange thing, dis heah, who chillun takes arter. Sometime dey breeds back an' back. It's like a fine stallion my ole marster — de judge's father, sah — brung frum Inglan. He was a great racer, sah; an' in dem ole times he jis beat every hoss in de State, an' he won ole marster a power o' money; but he had a glass eye. An' all his colts arter two ginerations frum dat day to dis kin be tole anywhar in Firginny, sah; it broke out in 'em. Dey's all got glass eyes, — leastwise all dem dat ain't crossed wid scrubs. Now, dar's our little Miss Rue, sah; she ain't one bit Cart'ret like Miss Marg'ret, needer am she a Mason —"

"She has the Leszinksky glass eye," laughed Captain Moore.

"No, sah, not quite *dat*, but she *am* a Desinksky out an' out. Sometimes I see ole Gin'ral Desinksky — dat's Marse Stan's gran'father, sah, de king's son — look right straight outen her eyes. Dat, sah, is when she wants her own way, an' she *mean* to have it, an' she mus' have it, an' she Do have it."

Both gentlemen laughed, and Leszinksky interrupted Uncle Abram's discourse on heredity by an inquiry:—

"Has your Miss Margaret returned?"

"No, sah; but we's a lookin' fur 'em to-day. De doctor cum frum Marse Cas'lar's yestedday; he cum by heah dis mornin' on his way to see dem sick Injins up de riber, an' he's a comin' back heah to supper, sah. He said Miss Mar'g'ret would be home befo' dat."

Captain Moore pulled his moustache nervously, and asked: "Do they cross the river, coming from Castalar's, at the ferry or at the upper ford?"

"Neither: they come the old trail — the road through the prairies — and by the south bank. It crosses the Canadian a few miles above its confluence with the Arkansas, and the Arkansas four miles below here."

They rode on up the hill. Leszinksky, leading the way, did not see the clouded face of the dragoon. When they reached the house they found Solomon ready to take charge of the horses. Captain Moore said hastily:—

"Do not put my horse in the stable. Take off the saddle and strap the blanket on, and let him rest out there in the shade. I shall want him immediately."

"But, Moore," said Leszinksky, "you are not going back to the garrison until evening. Why, you half promised to stay all night. The doctor and Margaret will be here, and we can have a game of whist. Be reasonable, old fellow; they will all want to see you."

"It may be all nonsense, Stan, but I was going to propose to you that as soon as we get some luncheon — which you had better tell them to hurry — we go on and meet Mrs. Leszinksky. A Delaware runner, in from the Trading Post near the North Fork, overtook me some ten miles from the fort this morning, and he reported both North and South Fork as rising rapidly. It is the June freshet, somewhat delayed, but now nearly bank full. I had forgotten until I heard that Mrs. Leszinksky was at Castalar's and was coming home to-day. I trust they have heard of the rise and are coming by the ferry."

"No, they are not likely to hear of it. Castalar's ranch is shut in between the hills, out of the way of passers by. Margaret has gone over the ground so often that she will be fearless. Oscar and Sara are with her, and some of the family will come with them to the ford of the Canadian, — Castalar himself, I hope; he would be quick to see any change, as he is an accomplished frontiersman. But we will go at once, only you must excuse a hasty snack. Mead will give us whatever he has. Solomon, is your Miss Margaret's horse in the stable or in the field?"

"In de field, sah."

"Then see how quick you can catch him. Oh, here's Uncle Abram. He will get us a snack, and Mead can go with you to catch Sultan. Be off this instant."

"Yes, sah; we'll be back wid de hoss 'fore you's done eatin', sah."

In half an hour they were mounted and off, leaving Solomon on top of the new gate, looking after them and pulling up the weights and pulleys from below, until a voice behind him brought him with sudden fright to the ground.

"What yer doin', yer lim' o' Satan, meddlin' wid dem 'ventions? Ef I eber cotch you top ob dat gate agin, I'll give you sumfin to make you 'member it! Heah's de whole family upsot, an' mebby Miss Marg'ret an' yo' mammy drownded, an' yer takes de kashun to be a breakin' dat gate."

"I wah n't a hurtin' de gate, gran'daddy. I got up dar jes to see how fas' Marse Stan an' dat hossifer gentleman ride. Den I thought mebby dey went froo in sich a hurry dat dey mout a spiled some o' yo' fixin's, an' I was lookin' so I mout done tole yer."

While the old man investigated any possible injury that might have befallen his invention, Solomon prudently retreated.

CHAPTER XI.

THAT he is gentil that doth gentil dedis.
CHAUCER.

AN accident to their light wagon had delayed the party at Castalar's several hours after the time intended for the start. The repairs completed, Margaret insisted upon immediate departure. To the entreaties of the entire family that she would remain another day, she answered, —

"I cannot stay. My husband may return from the Osage to-day. He has never yet crossed his own threshold without the welcome of his wife and child. You will forgive my obstinacy. I must go."

Castalar glanced at the patient, worn face of his wife, who, without another word of remonstrance, commenced to gather up the little packages made ready for the travellers, as he said, "Then we must hurry your going. It is a long day's drive, and now late for a start. I will see you across the Canadian, and Stephen will go on to Bouie's Hill with you. An outrider is always needed in the bush."

"No, you shall not go, — neither you nor Stephen. I am a good enough frontierswoman to know that the herders will not soon recover the strayed cattle they reported this morning without your assistance. Oscar drives well, and the mules are gentle. There is not the slightest danger, and I know the way perfectly. We can reach the Arkansas River before sundown, and from there home is not an hour's drive."

"The herders do need me. If you will accept Stephen

as escort, I will say farewell here. Marie would imagine a thousand misadventures to you and her goddaughter if the '*gars*' did not go to bring her a faithful report of your safe arrival at home."

Adieux were said. Castalar rode off up the valley. Madame Castalar, her daughter, — a pale, slight child of thirteen years, — and two younger children stood in the doorway of the substantial log house, watching the wagon and its boy-escort down the valley until they passed through an opening in the hills and were lost to view.

Two hours brought the party to the ford of the Canadian. After leaving "Castalar's Valley" they had gradually ascended the rocky divide that separates the headwaters of the San Bois from the Canadian. To the bank of the latter the descent was abrupt, down shelving, sandy inclines, covered in patches with broad-leaved cactus and prickly pear. Below the ford, the shelving bank, with its strata of colored clay, inclosed in a sweeping curve a little stretch of alluvial soil, covered with a dense cane-brake that grew to the water's edge. Above the ford the bank was steep, its ridges ending at the base of a lofty chain of broken hills, presenting an alternation of terraces and cliffs covered with scrub-oak and stunted pine. On the opposite side of the river, which was nearly one quarter of a mile wide, the trail wound upward through tangled thickets to a ridge five or six hundred feet in height, covered with yellow pine and fragrant red cedar, that gradually dipped in broken swells, inclosing lakelike little prairies of wavy blue grass, to the valley of the Arkansas.

On the divide above the ford Oscar had stopped to breathe his mules and lock the wheels of the wagon. Stephen, a handsome boy of sixteen, was on a mettlesome mustang that he managed with the ease and grace of a Comanche. Unfortunately in his curvettings around the wagon, whilst talking to Margaret and trying to catch the attention of Baby Rue, he had disturbed a hungry hornet. The winged warrior struck the mustang fairly between the eyes, and the animal, wild with fright and pain, executed a series of leaps that would have unhorsed the best rider of the most famous cavalry school. But the spirited young Franco-American had learned the *manège* in the wide arena of the prairie under a Comanche tutor. "Bucking" was to him a familiar experience. Mustang and *métif* were fairly matched. Moreover, the boy had spectators before whom he felt failure would be disgrace. What boy of sixteen could bear failure in the presence of women and servants? Now a *man* might understand the odds against him, but these inferior people would only know the fact of defeat. Then add to the feeling of the ordinary boy the conceit of Young France, the deeper pride of the Indian who feels the blood of a chief in his veins. As we said, in a mere physical contest mustang and *métif* were fairly matched. Add the mental process and the moral result of such factors as pride of race and boyish conceit, and you will see that our statement was in a measure incorrect: the mustang was handicapped, the overweight told. Through vault and demi-vault, despite flying heels that struck out like a lightning flash and then gathered as rapidly in a game of "all fours," the boy stuck. The mustang was conquered in one point: he could not unhorse the rider, who, in the ease and grace with which he swayed to every movement, proved that out in the forest and the plains, where gloomy depths and arid stretches repel civilization, there is a more splendid centaur than the fabled monster of the Greeks, — a centaur which is the perfect unity of two distinct organizations controlled by a will that executes its mandates with the iron hand of the autocrat whose throne is the saddle. The mustang's final effort was expended in a rushing gallop toward home, and before the boy could force an acknowledgment of submission and change his course, the wagon was down the divide and at the river bank.

Rue was fretful and impatient. Margaret, already anxious to go on, ordered Oscar to cross without waiting for Stephen. Oscar called his mistress's attention to the deep reddish-chocolate color of the water, adding, —

"I don't like the look o' the river nohow. It's a

heap fuller 'n 't was las' week. Them cane-brakes was clar out o' the water when we crossed las' week. Sandy-bottomed rivers wash into holes mighty quick, an' thar's always a mighty deep one out thar jes' t' other side o' the big san'bar. Can't see the san'bar now, it's all covered. I think, Miss Marg'ret, you better let me go over an' try the ford on one o' the mules. It's a heap safer."

"No, there is no danger; the river is always a muddy red. It is too late in the season for a freshet. Drive on."

As they entered the water a gaunt, haggard man, bareheaded, with long, matted hair and beard, and clad in a few loose rags, came out of the cane-brake about a hundred yards below the ford, shouting to them. Sara screamed. Margaret, looking back hastily, saw the man running toward them followed by two others, one a nearly naked Indian. She called to Oscar, —

"Drive on! Quick!"

Oscar drove steadily, although he knew the river was much above its usual level. One hundred feet from the shore was the now hidden sandbar. Beyond that the current swept by at its greatest depth. When they gained the shallow water of the sandbar, Margaret again looked back. The man with the long, tawny beard was in the water, following the wagon; the other, a slow-motioned giant, had thrown his leggings and moccasins on the bank and was leisurely wading into the river. The Indian had disappeared. Margaret called out, —

"Faster! Drive faster!"

Oscar struck the mules; they sprang forward into deep water, slipped, struggled an instant to gain a foothold, and then fell, tangled hopelessly in the harness, rocking the light wagon from side to side in their efforts to get loose. Without hesitation, although he could not swim, Oscar did the one thing he thought would save the lives intrusted to his care: he climbed over the dashboard with an open pocket-knife in his hand, to cut the drowning animals loose from the wagon. Sara's screams rang over the water; whilst Margaret in speechless agony held her baby to her heart.

At this moment a hand was laid on the wagon, and the firm hold steadied its swaying. As Margaret turned her head, a pair of kindly, reddish-brown eyes looked into hers. The face to which they belonged had a suffering, half-starved, weather-beaten look, and water was dripping from the tangles of hair and beard. The owner of all these called to his companion, —

"Hillo, Pike! Swim 'round in front thar and holp the nigger get them mules loose. Let 'em go; you can't save 'em nohow. If the boy can't swim, pull him out; then come back. I'll steady this steamer till you get here. Maybe we can get her off the wheels and pull her on the bar thar."

Then he added, talking to Margaret, in a voice with honest intonations a child or an animal would have trusted, "Don't be skeered. You didn't hear me time 'nough to stop. You see I wah n't a-comin' out of the canebrake if I could a-holped it. I thought maybe you'd see for yourselves the river was on a bust; but you didn't. 'T was my fault not tellin' you sooner; so you see we are boun' to get you out of this. On'y don't be skeered at us. We are white men — leastwise two on us — and we've got mothers — or if we ain't now, we had — and you and that little baby's just as safe with us as you would be in heaven. We couldn't let you two drown, so be and we all went down. The Delawar' too, if he is a Injin, he's got a white man's heart. He's gone down the river thar, whar we hid the canoe, and he'll be here with it direckly. Don't be skeered; you look a good plucky one, and so does the baby."

For Rue had reached out her little hand, and pulled at the tangled beard, laughing as she did in her romps with her father.

Margaret saw tears in the reddish-brown eyes, as the baby kept up her play and laughed and crowed, as she would with a shaggy Newfoundland. The man shook the water from one rough, hairy hand, and caught the dimpled little fist and hid it for an instant in the billowy wave of his tawny beard; and a new light shone on the haggard face as he kissed the baby fingers.

"Pike" literally followed instructions. He had cut the mules loose from the wagon; fished out Oscar, who was half drowned by the struggle and the water he had swallowed; towed him ashore, and waded back to the bar, from which a few powerful strokes brought him to the still floating vehicle.

The two men now united their strength to tow it into shallow water, but the current was too rapid. All they could do was to keep it steady and afloat. Again the leader spoke to Margaret.

"I don't know what keeps the Delawar' and the canoe; but you give me the baby, marm, and then climb out here and hold on close by me till Pike can swim round to you. Don't cotch hold on him, but jus' let him take you out: he'll do it — he's a powerful strong sure swimmer. The wagon-bed will float the nigger woman till we get you out and come back for her."

At this proposal Sara commenced afresh.

"Good Godamity, Miss Marg'ret, doant leave me heah! Lemme go wid yer!"

Margaret quietly kissed Rue, and put her in the man's arms. The baby, thinking this a part of the frolic, clutched the shaggy head, and screamed her delight. For the first time Margaret spoke to the man.

"Take my little daughter to Oscar. God bless you for coming to us! I will wait with Sara until you get back."

"I'll come, marm; don't be skeered. The baby's all right. So holp me God, she and you can trust Bob Stearns!"

"I know it. I trust *you* and the mercy of our Heavenly Father."

The baby, dripping wet, but still laughing, was placed in Oscar's arms just as the now completely conquered mustang came down the divide. One look revealed to Stephen the accident. He was off his horse, threw off coat and boots, and was in the water as Bob Stearns reached the bar. Again that stout-hearted fellow was in the deep water, just in time; for the wagon, caught by the swift-increasing current, turned on its side as he reached it, and drew Margaret out. Then the slower Pike loosened the vise-like grip he had kept of the front boards, and, with a water-dog's dip and plunge, brought up Sara, who was fortunately too limp to resist or embarrass him. He swam to the bar and placed her firmly on her feet, and then turned to look for his comrade. What he saw brought out all the latent energy of the giant. His comrade, although near shallow water, was slowly sinking, overweighted, exhausted. Notwithstanding the most desperate efforts, he was going down. Margaret, understanding how she endangered her would-be deliverer, clasped her hands as she broke from him with a murmured prayer, —

"My baby — my husband — God bless —" and was swept under the muddy current.

Stephen and Pike reached the fatal spot at the same moment. Both dived — came up — dived again. This time they won salvage from the waters. Pike had tangled his hand in Margaret's brown hair, whilst Stephen had clutched the tawny mane of Bob Stearns. Pike swam ashore with his burden, and turned to meet Stephen and the Delaware pushing before them the canoe which held the apparently lifeless remains of his comrade.

CHAPTER XII.

> He had got a hurt
> O' th' inside, of a deadlier sort.
> BUTLER.

AT the moment Baby Rue was placed by Bob Stearns in Oscar's arms, Leszinksky and Captain Moore were riding rapidly down the trail which wound in reverse coils from the top of the ridge on the opposite side of the Canadian to the bank. On a little plateau overlooking the river, Captain Moore halted long enough to take his field-glasses from their case and inspect the stream. Seeing Oscar with the child in his arms by the river side, and Stephen dismounting from his mustang, he said, —

"It's all right. They *are* on the other side, but certainly not going to try the ford."

Mechanically he handed the glasses to Leszinksky, and awaited. Suddenly Leszinksky dropped the glasses, with a quickly exclaimed "God save my wife!" and rode off at Sultan's best speed. Captain Ben, rather dazed at the prayer and the action, dismounted, picked up his glasses, and from his recovered seat in the saddle again examined the shore and the river. Leszinksky had seen the wagon as it upset, and, as the curtains were up, saw that Margaret and Sara were in it. Captain Moore looked as Pike placed Sara on her feet in the shallows of the sandbar, at the instant Bob Stearns and his burden went under.

Never had the spurs of the bold dragoon raked so pitilessly the flanks of his good horse. With a mighty oath (I am sorry to record it) and a yell that was half dismay, half encouragement to his comrade, he came thundering down the bank.

Leszinksky, already in the river, was stemming the heavy current as Pike waded out with his senseless burden; and Stephen and the Delaware, who had arrived just in time to pull into the canoe the heavy weight of Bob Stearns, pushed and paddled ashore. Sultan clambered up safely with his rider, a few minutes after Pike had laid Margaret down beside her baby, on a shaded spot high up the bank. Sara, completely overcome with fright, was in violent hysterics; while Oscar, in speechless agony, knelt by his mistress, wiping the muddy stains from her fair face. As his master arrived, he looked up, and moaned, —

"O Marse Stan, Marse Stan, God has took back his angel! They did all they could, them poor men thar, but they could n't save her for us. O Marse Stan, we's on'y got her chile lef'!" And the poor fellow burst into a storm of sobs as he saw the grief-stricken face that bent over Margaret.

The young wife was lying with her hands clasped over her breast, as she had gone down in that supreme effort to liberate her rescuer. The sweet face, lit by the slanting rays of the descending sun, was of a death-like pallor. The blue eyes, partly open under violet lids, had lost their light. The white lips were closed, and ashen shadows had gathered around the mouth.

Into this group on the bank strode Captain Ben. He had had a hard fight with the rising waters. Accoutred as he was, he had plunged in, and, when his good steed was about to go under, had slipped from the saddle; and the horse, relieved of the overweight, swam easily; but his own heavy cavalry-boots would have taken Captain Ben to the bottom, had he not held to his horse's tail, and so been towed ashore. Fortunately for the sufferers to whom he arrived, his helpfulness in disaster was a quality to be counted on. Danger and reverse brought him to his best. The careless, gay dragoon of the garrison had a graver side, — a cool, collected, resolute side, — to front danger or mischance. After shaking himself like a water-spaniel, he knelt by Margaret, and slid one broad, strong hand under her shoulders, and pressed firmly the pulseless chest with the other; then spoke cheerily: —

"She's not drowned: she fainted before sinking. Run, Oscar, and look in my saddle-pocket, and bring the flask you will find. Don't be unmanned, Stan: she'll get over it; there is no water in the lungs. Here, Oscar, give me the flask. Get her feet bare, Stan, and rub them with the brandy."

All the time he was rubbing the cold hands and bathing the pale face with a touch that was as gentle as a woman's. A feeble pulsation was soon perceptible; then long-drawn, pained sighs told the suffering that came with resuscitation. In twenty minutes more they knew she would live. Then, with a final administering of his favorite remedy, Captain Ben left her lying in her husband's lap whilst he looked after the others. Stephen was soon mounted on Sultan, and started to the ranch for help. (The mustang had escaped for home the moment his rider dismounted.) Captain Ben's orders to Stephen were: —

"Ride like the devil! Bring back dry clothing and any conveyance you can get the quickest, for Mrs. Leszinksky must be out of these wet things before the evening chills her; and don't fail to bring whiskey enough for all these water-logged people. How soon can you get back?"

"As soon as zis horse he can run ten mile, I shall at home be, *mon capitaine.* It will take ten mineits to give ze or*ders* and saddle l'Empereur; he will me bring back me in twenty mineits more wiz ze whiskey and clozing for Madame Leszinksky and ze *bébé.*"

"Good! Give Sultan the spurs. I shall expect you in an hour."

"I will here be, *mon capitaine,* if it kills two horse."

Captain Ben now turned to where the gigantic Pike worked, in concert with the Delaware, for the restoration of their well-nigh-drowned comrade. They had turned over the canoe, and laid the body face downward across it. The Delaware rolled it from side to side, whilst Pike worked the lifeless arms like pump-handles above the limp head, great tears rolling down the giant's cheeks and washing furrows in the stains left by the muddy river, as his grief found expression in porpoise-like sighs, that seemed blown from the vent of a tired whale. The captain aided, slightly changing the treatment, — simulating respiration, pressing the lungs into regular rises and falls, blowing into the nostrils, and, at last when a feeble pulsation came, giving all that remained of his panacea in small doses that acted like magic. When Stephen returned the drowned man was sitting on the canoe, looking with unqualified regret at the flask he had just emptied of its last drops. His face brightened when the newly-arrived supplies were unpacked, and Captain Ben approached with a leathern drinking-cup full of whiskey, although the words that accompanied the gift somewhat damped his delight: —

"Here, Stearns. I see you have n't given up the old habit that brought you to grief before you deserted. There's some excuse for your cups now. You have swallowed more water to-day than you would like to drink in a six-months' march over the plains."

Bob hesitated an instant; then, thinking that words would keep longer than unbottled whiskey, emptied the cup first, and replied: "I see you know me, Capt'n, and I ain't sorry for it. What with the Pawnees robbing on us, and dodging soldiers and white men from the settlements, we 've had dogs' lives on the plains. It was all my doin's, — our desertin'. You know Pike always sot great store by me: he would n't let me go by myself. We ain't had but one piece of luck sence we left, and that was gittin' Black Beaver here outen the clutches of a party of Navahos who was about to brile him standin'. I s'pose you 'll take us to the fort. Now, jus' you say what you can for Pike; he wah n't to blame nohow. I 'd ruther be shot than be in the garrison with Capt'n Hartley."

Oscar, who was listening, started forward, and then suddenly stopped; whilst Captain Ben said: —

"Captain Hartley has resigned. I will have to take you to the fort. But you have behaved like a brave man to-day. You would have made your way to the Mississippi safely, if you had n't come out of that canebrake to save the wife and child of an officer. By God, they shall not shoot you, if I can help it! Give me your word that you will go to the fort, and I will leave you free to go without arrest. It will be better for you."

"Yes, Capt'n, I 'll go. I *was* a-goin' to the Mississipp', and home to Missoury; but I 'd a-always felt mean hidin' about like a thief or a Pawnee. I s'pose I 'll have to take the chances of shootin'."

"You are not shot yet, and after what you 've done to-day, 't will be damned hard to get a court-martial that won't let you off easy. Lieutenant Leszinksky, whose wife and child you have saved, belongs to 'Ours.'"

Captain Moore walked back to meet Margaret, who, with dry clothing on, now came with her husband from her dressing-closet among the scrub-pines. Pike and the Indian had gone down the river to try and secure the wagon, which was lodged against the branches of an overhanging willow. Oscar hesitated an instant, then ran to Stephen's supplies, and came back to Bob with bread and meat. Bob thanked him, and ate with the appetite of a half-starved plainsman. After he had finished, seeing that Oscar still waited, Bob asked:—

"Have you got any more of that whiskey? My bowels is powerful watery yet."

Oscar ran to the captain, and came back with the cup half full, saying apologetically, "Captain Moore say 't ain't safe to give you too much, an' you jes drownded; but I 'll try an' get you some more after while. An' I jes wanted to say to you, if thar 's anything Oscar (that 's me) kin do fur you, he 'll do it. If you don't want to go to the fort, you need n't. If you has cause to hate Captain Hartley, so has Oscar. An' to-day you brought us back the angel o' the fam'ly when she had started for heaven. If you ain't no kashun to go to the fort, *don't go.* We's all got to go back to Marse Caslar's; but Marse Stephen an' me will fix it so you kin go your own way 'fore the week 's out."

"So be and 't had been yesterday you'd a-offered to holp us, I'd a been glad and thankful; but you see I 'm a soldier, if I did desert, and I 've jus give my parole to the capt'n. I must stay here now, and I must go to the fort to-morrow. I 'll keep my word to the capt'n. I 'd like to be with the regiment, if Capt'n Hartley's gone."

"What did he do to you?" asked Oscar, with the *naïve*, straightforward manner of a child.

Bob's face grew black and angry; but after a moment he answered, simply: "He bucked and gagged me the fust time I was drunk when he commanded. That wah n't so much. The next time he give me thirty-nine lashes and chained me by the thumbs to a wagon for a two-days' march. You can see the marks yet; a piece of this left thumb sloughed off. Pike unchained me when he see it had cut through the flesh, and he had Pike bucked and whipped. *Then* I deserted."

Oscar drew a deep breath.

"He did worse fur me. Somehow, when I think of it, I know I 'll kill him yet. Leastwise, I 'm sho the Lord 'll deliver him into my han'. If it had n't a-been fur Miss Marg'ret, I 'd a-killed him that day."

The negro walked away: Leszinksky was coming.

"King Stan" offered his hand to Bob, saying, "I owe you a debt I can never pay, but which I shall never forget. Captain Moore has told me your troubles, and we hope to get you out of them safely. You may count on all we can do."

"Thank you, Leftenant; but you don't owe me nothin' for what I did for yo' wife and that little baby. I oughter a-come out of the cane-brake sooner, and saved them a-gettin' in. I mought a-knowed they would n't know the river was up. Howsomever, I did my best arterwards, and I 'm powerful glad they 're safe. I ain't seen a little child like that sence I left Missoury. If my wife had a-lived, and I 'd a-had a little child like that in my cabin, I would n't a-been the worthless cuss I am. She 's a good, plucky one, that little one, Leftenant; and that nigger ain't fur wrong when he calls her mother a angel. When she give me her child, and said she trusted her to *me* and God's mercy, I did n't know what *God* mought do, but so be and a man could save 'em both, I knowed I would."

CHAPTER XIII.

*To be weak is miserable,
Doing or suffering.*
      MILTON.

MARGARET was ill at Castalar's for some time after the accident. Before her arrival at Bouie's Hill, Bob Stearns and Pike had been tried, sentenced, and then pardoned " in consideration of their gallant conduct and voluntary return to the regiment." Black Beaver was enlisted in the corps of scouts. So the Leszinksky's had frequent occasion to bring to their home these men, whose well-being and well-doing had for them deep personal interest.

The Fourth of July, Oscar came back from the fort early in the afternoon with some things needed for the dinner, to which all our friends were invited, and this one piece of news: —

"I's sorry, Miss Marg'ret, to have to tole you, but when I went to tole Black Beaver an' our soljers as you'd expect 'em to eat thar Fourth out heah, I foun' Marse Bob Stearns too drunk to come. Marse Pike an' the Injin has to stay to keep him outer trouble. They say he's a powerful han' to quarrel when he's a-drinkin'. That's what's always gone wrong with him. If he can't get no fightin' of his own, he's sho to get somebody else's. Jes now at the fort he done knocked down Mike O'Dowd, 'cause he was disrespeckful talkin' 'bout me and my — my misfortshun."

Either Pike and Black Beaver had drunk too much themselves to be efficient guards, or else in some way

Bob flanked his friends. Before sundown he got into a "free fight," and spent the night in the guard-house, where, the next morning, by some process known only to himself, Oscar furnished him a comfortable breakfast. The jug of strong coffee had its effect, for when released Bob came out sober, sorry, and ashamed at the violation of the pledge he had only a week before made our saint. The certain result, if left to himself, would have been a fresh debauch. Remorse and shame go against a man of weak will; and poor Bob's good resolutions were as yet untwisted flax, powerless to resist the pull of habit. This day Bob had a new experience: he was not left undefended to the fierce thirst that had hitherto led him, helpless and unnerved, into the power of the enemy that was spoiling him of his manhood. A friend stood in the way of the tempter. A peerless Sir Galahad, all the more pitying because of his own perfect purity, waited at the guardhouse door to save him from a fresh assault, — a stainless knight, whose heart was the shrine of the Holy Grail; for in it burned the strong love of humanity that had taken Jesus of Nazareth into the haunts of publicans and sinners.

At the first sight of Leszinksky, Bob recoiled, and then turned the other way, pulling his cap low over his eyes. A kindly hand was on his shoulder. Though at first he looked down abashed, he felt the eyes that finally drew his own and held them, as the words came slowly and with a sympathetic intonation that seemed to the rough soldier a voice from heaven.

"We are all grieved at this new trouble, Bob, — we who love you and who owe you so much. But for you, I should have neither wife nor child. Whenever I thank God for their spared lives I am thanking Him for your unselfish courage, for the manhood that is in you. I do not think you know how we suffer in the fall of a friend we fain would respect. Any stain upon you, any failure in that brave nature of yours, grieves and hurts the family you saved. It also shames us in that we are so heavily your debtors, and yet cannot defend you from the evil that pursues and ruins you. You must come home with me. I have waited for you, and my wife is waiting for us both."

"Please, Leftenant, I can't go now. I ain't fit. I don't want to see *her* nor the baby jus' now. I ain't wuth the trouble you've done took a'ready."

"You must come, Bob."

"I'll come in the mornin', sir; I've got to go on duty, sir, this evenin'."

"No, that is arranged. I have an order from Captain Moore. You are to stay at Bouie's Hill until the company changes quarters."

"Please let me come in the mornin', sir. I don't want to go thar like this."

There was repentance as well as shame in the eyes that looked into Leszinksy's; but the evil habit clutched the sensitive nerves until they quivered with longing for the poison that "doth mock the meat it feeds on." The poor drunkard felt that nothing but the devil's fluid could quench the flame of remorse. The trinity in man was disturbed: mind and soul had succumbed to the bondage of the flesh, and the anguished heart would fain have sought forgetfulness of its pangs in a fresh insensibility of drink.

"I dare not trust you, Bob. You are not in a state to resist the craving that is even now upon you."

"No, Leftenant, I ain't. I must have a drink. My nerves is a-shakin' for it. If you'll let me get one, sir, I'll come."

"No: come with me now."

Bob followed. At the doctor's quarters Leszinksy stopped, and bade the soldier come in. Leaving him in the office, Leszinksy sought the doctor in his private room.

"Doctor, I have brought Stearns to see you before taking him to Bouie's Hill. He is shaky and nervous, and begs for a drink. What shall I do?"

"Give him one. Without it, after such a debauch, he risks *delirium tremens*."

"Would not that be feeding the appetite for alcohol? Captain Moore tells me that Stearns is powerless to resist this mania after the first drink. Have you no tonic that will strengthen the nervous system sufficiently to permit a short stop?"

"I can give opiates, which are dangerous; or emetics, that will relieve the strain on the nerves, but then the penalty may come upon the stomach and bowels. I had one case that resulted in a fatal hemorrhage."

"Is medical skill, then, powerless to repair the physical derangement that follows debauch?"

"It has as yet found no antidote to the subtle poison of alcohol, — a poison that thoroughly impregnates the brain, breeding the most fierce and craving desire for reindulgence, whilst it stupefies the moral quality of resistance to evil."

"There must be a physical cure for its physical effects. Nature is too richly endowed by the All-Father to fail where failure wrecks so many of her children."

"I trust the discovery will reward a greater than Hervey. There is no puzzle to medical science like this presented by the drunkard. Year after year men die by thousands, poisoned by alcohol. Prisons are filled with criminals whom law has held to account, although their crimes were committed under the sway of the most fatal and uncontrollable insanity known to physicians: and this very poisoning, which always ends in death (sometimes long delayed, but then more terrible in suffering), madness, or idiocy is in a measure legalized. The sale of alcoholic drinks is unrestrained; the profits enormous: human vampires fatten on the blood of its victims. Law, which in England condemned the suicide, and in this country punishes the vendor who sells him quick oblivion of the ills of life, lets the distiller and trader in alcohol, who put a criminal or a madman in nearly every family in the land, go unwhipt of justice."

"Then, Doctor, you do not believe in the moral accountability of the drunkard?"

"In the main, no. In the beginning of the evil, society is responsible for the custom that commends a brain poison to the untainted palates of the young; and then society is again responsible for the condemnation of the victim who has lost all will-power to resist the destroyer."

"Then there is no hope for this poor fellow to whom I owe so much, and for whose redemption from this slavery to hell-fire I would give all that a man may give to save a friend?"

"Yes; there is always hope in the power of human love and human sympathy. In Stearns's case the habit is spasmodic. There are intervals for patient affection to work a moral cure. Find a motive for regeneration stronger than the physical appetite, and his case is hopeful. Nothing short of a miracle will stop the regular drinker,—and miracles do not occur in the nineteenth century. The spasmodic drunkard can cure himself if will is strengthened by an unselfish desire to save from pain and suffering some one dearer than self. I know of nothing else that will insure the victory. The first difficulty in this case is tiding over the tendency to *delirium tremens*."

"With God's help I shall struggle for his salvation point by point. What shall I do first?"

"Give him a simple but nourishing diet, plenty of milk, constant but light exercise in the open air. If he cannot sleep—then opiates: but still keep him in the air, on horseback when possible; that is of itself a narcotic. *Above all, give him a motive to reform, a reason for self-control.* I fear you will find that you have set yourself a Herculean task."

"Doctor, you forget what I owe Stearns. With my great debt in the balance, any task that may do him good will seem light. Moreover, I feel sure of help from the Father who watches over us all."

"Ah, Leszinksky, if faith were contagious, and you could infect him with your beliefs, cure would be certain! Even I am ready to admit that such 'faith can remove mountains,'—not by abstract thought and wish, but by its constant striving with the little things, with the trivialities of a very material universe."

"Doctor, would that I might infect *you* by so much as 'a grain of mustard seed.'"

"You have, in so far that I believe in the earnestness of your beliefs. They are not mere beliefs, barren of effect; they are something more: they are motives for action that are fruitful of result. Yours is a kindly infection. I hope it may spread."

CHAPTER XIV.

> For years the Indians clung to the homes of their forefathers, and it was at the cost of much blood and treasure that they were finally expelled from that country.
> BRACKETT.

LATE in the fall of '45, a little more than a year after the accident at the ford of the Canadian, the 1st Regiment of Dragoons was in almost constant service in the Indian Territory: consequently Leszinksky was frequently absent from Bouie's Hill.

The dismounting of one regiment in 1843 — through the false economy of the lip-patriots in Congress, who were constantly meddling with the details of the War Department — had caused such a weakening of the little army on the frontier that every mounted officer and man of the small force left was almost continually in the saddle.

The vacillation of the Government in its Indian affairs was then, as now, the curse of the savage as well as of the frontiersman. Its revocation and modification of treaties which had been signed as final adjustment of real grievances; its constant changes of policy from the tyranny of the autocrat to the subservience of the trader; the causeless arrest and equally causeless release of friendly chiefs, — to say it in the very mildest form, *seemed like treachery*. Naturally, the savage became exasperated and distrustful. The entire history of the Seminole War, and the removal of the feeble remnant of the broken tribes across the Mississippi, was a disgrace to the nation, — but not to the army, which simply obeyed orders, after its wisest and bravest officers had remonstrated in vain against their execution. At the close of a campaign in which the Seminole chiefs had shown courage, endurance, and patriotism that Greece would have rewarded with monuments, and Rome with civic triumphs, General Jessup thus writes to the Secretary of War: "In regard to the Seminoles, we have committed the error of attempting to remove them when their lands were not required for agricultural purposes; *when they were not in the way of the white inhabitants.* We exhibit in our present contest the first instance, perhaps, since the commencement of authentic history, of a nation employing an army to remove a band of savages from one wilderness to another. As a soldier, it is my duty, I am aware, not to comment upon the policy of the Government, but to carry it out in accordance with my instructions. I have endeavored faithfully to do so; but the prospect of terminating the war is anything but flattering. Unless immediate emigration be abandoned, it will continue for years — and at constantly increasing expense. Is it not, then, well worthy the consideration of an enlightened government whether — even if the wilderness we are traversing could be inhabited by the white man, which is not the fact — the object we are contending for would be worth the cost."

To this the Secretary replied that the Government desired "their removal *or extermination.*" The first act of obedience to this order was an invitation to a friendly council. Five hundred and thirteen Indians accepted, hoping for peace and trusting the Government. Colonel Twiggs was ordered to "seize the whole party." The leading chiefs and warriors had refused to come. Osceola, Coacoochee,[1] Hospetarke, with their tribes, and the little remnant of valiant Mickasuckies — who foot by foot had defended their country upon the Swa-a-nee from the time of the landing of De Soto, — had learned to distrust such invitations. Osceola and Coacoochee had been taught by personal experience that the council-chamber of the white man was the ante-chamber of a prison. The escape of the latter from San Augustine was a marvel of adroitness and courage.

[1] Co-a-coo-chee, — Wild Cat.

The son of King Philip, exceedingly handsome, mild and amiable in manner, a fearless and daring leader, a generous friend and magnanimous foe, endowed with great personal bravery,—Coacoochee was the idol of the younger warriors. Although determined to resist the forcible removal of his people, he had been the friend, and would have been the ally, of the white man.

The seizure and forcible emigration of these Indians, who had hoped by prompt submission to secure for their tribes the privilege of living and dying in their native villages in the Everglades, and the enslavement of their allies, had the immediate effect of uniting for common defence against the aggressors the younger chiefs — whose petty jealousies had fallen before the common danger — and Ar-pe-i-ka (better known as "Sam Jones, the fisherman"), who had sworn eternal enmity to the white race.

The war was now fierce and earnest; the newly established trading post on the Caloosahatchie was attacked, and, with the exception of Colonel Harvey and thirteen men who escaped, the entire garrison massacred. In revenge, Harvey organized an expedition to the Everglades, and utterly destroyed the tribe to which the marauders belonged. Chikika, the chief, and twelve of the leading men of the tribe were left hanging in chains, as warnings of the vengeance of the white man. The warning had no effect. Coacoochee, with two hundred warriors, attacked a fort garrisoned by detachments from the Second, Third, and Fourth Artillery, and four companies of dragoons. The boldness and desperation of the assault, which lasted three hours, obstinately repeated after each fresh repulse, convinced the Government of the determined character of the leader and the resolution of his followers. More troops were sent to Florida. The Indians, heavily outnumbered, retired to the fastnesses of the Big Cypress Swamp, the desolate islands of which afforded refuge to the women and children, whilst the warriors defended, from the hummocks, its outposts; occasionally making predatory excursions through the very camps of the enemy who environed them.

The Government now brought fresh allies into the field. At great expense, it imported bloodhounds from Cuba, bringing with them their Spanish trainers. Atrocious massacres were followed by atrocious reprisals. The first publicly to denounce the use of bloodhounds as allies was Mr. Wise, of Virginia, who, in the House of Representatives, made the inquiry: "Whether the general Government had been a participator in so infamous a mode of exterminating human creatures."

More determined in their defence grew the chiefs, who made their last desperate stand on the hummocks of the Big Cypress. These hummocks, surrounded by water from two to three feet in depth, swarming with reptiles, were made more impassable by fallen trees and brushwood. The need that had made warriors, now taught engineering. Advance after advance of the United States troops was repelled. But numbers and the murderous weapons of civilization told. Even then success was delayed; so, finally, a spy was found who knew the secret passes; a traitor was bought; a path to the last shelter of the broken tribes was open. There was a final assault, a terrible butchery. The dragoons, whose feet and hands were cut and bleeding, by the swordgrass (the only ally of the Seminoles), were not in the humor to be merciful: they were men, and men are cruel when resistance has enraged them. The very officers, whose honest opinions, when expressed in private discussion, had justified the Seminole chiefs in the brave defence of the land of their ancestors, now cried, "Kill!" as they remembered the comrades dead in the fatal hummocks, the friends shot by the watchfires in the camp.

The Secretary was obeyed: they were nearly "*exterminated.*" There was to be *peace* in Florida, and, to secure it, her children were to be torn from the soil or destroyed.

A captive for the second time, loaded with chains, in the midst of enemies, and threatened with an ignominious death, the bearing of Coacoochee was that of a king. He awaited his doom with composure and dignity. The only threat that drew from him reply was " that unless he submitted to the will of the Government, and removed, with his people, peaceably across the Mississippi, every captive warrior would be hung to the yards of the vessel" (broken and in chains, they had not dared trust to imprisonment on shore), " for he only could and *must* end the war." His reply is a complete and eloquent epitome of the relative positions of the white and red races in North America. It depicts the first childlike trust of the Indian, — a trust from which he was driven by repeated and cruel wrongs — and how his just resentment of outrage was made the excuse for pillage and extermination.

" I was once a boy," said he, in subdued tones; " then I saw the white man afar off. I hunted in these woods, first with a bow and arrow, then with a rifle. I saw the white man and was told he was my enemy. *He said he was my friend.* He gave me his hand in friendship. I took it. Whilst taking it, he had a snake in the other. His tongue was forked. He lied, and stung me. *I could not shoot him as I would a wolf or a panther; yet like these he came upon me.* Horses, cattle, and fields, he took from me. He abused our women and children, and told us to go from the land. I asked but for a small piece of these lands, enough to plant and to live upon, far south, — a spot where I could lay the ashes of my kindred. This was not granted me. I was put in prison. I escaped. I have again been taken. You have brought me back. I am here — *in chains. I feel the irons in my heart.* You say I *must* end the war. Look at these irons. Can I go to my warriors? Coacoochee chained! No: do not ask me to see them. I never wish to tread upon my land unless I am free."

His captor, Colonel Worth, was only the mouthpiece of the Government when he made the chief understand the inevitable, —" Submission to removal, or extermination." The Indian was then being taught the lesson so often repeated: *that his land was his only until the white man was ready to claim it.*

The Seminoles submitted. The remnant that had escaped the butchery of the Big Cypress came in voluntarily when they heard of the danger which menaced their chief. They consented to emigrate. With their wrongs rankling in their hearts, they were removed to the territory west of the line of military posts that guarded the Arkansas frontier.

The 1st Dragoons, who had fought them in Florida, were now their neighbors at Fort Gibson. So were their late foes, the Creeks. Forty refugee Creek warriors (whose homes had attracted the greed of Georgia settlers) had fought as allies of the Seminoles and Mickasuckies in the battle of the Big Cypress; although there was opposed to them a Creek regiment, whose major, a Creek Indian, had graduated at West Point. Surrounded by these discordant elements, one mounted regiment of dragoons, three companies of infantry, and a small detachment of artillery were to keep the peace upon a long line of frontier.

As stated in the beginning of this chapter, in the fall of 1845, officers and men of the 1st Dragoons, stationed at Fort Gibson, were almost constantly on scout. True, the dismounted Second Regiment had been restored to that acme of all hope to a cavalryman, — a seat in the saddle; but the mutterings of war on the Mexican border had compelled a gathering of Taylor's "Army of Observation" at Corpus Christi, in readiness for any contingency. The reserves at Fort Gibson had been called for; so the force actually there were kept at hard and constant work. There were rumors of incursions of hostile tribes. A large party of young Seminole braves had ostensibly gone on a distant hunt; but old Indian fighters among the officers and men began to examine the trails more curiously. They knew the war-path was open.

PART IV.

BABY RUE.

But oh! as to embrace me she inclined,
I waked; she fled; and day brought back my night.
JOHN MILTON.

PART IV.

BABY RUE.

CHAPTER XV.

CALAMITY is man's true touchstone.
BEAUMONT AND FLETCHER.

EXCEPT the frequent absence of Leszinksky and the two soldiers, who now belonged of right to the family, there had been few changes at Bouie's Hill. The one likely to prove most grievous to that loving little circle was, as yet, scarcely perceptible to a casual observer. Margaret's health was gradually failing. No apparent disease; but ever since that illness at Castalar's, after the accident, she had slowly succumbed to a growing feebleness and delicacy which the doctor had watched with anxious solicitude. Leszinksky, ordinarily so clear-sighted, so observant, and carefully tender of his wife, was completely deceived by the bright color and gay spirits that marked, at his return, the feverish reaction from languor during his now almost constantly enforced absence.

The rest of the family news can best be gleaned by an evening with Uncle Abram. It was the twenty-fourth of December. A bright fire of pine-knots, which the old man had gathered in the hills "up the river" to make a hospitable light when the comfortable cabin held guests the patriarch delighted to honor, gave the high lights and deep shadows of a Rembrandt. In front of the fireplace was a table upon which Solomon was arranging a medley collection of delf, the last pieces of many sets that had adorned hall and kitchen at Mount Hope through the changes of four generations. The light-wood knots were burning in the end of the huge fireplace near where the guests were sitting, whilst in the other Mead was watching the red coals that covered his 'possum roast, while he carefully turned the hoe-cakes that both sides might have the required color of golden brown. In a sheltered corner the coffee steamed slowly. Near the pot sat Uncle Abram, and from his coigne of vantage in the shadow he could watch his aids at their work, and yet not lose the admiring looks his guests gave the preparations for the evening feast. These favored guests were the gigantic "Pike" and Black Beaver. The giant sat in the corner near the bright blaze which bronzed his yellow hair and ruddy complexion, deepening the blue eyes until they looked like purple amethysts set in the huge face of some roughly-sculptured Viking. Near him Black Beaver reclined at ease upon a shaggy buffalo robe, his blanket thrown aside for the greater luxury of the fire. Moccasins and leggings removed, the shapely limbs showed their network of compact, sinewy muscles. The *ensemble* of light and shade, the rough walls with their mixed ornaments, — here a hideous print in the style of art known to the decorative department of the travelling showman, there a magnificent pair of antlers, — a dresser decked with the dishes Solomon dared not heap upon the table, an old musket, and numberless strings of onions and dried pumpkin, with here and there bunches of savory herbs hanging from the rafters, combined to form a picture that would have delighted an artist.

The taciturn guests left to Uncle Abram the delight of a continuous flow of talk. Mead's occupation was too serious for conversation, and even Solomon rarely found time to interrupt the patriarch with question or correction; so the stream ran freely.

"Yer see ef Marse Stan has to go wid de army to Mexiker, ef dey can't do widouten him, fur he's de on'y one ob dem ossifers dat wus bawn a gineral, — least ways his gran'fadder was one, — den I dunno what's gwine to become o' Miss Marg'ret. She's a gittin' dat peekid an' white dat I 's mos' 'fraid she 's got de ager an' fever consumshun. (See heah, Mead, you 'tend to dat 'possum! I s'pec' he 's a burnin'. I smell de cabbage leaves dat 's roun' him a scorchin'.) Well, ef she don't go wid Marse Stan, den she 'll git wusser every day. I 's noticed dat 's what she 's a doin' all de time. Now dis very day befo' Marse Stan cum home she look white as my Miss Mary did dat summer she lef' us, an' jes as soon as he got heah her cheeks is like dem big damas' roses at Mount Hope, an' her eyes as bright as dat light-wood a burnin'. I tell yer she 's got fever an' ager consumshun sho. (Solomon, don't yer touch dat big dish; yo' 's too rambitious fur yo' size.) It 's a good thing Miss Cas'ler tuck little Miss Rue wid her to de ranch. She was a-aggravatin' her mother an' makin' her wuss. I never did see a chile like her nohow. She ain't quite three year ole an' she sticks on dat little Injin pony Marse Bob Stearns brung her, jes like a monkey. I s'pec' dem ole Desinkskys mus' a had some Injin blood. She ac' like it, she do. I don't mean no 'fence to you, Black Beaver; but she ar' *dat* cantakerous when yer try to make her behave like a little white lady. Not as I kin say she cries or hollers; fur she don't dat. But 't ain't no use wurritin' her. I see Miss Marg'ret done guv up tryin' to break her in. Not dat she don't lub her mother needer, but yer see she 's jes bawn havin' her own way. She do mine her father, now she knows he 's a Desinksky too; but she ain't 'fraid o' *him* one bit. She go 'bout doin' what he say in sich a way, so proud-like, dat it 's jes sayin', ' I mine yer, cos I want to ; ef I did n't, I would n't.' An' she would n't. But fur all she so proud-like, she ain't got one bit o' proper seristocratic notion; she ain't. Now she don't take to *me;* but she 'll do anything for Oscar, cos he don't never 'tradict her in nothin'. An' Marse Bob Stearns, drunk or sober, she 's his frien'. Now dat time las' Easter, an' she wah n't but two year ole, when Marse Bob got on dat big spree an' rode up de steps ob de porch dar, an' ax her to clum up in his lap, she did it, an' on'y laffed an' hollered when he made de hoss jump offen de end ob de porch an' flinged bofe ob 'em. An' when Miss Marg'ret run out all tremblin' an' pick her up, befo' Oscar heerd de noise an' could get dar, why, she jes would n't go in widouten Marse Bob; an' I *mus'* say, it sobered him, an' he ain't been drunk since. (Mead, I know dat 'possum's done; did n't I tole yer long ago? Now jes' look at dem cabbage leaves yo's a peelin' off; dey's burnt all to rags; but I mus' say it do smell good. Now take dem 'taters outen de fire. *Solomon!* let de table 'lone. Don't do no good to keep a fixin' de dishes an' yo' all de time stealin' dat sugar.)"

"No, I ain't, Grandaddy; I on'y spilled a little on my han' a moovin' of it. Dat's all I eat."

"Well, yo' quit a movin' of it, or I 'll move yo' up de lof' widouten any supper. Now, Marse Pike, ef you 'll sot at dat end ob de table dar, an' 't ain't no 'fence to you, Black Beaver and me 'll sot here at dis side."

And so the Viking was throned above the salt: thus the rude courtesy of a negro cabin defined the difference in race. Pike and Black Beaver now opened their mouths to some purpose, and Uncle Abram was silenced by the savory morsels the two attendants heaped upon his plate.

There were also guests in the dining-room of Bouie's Hill. At the fort, Leszinksky, newly arrived from an expedition up the Arkansas in search of a band of marauding Pawnees, had met Carson and Captain Ben just in from the Creek country; they gladly accepted his invitation to accompany him home. Another welcome addition to the party arrived at sundown, — the doctor, who had been on a visit to the family of the Cherokee chief at Talequah. Margaret's hot, feverish hand determined him to warn Leszinksky. Glancing from her burning cheek to her husband, he said, "It is well you are home, Leszinksky. I do not like Mrs. Leszinksky's languor when you are away any better than I do this very high color, which is certainly feverish."

"Don't believe him, Mrs. Leszinksky," broke in Captain Ben's cheery voice, "you were never looking better. Randall's getting to be a regular calomel croaker. He has certainly frightened the color out of Leszinsky's brown face; so, to get even, keep yours. Why, Miss Stephanie has a little pale-rose bloom in her cheeks this evening, because Randall's pill-bags have been at Talequah for a week"; and he pinched the shell-like ear of the daughter of Paul Castalar, and went on with a merry teasing which the little child-woman resented with a gravity that delighted him.

Leszinsky's fears *were* aroused. All through the supper he watched Margaret's face, and grew more grave as he began to understand the story it told: she was much thinner, and that deep circle around the eyes and the blue veins of the pale temples, were all parts of the history. Carson, too, was observant; and Margaret, feeling the watching, blushed and paled visibly. Then somehow Captain Ben caught the prevailing infection of fear; and, to hide it, grew more noisy. The doctor led the conversation into another channel of anxiety by an inquiry: —

"What of the Seminole hunting-party, Captain Moore? Has it gone to Mexico?"

"Yes; it is impossible to believe anything else. Black Beaver and Stearns followed them to the Washita River, whilst we waited in camp on the South Canadian near their village. They were positive that it was a war party. Black Beaver is the best trailer I know, and Stearns's judgment as a frontiersman is simply perfect. Moreover, I learned from some friendly Indians that the party was composed of young Seminole braves and the disaffected Creeks who came with the Seminoles from Florida. I know what they are up to. The Indian women were all left at the village, provisioned for the winter, whilst the negro settlement is deserted, — which proves it was no hunting expedition. The young braves are burning for martial fame and a seat in the council. I saw Coacoochee and saw that he had no love for us. He has not forgotten old scores, although he has learned that peace is the policy of his people. It is possible that he could not control the young men. It is also possible that he did not care to, if they were sufficiently prudent in the start not to inculpate those who stay at home."

"Do you think there will be trouble here?" asked the doctor.

"None; unless from the Pawnees, who will naturally grow bolder as our force is weakened. Leszinksky can tell you news of them."

"Very little that is certain," said Leszinksky. "We only learned that there are small marauding parties out along the frontier. We heard of two which were going toward the Canadian and probably further south. The most alarming rumor is that they have made, or are about to make, an alliance with the Comanches of Senaco's band. I know they are in motion, — their signals were always before us. We saw the smoke rising from peak to peak of every hill-top on our way out. The signals multiplied behind us as we returned."

"You did not tell me of that, Leszinksky," said Captain Moore. "I don't like the idea of these signals following you. Where did you leave them?"

"At the junction of the Red Fork."

"What direction from you?"

"South. Nearly all the hill-tops south caught the signal and answered."

"Did you report that fully to Colonel Kearny?"

"I mentioned the signals, but possibly did not give them the importance they deserved."

"They are all-important when the hostiles are out on a foray. I should not wonder if they struck some outlying ranch near us. Who is at Castalar's?"

"My baby — Rue is there!" broke in Margaret excitedly. "She is coming home to-morrow."

"Calm yourself, my dear Mrs. Leszinksky. She is in no danger. We are just in from the suspected districts; but in a week or two it might not be quite safe. Fortunately I sent Stearns to Castalar's to tell him to guard his cattle from thieving parties, and also to advise that he send the non-fighting part of the family here. I do not know that Rue belongs to the peace party, but still she will come with the non-combatants." And Captain Moore laughed heartily, partly at Rue's well-known peace principles, and partly to calm her mother.

Before the ring of the laughter died the door opened, and Bob Stearns staggered in, more haggard and wild in appearance than when we first met him at the ford of the Canadian. He looked at Margaret, and then dropped on his knees with his face covered by his hands. All sprang to their feet. Leszinksky put his arm around his wife, who paled and trembled like an aspen, before the coming storm.

"What is it, man? Can't you speak?" said Captain Moore.

"Take *her* out of here before I tell it. God o' mercy, take her out!"

"My baby — Rue — my darling! She loved you — tell me what of her? It is *that* I know. Oh, tell me! If God has taken her I can bear it. She is safe with my Heavenly Father — tell me it is THAT!"

"Tell her," said the doctor, forcing Bob to speak. "This suspense is worse than what you have to tell."

"She ain't dead, marm. I wish to God she was, so be and you could bar it. She's a prisoner with them damned Pawnees. She's the only human thing they spar'd outen the butchery thar at Castalar's."

The bolt had gone straight to the mother's heart. There was no outcry, — only a pitiful white face, with a wan, unmeaning smile upon it, turned from one to another, and then with a murmured "My little daughter, you said — I do not understand. Rue? Baby Rue! She is coming to-morrow, for Christmas — my baby. She will come, Stan. It is her *fête* day. You remember, Doctor, she was christened on Christmas. You are all here in time. Her god-father, too — just in time. Madame Castalar will bring her. Don't cry, Bob — she loves you. I always can trust you now. You have not been drunk since that day I thought you had killed her. What is wrong with you all? Rue is coming — Baby Rue! Are you not glad, Stan?" then a burst of hysterical tears and mad laughter, calling her child, always calling her child, — "Baby Rue, little daughter! Rue! Rue! Baby Rue!"

8

CHAPTER XVI.

O the difference of divers men in the tenderness of their consciences! Some are scarcely touched with a wound, whilst others are wounded with a touch therein. — FULLER.

IT is needful for the understanding of this history to go back to the moment when, in obedience to Captain Moore's order, Bob left the command to warn Castalar of the probable incursion of thieving parties of hostiles. A few weeks previous Bob had met at the fort a trapper, an old comrade, in from the headwaters of the San Bois. The trapper had given a very accurate description of the situation of his camp; and a cordial invitation to Bob to visit it, if at any time his duties as scout led him to that neighborhood. Remembering the solitary condition of his old friend, who had no idea of any immediate trouble with Indians, Bob thought it no violation of orders to make a slight *détour* from the direct route to Castalar Valley and give the trapper the benefit of the warning he was taking to the ranch.

The camp was at the head of a secluded little ravine, through which flowed one of the smallest tributaries of the San Bois. The judgment of the old Indian fighter had ruled in its selection. The winding path that led up the ravine was on a low ledge of broken rock overhung by jutting points fringed with lengths of trailing vines that touched the tops of the swamp-willows that formed a dense thicket on the south side of the boggy banks of the little rivulet. Across the narrow stream on the north, pond-lilies grew to the very edge of the abrupt and perpendicular cliff. At the head of the ravine the bluffs widened suddenly, and then joined at the point where a little cascade issued from a clear, cold spring in the cleft rock; thus forming a circular setting of wooded heights to a lovely little valley which the spray had kept fresh and green up to this late season.

It was after sunset: the trapper had not yet returned from his rounds, but, sure of his welcome, Bob unsaddled and tethered his horse, and, finding in the Comanche-like lodge of his friend ample provision, commenced the preparation of the evening meal, chuckling with quiet glee as he thought of the surprise he was about to give his old comrade of the plains. The meal ready, Bob waited until hunger got the better of courtesy. After eating his supper, he remembered a package of tobacco he had seen on an upper shelf of the lodge, so he added a few logs to the fire and took a burning brand of dry pine to light his search. Unfortunately, behind the tobacco was a large flat bottle of whiskey. Resolutely Bob turned from the temptation, but out in the growing darkness, try all he could, — and he did try manfully, — the bottle, like Macbeth's dagger, was palpable to sight. The pipe no longer soothed: it only suggested a greater pleasure. One habit indulged, the suppression of the other grew more difficult. The old, mad longing for alcohol came upon him in his loneliness. One by one the sophisms of the drunkard hushed the voice of reason — of conscience. "He would take just one drink, only one. That could do no harm. He was tired and sleepy. He would only take a moderate drink, and then doze out there under the stars until his friend came. He had been with Black Beaver on that long scout to the Washita. He needed a drink; people always needed anything they craved like this; he had heard the doctor say as much long ago, that time he had the fever in Florida. *Only one drink*, and then he would wrap up in his blanket and sleep out here by the fire. That would do him good. He would then be all strengthened and ready for that long ride to-morrow. He could get to Castalar's to breakfast, and report at the fort in the evening. He was not ordered to be there sooner." And so the fiend conquered him.

It was nearly midnight when the trapper returned, and found Bob lost to consciousness in the deep, heavy sleep of the drunkard.

The sun was shining brightly in the little valley when Bob awoke. Sleeping in the clear, crisp air had nearly sobered him. The sight of his friend and the smell of the freshly made coffee brought him to his feet.

"I say, Tisson, if you had n't a-told me all about the windin's of this little creek I never could a-found yo' place up here. It's a mighty good thing it's so well hid, for I jus' come to tell you them damned Pawnees is up agin."

"I know it; I seed 'em: but hurry up now, and souse yo' head in that trough thar to git the kinks outen it. Yer mos' finished all my meddysin fur me las' night."

Looking like a school-boy who has deserved and awaits punishment, Bob obeyed. Two or three times he plunged his head in the trough of running water, which seemed warm in that sharp December air, and then rubbed it vigorously with a rough towel, that hanging upon a pole above the trough made a luxurious toilet equipage for a backwoodsman.

The hot coffee and venison steak in a measure repaired the effects of the debauch, which had not lasted long enough to get the nerves fully in the toils. Tisson soon cleared away the remains of the breakfast, and, producing pipes and tobacco, was ready to exchange news. The trapper began : —

"I knowed thar must be mischief up. I was down thar on the San Bois yesteddy about sundown — below the mouth of this here branch. It jus' happened I had tied my hoss about a half mile furder up in the bushes, and was a lookin' along at my traps thar, when I heerd somebody comin'. I thought fust about you, and then I thought maybe it mought n't be you, and I better not show thar was any traps thar. So I stooped down in the bushes and presently one o' them cussed Pawnees come ridin' along in his war-paint. Now, that tuck me all aback. You see the imperence o' the varmint, way over here outen his beat, right under the nose o' the fort you may say, and I was jus' a-goin' to fetch him (I had a cl'ar bead on him) when I seed the bundle he was carryin' was a little young un. Now, you see, if 't was a white child he had stole I mought a hurt it, and if 't was a pappoose and I killed him I would n't know what to do with it, cos, you see, I could n't brain it like a Injin would. So I was kinder kumflabbergasted. He was a powerful mean-lookin' Injin. I saw him close, fur he brushed the bushes whar I was. His nose was cut bad, and thar was a long scar clar across the side of his face. I 'm sho' some dragoon must a done it, fur it looked like a sabre-cut. Jus' when he passed me the young un kicked and fit, and give a mad-like little cry, and somethin' dropped right by me. It was on'y a little moccasin, so I knowed it was a pappoose and I let him go on. And it was mighty well I did, fur ten minutes arter I saw a whole pack o' them red devils ridin' 'long the other side the creek, all in thar war-paint and a drivin' a lot o' hosses and mustangs, haltered together, that they mus' a stole. If it had n't been fur this little moccasin, that I kep' cos 't was so purty, I 'd a-been sho that young un was a white child they 'd stole."

"Lemme see that moccasin," said Bob, with a face so scared and white that Tisson sprang to his feet in alarm as he handed the tiny thing to Bob.

"Yes, it 's hers; I brought 'em to her from up the Osage country. That 's two weeks ago, and she would n't war anything else"; and the poor fellow looked at the little covering of a baby's foot as if his sense of all else on earth had vanished.

"Who? What do you mean? Why, Bob, I believe you 're drunk yet."

"This is the wust cuss the liquor 's brought me yet. It 's jus' that, and I swore to myself the day I mos' killed her that I 'd quit. If I had n't been drunk when you come last night we mought a-got her out o' thar clutches. And now — now I can't tell what devils' doin's has been at Castalar's; and I did n't know she was thar; and her mother — they must a-killed her mother 'fore they got *her*."

"Who is she, Bob? Are you drunk or crazy?"

"It's the little capt'n's moccasin, — little Miss Rue, the leftenant's little baby. They've been gooder to me than God. Her mother come straight from heaven, and her father's the best and bravest man sence Julius Cæsar or Jesus Christ. But we ain't got no call to stop here. Tisson, you're a man, and so am I, — leastways when the devil of drink ain't got me. We'll get her agin, so be and all the Pawnees in hell was back in the woods here between us and her. I swar by my ole mother and my dead wife, and the chillen I mought a-had, and *her*, that I'll never put another drop of cussed liquor in my mouth till I see her safe and sound with her folks."

Two hours' hard riding brought them to Castalar's. Tisson had persuaded Bob to go there first. The trail of the marauders was easy to find: they were a large party, and evidently did not expect immediate pursuit. Bob had listened to reason; and, seeing the trail might lead into the Indian country, knew it was the best and only safe and right way to go first to Castalar's, find out the extent of the misfortune, and then send or go to the fort for assistance.

The first glance down the valley told the tale of horror. The house was a heap of smouldering logs.

CHAPTER XVII.

He cometh unto you with a tale which holdeth children from their play and old men from the chimney-corner. — Sir Philip Sidney.

MARGARET had been taken to her room in violent hysterics, when Stephanie Castalar, who had listened to Bob's announcement of the tragedy without an outcry, suddenly dropped, like some wild thing who has vainly tried to repress the pain of a death-wound. Captain Moore threw open the window, and let in the clear, cold air, whilst Carson chafed the girl's hands.

All this time Bob Stearns stood looking helplessly about, listening to the wild cries that came through the closed doors from the room where the stricken mother lay in her agony.

The stooped and relaxed pose of the soldier expressed his crushed, hopeless condition. Every muscle was unstrung. His very sorrow seemed to shrink out of sight in the presence of a deeper grief. The manliest part of Bob's nature came always in action rather than endurance; and now he must wait for the decision of his superiors. There was nothing more trying to him than to wait. He wanted to tell the whole story, — to have done with the questions that would be asked. His conscience pressed him sore, and he had the vague hope of a child who trusts to get rid of the burden of a repented fault by confessing it. Even penitence with Bob expressed itself better in action than in words. He wanted to be off, following the bloody trail up the San Bois. He wondered how any one could delay a moment, now they had heard of Rue's danger. The child was everything to him. *She* was his conscience. The danger he had saved her from, the danger he had placed her in, led all his thoughts to her. He had tried hard to keep sober for her sake; and now there was a tinge of superstition mixed with his sorrow. He had only been drunk twice since this Christmas eve a year ago, and both times he had put Rue's life in danger; for he could not rid himself of the belief that, if he had not drunk Tisson's whiskey, he would, single-handed, have followed the baby and saved her. He felt now that the hour for saving her had passed. It was the night before — the night he had lain like a log, whilst she moaned and fought in the hands of her captors — the recapture should have been attempted. Then the Indians rested, fearless of pursuit, in a country where he knew every foot of the ground. Where he could have turned every accident of formation in hill and ravine into a helper, with Tisson to assist, he could have brought her unscathed out of the midst of the savages. But now he must wait. He was no longer a man free to think, to plan, to act: he was only a dragoon waiting for orders. His aimless thinking had at length resolved itself into the resolution to desert again, and follow her through the trackless wilderness like a faithful dog, when Sara and the doctor came from Margaret's room, where the cries had sunk to low moans. They carried away the unconscious Stephanie, who had been so suddenly bereft of home and kindred. Then, as Bob's questioning commenced, Leszinksky returned.

"What did we see at the ranch? Why, 't was a sight to make a Quaker swar he 'd kill Injins the rest of his life. The house had fell, and was still a-burnin'. We pried up some logs, and found a lot of half-burnt bodies, — Madame Castalar and the little children. I thought Mrs. Leszinksky was thar too till I got here. In the kitchen and cabins the nigger women and children was butchered. Some little ones was a-lyin' dead outside, smashed — well, you know how Injins kill 'em. Castalar and three of the nigger men was killed and sculped in the corral; two more niggers was a-lyin' dead, and sculped, down by the sheep-pen. Thar's whar Stephen was killed, and thar's whar they got *our baby!*" Here his voice broke into pained gasps.

"How do you know?" asked Leszinksky, whose face was as colorless and pained and sweet as that pictured of the Sufferer in Gethsemane.

"Why, that's the on'y place any fight was made. The rest on 'em up at the house was killed sooner. Them two men was thar fixin' the shed for the lambs. We could see whar they left thar work. Stephen had the little capt'n with him. He had put a board, with a piece of sheep-skin over it, in a crossed place in the fence-corner whar she could see the lambs. When he saw the Injins, he tuck her and run with her to a pile of logs. I could see his steps runnin' in the soft mud down thar. He drapt his hat inside the pen when he reached to get her outen the little seat she was in. Then he must a-seen more comin' the other way. He was unsartain like; for he put her in between the logs and stopped. Thar I found this little bonnet o' hers." And he took out a blood-stained little blue hood, and gave her father, who put it in his breast with a groan. Carson turned to hide the tears that would come; whilst Captain Ben, with a half-smothered oath, strode up to the open window, where Black Beaver and Pike were trying to hear the story.

"Come in here, and listen to Stearns's description. You must know just where we have to look for the child. Black Beaver, see if you can make out who has taken her."

The giant swung himself into the room; after him, with a light bound, sprang Black Beaver.

Calmly, but with a low, vibrating tone that told of repressed feeling, Leszinksky said: "Do you think my child was unhurt?"

"Yes, Leftenant. The blood on her little bonnet is Stephen's. Thar was a pile of logs, and he put her in among 'em, whar a bullet would n't strike her. He must a-called to the niggers, for they come to him, runnin'. Thar long jumpin' tracks was easy to see; and they had the axes they was a-workin' with. Stephen fought mighty cool for a boy. He had them derringers you give him, and he waited till the niggers was by him with thar axes. - I could see thar tracks all together, standin' squar' and steady like. The niggers fought like white men, and brave men at that. Stephen must a-killed the fust Injin he shot at close by the logs, and one of them niggers clove another red devil most in two with his axe a few feet closer in. That's how I know Stephen waited. He knew from the fust 't was a losin' fight; but he tried his best for the baby's sake. They all fought outside the logs 'cause of her bein' in 'em. And just at the last, when the niggers was dead, and Stephen was shot in the leg and settin' on the log by the baby, he cut down another Injin with a axe, and then shot down one that was gettin' in behind the baby with the loaded derringer he had kep' for the last. He must a-been mos' faintin' when he shot, for he lay with his hand restin' on the log, jus' by the baby, to shoot; the powder scorched the bark. I could see whar' he caught her and pushed her down in the damp thar. I could see she had been standin'. I reckon she got up to look; she ain't 'fraid o' nothin'. The little moccasin tracks was plain, and then I saw whar she had been pushed over, — and it must a-been Stephen, for his arm was lyin' close to the place, and the derringer in his hand, when we found him. He was riddled with arrows, and cut with a tomahawk, and sculped. A big Injin got the baby. His tracks was thar, in between the logs. I dunno how it come he did n't kill her; but he did n't, for when Tisson saw her she was hollerin' mad-like, and scratchin' and kickin' like a young catamount."

"Who is Tisson, and where did he see her?" asked all the officers in a breath.

Then Bob told the story of his visit and his friend's account of the marauding party, not shielding his fault from blame, but adding: —

"'It's the hardest of all, Leftenant. I mought a-got thar and warned 'em, if I had n't a-gone by Tisson's;

and I mought a-been arter 'em and Tisson here to tell you 'bout it this mornin', and we could a-had a better chance follerin' 'em, if I had n't a-got drunk last night. It 's stopped me this time. The devil 's lost his chance at me, — leastways till the little capt'n 's back here safe."

Black Beaver gave a significant " Humph ! " and then asked : " You say him big Pawnee got heap long cut off his nose on um face ? "

" Yes, a sabre-cut, Tisson said."

" You see him track ? "

" Yes ; whar he found the baby : then we follered it to his horse. He limped on one foot."

" Humph ! How you know ? "

" One foot dragged always on the same side. You have seen me trail Injins. You know I can see."

" Yes, white man got eyes heap good. Sometimes see too much — see tings never was. Dis time no see nuff — no see which foot go bad."

" Yes, I did. I follered the trail going south. The right foot dragged."

" Humph ! Right foot go lame — heap long cut on nose : which side ? "

" The right side. Tisson told me that, I remember now."

" Humph ! Good ting — heap 'member sometime." Then he turned to Leszinksky : —

" Lo-loch-to-hoo-la, Big Chief — got um pappoose. Wolf Pawnee on em war-path."

The doctor had returned in time to hear the questioning. Leszinksky said to him : —

" Doctor, I leave my wife in your care. It is hard to leave her, but my first duty is to follow my little daughter. We may have to go into the heart of the Indian country. If it please God that I do not return, you will take my wife to her friends in Memphis. I rely upon you as I would upon a brother."

" Thank you, Leszinksky, for the trust. I will try to deserve it. I have given Mrs. Leszinksky a composing draught, and can leave her with Sara until I go to the fort. . I must arrange for Coolidge to go with you. A surgeon may be needed in your party."

Captain Moore interrupted : —

"Stay here, Leszinksky, with Stearns, Pike, and Black Beaver until the doctor returns from the fort. After this daring piece of deviltry we cannot risk Mrs. Leszinksky here without an efficient defence. I will go to the fort with the doctor and report to Colonel Kearny. I shall ask for my company to go with you. The doctor will return in time for you to meet us at the ford of the Arkansas. We will try to be at Castalar's by daylight. From there we shall follow the trail of these devils. As sure as there is a God, we will get Rue out of their clutches!"

CHAPTER XVIII.

These let us wish away;
And turn, sole-thoughted, to one lady there.
                                                    Keats.

AT the quarters of the commanding officer, Colonel Kearny, the Whist Club was in full force that night. The best players of the 1st Dragoons were pitted against an adversary, not only famous in the army, that school of whist, but among the masters of the game in Washington; where he and the gallant young *aide* of the commander-in-chief won three successive rubbers that famous night when they played the champions of the Congressional Club, — a victory not counted in official reports nor inscribed upon regimental banners; but one of which every young subaltern and "old mustache" in the service was justly proud. After that night the newest fledged cadet from West Point never touched a pack of cards in the presence of base civilians without some knowing reference to *that game*, — " where old Ben Beall and little Phil Kearny taught those 'nobs' in Washington a few army points"; or, "You have heard, of course, of that night at the Congressional when the last rubber was played at thousand-dollar points; when the army, from the general-in-chief down, backed their players with every cent they could raise. Why, they say old S. bet W. of Massachusetts a year's salary in advance. C., one of the Congressional champions, mortgaged his plantation the next day to take up his I. O. U's. They've fought shy of the army ever since."

The first rubber was finished, and the host, in a testy

way, that showed the loser's temper, although it did not conquer his hospitality, was mixing a generous bowl of steaming punch, throwing occasional expletives at his late partner, who persistently tried to explain.

"If you had understood my play, and forced trumps once more, then my long suit at spades was good for the odd."

"Damn your long suit! Beall played after *you*. He had a fist full of little trumps, and trumped spades every time. You cut my hand like hell all through the game."

Then, relenting in temper, and anxious to make *amende* without formal apology, he turned to their smiling opponent, the ideal cavalry-man of his time.

"I say, Beall, sing us one of your old Florida songs while the punch is brewing. Old McKenzie at Fort Snelling taught me this Scotch brew. It's the secret of 'Ours.' I'll bet you a cool hundred there isn't a man in the Second, unless it's some fellow transferred from the First, can compound such a bowl of nectar."

"I will sing the song and take the bet. It's the only way to harmonize you with that unlucky partner of yours. Why, the poor fellow is in a cold sweat with the tickle of your sugary compliments."

"Damn his sweat,— and his spades!" growled the colonel. "Let us have the song." And the half-smothered laugh hushed as the *beau sabreur* began.

> Wrapt in his blanket, the soldier is sleeping
>   Under the stars, and the pale crescent moon ;
> Out in the hummock his brother is keeping
>   Watch, near the slumbrous and silent lagoon.
>
> Far to the North is the home of their mother,
>   Set where the hills catch the song of the streams.
> She prays for the picket ; she weeps for his brother,
>   Who laughs with his love in the Palace of Dreams.
>
> A whir in the air ! The picket is lying
>   Prone on the moss. Is he taking his rest ?
> A bird — an arrow — which was it came flying ?
>   *Something* is sheltered or sheathed in his breast.

>The camp-fire flashes, the red cedarwood gleams,
>   As the scarlet flame catches the glistening bark;
>The soldier still sleeps in his Palace of Dreams,
>   Though some one is stirring, out there in the dark.
>
>From hummock, and swamp, and Everglade islands,
>   War-whoop and shot wake the slumbrous lagoon.
>Two hearts are desolate there in the highlands,
>   Two sleepers are sleeping here 'neath the moon.

There was a pathos in the manner of the singer, a thrilling quality in the round, full notes of the splendid baritone, that was magical in effect. Sung as only Ben Beall could sing an army ballad, the words made a picture every shade of which was distinct and palpable to these rough fighters. There was no outburst of applause, no *claque;* not only no prodigality, but no expression of compliment. The sentiment of soldiers is usually best defined in action; yet they understood each other, and the musician could read the effect of his song in the uneasy scrape of a heavy cavalry-boot or the sonorous blow of some arched proboscis. The colonel had forgotten his brew, and sat glowering in the fire, with a look on his face that told

>"From the present back to the past,
>   There is only a step to be made."

A break to his reverie came in the ringing clink of spurs, as steps hurried up, on, and across the porch to the door, left partly open to dispel the heavy currents of tobacco-smoke. The colonel looked up.

"Come in, Moore. You and Carson are too late for the first rubber. If you had been my partner — But what is it, Moore? You have brought a regular death's-head to the feast. What the devil is up? Nothing, I hope, with the Leszinkskys? Mrs. Leszinksky has been looking ill lately. But I see here is Randall: he would be there if anything was wrong. Why don't you speak? What the hell is it that *you* fear to say?"

By this time there was a general stir: the officers clustered around the late. comers, faces darkened, and hands instinctively clutched for the absent sword-hilts.

Hurriedly the story was told. Before the telling was over, the colonel was beset with impetuous offers from volunteers. There were prayerful entreaties, emphasized by deep oaths, that he would let them go at once.

All the old devotion of the regiment to the fair woman who had come to them a bride; their affection for and pride in the stainless gentleman, so modestly upright, so fearlessly true, who now suffered from this cruel blow, were intensified and made more personal from their feeling of proprietorship in the baby born in camp. To the married officers she seemed one of their own; to the homeless subalterns she was the representative of all they had left in those distant rose-gardens of Paradise, now dimly seen through the mists of fraternal and filial memories.

The story of her danger seemed to blot out all other claim. She was their first duty. She needed them. To the dullest imagination, the picture of the little prisoner out there in the forest was vivid and distinct. They saw the child in her pain and grief and anger. Even then there came a grim smile, as they thought of her passionate temper, her power of endurance, her elfin imperiousness. Then there was a longing agony to be off on the trail; to take her from the blood-stained hands of her captors, if it cost the lives of the entire regiment. Not an officer there would have held his life at an instant's value, if he could have bought her safety with that price.

The only question was, Who would stay in the garrison? Universal outcry settled that. All who were there to hear the story *must* go. There were others in the cantonment, — "*Les absens ont toujours tort,*" — they might stay. The colonel was carried in this rush of feeling. Yes, they might come, — the captains present, — with their companies. Well, yes: the young subalterns whose captains were so unlucky as to be absent might come as volunteers. He himself would leave Wharton in command. Wharton was ailing, and Mason would return before another week.

To this there *could* be no dissenting voice. Even Major Beall, the guest, who had taken the last week of his leave to spend Christmas with the 1st, before rejoining General Taylor in Texas, now insisted that his nearest route to his command was the path taken by the marauders.

All night long there was the tramp of horses, the clank of sabres, the ring of spurs, — the hundred noises that told of hurried preparation. The dawning light of the Christmas Day saw the rear-guard of the expedition, with its line of wagons and pack-mules, leave the fort. The advance column of Captain Moore's company — escorting the colonel and his staff, with whom rode Major Beall — had left at midnight. Mr. and Mrs. Page had gone with the doctor and the guard sent to Bouie's Hill.

Margaret was sleeping when Leszinksky and his little party left. The kindly drug had released her temporarily from the bondage of sorrow. The healing of sleep had come to the worn body and racked mind. Nature had opportunity to renew the strength that would be so sorely tried when consciousness returned.

With the earliest light of day came to Bouie's Hill the wives of Leszinksky's comrades. Later, as the needs of their daily life let them, one by one came the women of the garrison, — the veriest termagant and virago among them softened into gentle speech through the wide-reaching magnetism of sorrowing motherhood. Women, weeping silently in the house as consciousness came to the sufferer in that darkened chamber, as she moaned for her child, and would not be comforted; women on the porch; others out in the grounds, standing in groups with children in their arms, were drawn into the fold of a common sisterhood by their sympathy for the stricken mother. How true, how deep, how sincere the sympathy, I need not try to tell. Not a woman in all this land can fail to remember the painful shock, the quick thrill of agony, that made the grief of one family the common grief of the nation. Even now, when years have come and gone without lifting the veil of that mystery, there are mother-hearts in all the length and breadth of the land that ache with the burden of their helpless sympathy, whenever the thought of that lost child is uncovered in the treasure-house of memory, where it lies, only half-hidden by the daily fears and hopes of life.

PART V.

THE PURSUIT.

For one fair vision ever fled
. . . . . day and night,
And still we follow'd where she led.
                              Tennyson.

PART V.

THE PURSUIT.

CHAPTER XIX.

A stoic of the woods, a man without a tear.
CAMPBELL.

THE sagacity of the frontiersman had read as plainly as from the lines of a printed page the history of the affray at Castalar's. Baby Rue was the only prisoner the Indians had taken. An impulse of admiration for the courage of the little child, who, with unquailing look, silently struck at Lo-loch-to-hoo-la with her tiny fist, as he snatched her from the sheltering logs, saved her from instant death. Stephen's dauntless self-devotion was another factor in the count. The only little eaglet left of such a brood was worth a warrior's keeping. Courage is first and all in the list of Indian virtues; if we had time, it would be instructive to study the abstract question of how many qualities it is made to represent in the mind of the red man.

The blood that had come to our little heroine through the centuries, instinct with the haughty resolution and unyielding will of Milosch-Kabilovitsch, served her at need. The finer courage of the gentle Leszinksky would not have saved her. The fierce, aggressive spirit of the vengeful voyvode was more easily understood and more highly valued by the savage. Thus it happened that a chief on the war-path charged himself with the burden of the brave little child, who was now his own by right of capture.

The trail followed by the Indians crossed from the

headwaters of the San Bois, leaving Tisson's camp several miles to the left, to the headwaters of the Kiamesha (or Kimishi) River. At the junction of its three principal branches, in a secluded, rocky little valley, hid by the lofty ridges that bordered the river, the party made its first halt, and was speedily joined by detachments returning from equally successful raids upon the outlying settlements on the hills down the Kiamesha to Varner's ranch in the Red River valley, almost within sound of the guns at Fort Towson.

From the highest summit of the ridge, which was bare of all growth save a fantastically trimmed tree, — a beacon of the Osages, — the Indians sent up balloon-shaped columns of smoke to warn the stragglers of the party of their retreat. This is the red man's system of telegraphy. He builds a small fire, which is not allowed to blaze, then piles an armful of partially green weeds over the fire to smother it; thus a dense smoke is created. Having established his current, the Indian operator confines it by spreading over it his blanket; with one assistant he can cut off or almost wholly confine the smoke. Waiting until it begins to escape from the sides, then suddenly withdrawing the blanket, a beautiful, balloon-shaped column puffs upward, the smoke alternately interrupted and released until successive puffs ascend in regular order.

This warning given, the war party was soon in motion. Leaving the valley of the Kiamesha directly behind, they rapidly pressed on westward to the headwaters of the Boggy, in order to cross the Washita above Wild Horse Creek; whence the trail led south of the Witchita Mountains, where they could rely upon Comanche reinforcements as well as aid from the Mexicans, who, since General Taylor's occupation of Texas, had jealously watched the border. The Indians felt sure of one day's advance of any pursuers who might follow. Their work had been well done, — none had escaped to tell the tale of slaughter: so one day's advance was secure to them. Afterwards, their superior knowledge of the country, and the rapidity of their movement, would distance a hesitating enemy.

We know how false would have been their hope of a day's start, if Tisson's black bottle had not befriended them. Bob Stearns on their trail, and Tisson at Fort Gibson on the morning of the twenty-fourth, their *détour* to the Kiamesha would have cost them dear. The battle would have been at the crossing of the Middle Boggy, the apex of a triangle of which Fort Towson and old Fort Washita would have been the base. The dragoons would have had them hip and thigh. Unfortunately, Tisson's bottle had bridged the Middle Boggy: so that promising equation was lost.

At sundown, the evening of the twenty-fourth, they crossed the Middle Boggy, and after a few hours' rest were again in motion, turning northward toward the divide of the Canadian from the Washita. On Christmas Day they were beyond the headwaters of the Boggy, and now, feeling secure from pursuit that night, turned aside from their direct route to find a resting place for the coming day in a broad and fertile prairie which extends into the sand-hills of the Canadian, and where the Blue River has its source.

All this time Rue had borne herself bravely. She had kicked and fought, as Tisson saw, until she had nearly exhausted the patience of her captor. Fortunately, she was so worn and tired that she fell asleep at the critical moment, when longer dispute might have been dangerous. The charm of the helpless sleeping child completed the conquest her courage had begun. The rude warrior rode apart from the party, half-ashamed of the care he gave her; yet all the time she was stealing her way into the heart upon which she rested. One thought of the white man, which had heretofore been the most bitter grudge he held, — the remembrance of the death of his children by the fatal disease brought to his wigwam that summer the traders had spread the small-pox through the Indian country, — won the child his affection. The last one he lost was her age, a fearless "chincha," always delighted and happy when he returned from the hunt or the war-path. *She* had died in his arms, with her head on his heart, just as this little one was lying. The touch of nature that makes the whole world kin thrilled his pulse. In the gathering gloom the strong, sinewy arm held her tenderly, changing her position from time to time with wonderful thoughtfulness for so rude a nurse.

There would have been thanksgiving, not despair, at Bouie's Hill could Tisson have read and told the thoughts of the dusky warrior who passed him in the gloaming.

During the following day's ride the child's temper, resistant as it was, yielded to the seduction of novelty. There were surprise and curiosity, but — as her protector noticed with gratified pride — no fear in the glance with which she regarded these wild horsemen. Once she laughed outright, a child's sweet, clear, musical laugh, at the curvetings of a vicious pony which a gayly bedecked Indian was breaking to the heavy Mexican curb. From that moment Lo-loch-to-hoo-la was her slave. The laugh was the rippling laugh of the little "chincha." The Great Spirit had given him back the darling of his wigwam. At the next halt, the child, who had hitherto refused the food he offered, ate heartily. After this he had no difficulty with her: and so *her* Christmas dinner was a feast with Lo-loch-to-hoo-la. Then she slept the unbroken sleep of a tired, healthy child, through the long night-ride which brought them near the desired camping ground.

As they crossed the last bold, billowy roll that screened it, the advance party saw buffalo feeding in the prairie where they intended to rest. It was the crowning good fortune of their daring and successful raid. They had captured horses and arms and scalps in great numbers; but the Comanches, whom they were on their way to join, would have driven the buffalo from the country where they were to await the movement of their Mexican allies. Now, at the very moment of need, they could have food for the taking, with every circumstance in their favor.

They were leeward of the herd, — no small point of advantage. The prairie on the west and north was encircled by steep sand-hills, through which the only exit was up the pebbly bed of the creek in the little narrow ravine where Blue River has its source. The plan of attack was simple. Into the narrow gorge the buffalo must be driven; and, keeping out of sight as much as possible, their best marksmen were placed in every little hollow and cleft, whilst the "runners," mounted on fleet ponies, and armed only with bows and arrows, moved slowly and cautiously southward. When within the right distance a signal was given, and they all opened at once, like a pack of hounds, in a full chorus of yells, dashing up to the herd, and skilfully driving them to the desired point, — the cows in headlong panic, whilst an occasional bull would turn for an instant, with a frantic rush upon his pursuers, thus gallantly giving the weaker time to escape. All the time, these perfect horsemen of the plains were whirling and coursing among the frightened herd, selecting with the quick judgment of the hunter the fattest and youngest for their victims, frequently killing a cow with a single arrow, yet always directing the movement of the herd to the desired point, where the ambush waited. There, at length, the slaughter ceased, from very weariness in killing. The run of the hunt being over, the Indians proceeded to dispatch the animals they had disabled; then, cutting up the carcasses, they brought loads of meat to the camp, where the choicest pieces were soon roasted, and a cramming Indian feast began.

In the attack upon Castalar's Valley, Lo-loch-to-hoo-la had been one of the party at the corral when the massacre began. In a fight with dragoons on the Missouri he had learned the value of an American horse; consequently, to him "Emperor" was a prize to be won. It was the only one he claimed in the division of booty which was made at the ranch. The gray stallion was one of the strongest and fleetest horses on the frontier: of mixed breed, he had the speed and game qualities of the thoroughbred, united to the endurance and staying power of the wild mustang of the plains.

Burdened with his little captive, Lo-loch-to-hoo-la

had thought best to ride his trained war-pony until he should be free to try conclusions with his newly-acquired steed; so it happened that Emperor had been haltered with the drove until the last stop before turning aside to seek the desired camp. At that halt it had been decided by the chiefs to send on, with a party of the younger warriors, their long train of captured animals and the boys who were driving them, that in event of pursuit they might be free to fight or retreat unencumbered. The pony that had carried Lo-loch-to-hoo-la so far had begun to flag. A change must be made. At his command one of the drivers untied Emperor from the line to which he was haltered, and led him to the chief. At first the horse was restive and unruly, turning to eye the horseman who was directing the arrangement of the Comanche saddle and its trappings; when suddenly, with a snort of recognition, he gently stooped his head, as the little child in the warrior's arms held out her tiny hand and gravely rubbed his face. It was a caress to which he was accustomed. Stephen had often taken her to ride on Emperor, and had taught her this mode of salutation. The chief had no further difficulty with the stallion, which had always been proudly obedient to and gentle with the children seated upon his back, although he had invariably disputed supremacy with any luckless negro who chose or was ordered to mount him.

When the buffalo chase began the chief had declined to join it, merely riding to the top of the ridge, where the eager horse he rode was more amenable to restraint than the excited child, who laughed and shouted with delight at what she evidently regarded as a charming play in the valley before her. During their two days' journey, Lo-loch-to-hoo-la, with the quick observation of the Indian, had noticed the glances of his companions, first at him, then at each other, as they watched his gentle care of the little captive. From surprise their looks had changed to scorn; then a sullen, contemptuous manner or rude laugh when, at their halts, he attended to the child's comfort marked their disapproval of his conduct. The leaven of discontent had spread. Even the young braves and the boy drivers gave him hesitating obedience. He was now about to have a more decided proof of the disapproval of the band.

The warrior was holding Rue firmly as she stood up to watch the hunt, with one hand caught in the broad sash which tied the waist of the soft but now soiled dress, when an arrow cut through the folds of the skirt which the breeze had expanded. It had passed between him and the child: it could scarcely be an accident. All doubt was dispelled at the instant, for a second arrow touched the topmost arch of Emperor's neck; he had slightly moved at the moment the bolt was sped, and thus saved the child, who, as it was now evident, was the mark aimed at.

The horse reared and plunged, for the skin was cut, but the curb was pulled, and then, with a slight touch of the huge Mexican spurs and a turn of the muscular wrist, he was reined round and made to leap down the ascent just as a dozen arrows passed harmlessly above his rider. A derisive burst of laughter, as some one cried, " The old squaw must keep her pappoose out of the war-path," was another evidence of the intent that had speeded those arrows.

For the last twenty-four hours he had understood that a demand would soon be made for her life. It had been settled they should take no prisoners. He had violated the compact when he spared the child. The first day the thought had come that he might have to give her up to death if the chiefs demanded it of him; even then he had resolved that her death should be quick and painless — that much at least he would do for her; in no way should she be tortured or subjected to their cruel sport. The second day, as the wild imaginings of the superstitious savage identified her with the dead " chincha," he resolved to save her at all cost, — to save her, even if it brought him the disgrace that is attached to a chief who leaves his tribe on the war-path.

The time had come sooner than he expected, yet he was not unprepared. The change of horses had given him a fresh one, and its speed and endurance he felt he could trust. He had decided to leave the party that night: the act was likely to be forced on him before the sheltering night should come to hide the course of the fugitive. It might cost him his life. Well, that was nothing, he risked death daily; but he must make sure that she did not live after him. She should not fall alive into the hands of enemies who would then take double delight in her suffering. But he would save her if he could. He would even bear the sting of this last insult without resenting it, to save her. Any one who knows the Indian character will know he could give no costlier proof of devotion.

The only thing now was to gain time. It was midday: if he could only avoid dispute, and keep the child away from the enemies who sought her life, until evening, when the hunt and the cram of the feast would be felt, then he might escape with her unharmed. He had revolved this thought in his mind as he stood some distance from the camp, under the shelter of some cottonwood trees.

Rue was sitting on his blanket on the ground, eating a piece of the bread he had saved from the provisions they had brought from 'Castalar's. She broke off the half and handed him, saying, in her imperious way, "Eat it! eat it!" with a gesture that made him understand.

To gratify her he took it, but only to put it in a pocket he had contrived in the flap of his saddle, where he also had the forethought to place some jerked meat and a piece of roasted beef (the last of Castalar's slaughtered cattle) he had cooked for her, and which she had evidently relished at the morning's halt. If he had to leave suddenly they were provisioned for the flight. He was ready. His quiver full of arrows was slung on his back; his bow ready for use in his left hand; his shield on his arm; his gun in a buckskin cover hung at the pommel of his saddle, where a lasso was coiled and two folded blankets were tied with thongs. Constantly watching, as Emperor, picketed near, cropped the soft, succulent buffalo-grass, he saw every movement of the hunters as they returned to camp with their loads of meat.

After a time Rue fell asleep, and he carefully rolled her in the blanket on which she was lying, folding it in such a manner that her head was safely covered, though an opening was left through which the fair little face was visible.

The rays of the setting sun came aslant the ridge that divided the little hollow, in which was the camp, from the hunting ground of the wide prairie. The chiefs and warriors were grouped around the fires there to the south about five hundred yards below Lo-loch-to-hoo-la, in the hollow. Behind them to the east was the country they had devastated. By this time their enemies were aroused: the avengers were now, or soon would be, on their track. Lo-loch-to-hoo-la's judgment would have opposed any delay before crossing the Washita, where Senaco and his band of Comanches were to join them, — but his opinion had not been asked. At their last halt the chiefs had conferred apart from him. With the child in his arms he could not claim his place in council; and deprived of his care she would not have been safe an instant. Even then, he had been forced in a measure to surrender the interests of his tribe to her safety. If he had spoken, if *he* had urged the danger of pursuit, that moment the child's life would have been demanded of him. So the warrior's supremacy was lost; the chief tacitly resigned his leadership. He knew that if he claimed either, he must pay the price of a life he held above his own. There was nothing he could do but fly with her; and the only possible path of escape was up the pebbly bed of the little creek in the ravine where the hunt had ended.

There was a movement in the groups down by the fires, and at that distance the keen sight of the Indian saw they were watching him. The time had come. To delay them he must take the initiative. Their best ponies were blown with the chase, whilst Emperor had been fed at the morning's halt with corn from the pack-train, and now was fresh and rested. That long afternoon's grazing would tell when he came to measure the miles with flying feet.

The chief lifted Rue carefully, then vaulting upon Emperor's back laid her on the folded blankets he had tied to the pommel. Under and around the blankets and her, he coiled the lasso of twisted horsehair until it made a network that held her firmly and securely across the saddle.

The groups by the fires separated, and the warriors scattered in parties of two and three. Did they suspect his intent?

He rode slowly up the ascent which overlooked the prairie, turning his horse in the direction of the camp, and then stopping as if to look at the scene of the hunt. Thus, without seeming to watch, he could see every movement at the camp and in the prairie to the south, where the ponies were grazing by the creek. Two or three of the scattered parties were coming up the hollow, others sauntered on the ridge and down toward the creek. That was enough. There was no doubt now that the demand was to be made and enforced. What else but a thirst for blood could draw those *convives* from the feast that was preparing? Slowly he turned to the creek: his last look over the ridge as he crossed showed the warriors who had started up the hollow rapidly climbing the ascent behind him, whilst below them was a quick movement of the others out on the prairie southward. At the creek he paused to let Emperor drink. Again the warriors behind him stopped, while the movement to the south was hastened. Yes; they suspected his intended flight; but they supposed it would be across the Washita to Senaco's camp, or still farther, to the Comanche village. They had never thought of that bold venture into the Canadian Hills, and then northward through the country of their foes, the Osages, to the trackless wilderness of the salt plains, where winter had commenced in earnest. He was quick to take advantage of their error: he turned again toward the ridge. The few warriors who were on it disappeared down the hollow.

The path to the ravine was clear. This time Emperor was turned northward at a more rapid pace. The warriors near the ponies hesitated. Every instant was gain to Lo-loch-to-hoo-la. A few moments and he would be in the ravine with every advantage of the start. But the path was to be disputed. Two of the Indians had gone entirely up the hollow to watch his movements from a ledge in the hills near the entrance to the ravine. They climbed this ledge just as Lo-loch-to-hoo-la turned his head to see if he was pursued. He saw the Indians in the prairie running and mounting in hot haste, and then turning to pursue his course, there, not twenty feet from him, on the ledge to the right, were La-doo-ke-a and Non-je-ning-go, two chiefs of the allied bands of Ottoes who had most openly shown their contempt and disapproval of his conduct. In fact, it was Non-je-ning-go who had called after him so insultingly that morning, and now, to emphasize the insult, repeated it, with an imperious wave of his tomahawk, and an order to " go back to the camp and at once give up the white man's medicine child, who had conjured a chief into an old woman."

This last insult put an end to Lo-loch-to-hoo-la's patience. Snatching his tomahawk from where it hung at his belt, he sent it whizzing through the air at the very moment that of Non-je-ning-go was thrown. The weapons met mid-way, and, by one of those strange chances in which bystanders get a share in a conflict, one shattered the foot of Non-je-ning-go, whilst the handle of the other in its rebound laid La-doo-ke-a senseless. In the very act of throwing his tomahawk, Lo-loch-to-hoo-la had covered the sleeping child with his shield. Except for this self-devotion of the chief, here the history of our heroine would have ended; for at the very moment of his duelling exchange with Non-je-ning-go, a warrior on the ridge aimed at the child across the saddle in front of the chief, hoping thus to end the dissension without the loss of a renowned warrior, whose prowess had been proved in numberless fights with the "Long-knives." The arrow glanced from the tough buffalo-hide, the interposition of which had saved the sleeper, but cut the arm of the chief who held the shield. At this point Emperor took it upon himself to end the unequal combat: a plunging leap took him past the turn of the hill, into the ravine. Following the track made by the buffalo that had escaped up the bed of the now nearly dry creek, Emperor so completely distanced his pursuers that at the end of an hour's ride they returned sullenly to camp.

CHAPTER XX.

> ATTEMPT the end, and never stand to doubt:
> Nothing's so hard but search will find it out.
> HERRICK.

LESZINKSKY overtook the advance party with Colonel Kearny at the ford of the Arkansas. The warm grasp of each comrade's hand as they met him in the starlight, spoke their sympathies. Colonel Kearny briefly introduced Major Beall.

"Leszinksky, here is Beall of the 2d. You know him, if you have not met before."

"Yes, and I know how valuable an addition he is to our expedition. Major, I do not need to thank you for your kindness in coming with us. I knew you were at the fort, and when the news of this outbreak and my loss reached me, I knew you would come."

"Thank you, Lieutenant, for your kindly judgment. I am only too glad to be one of the party of recapture, — for I am sure we shall find your little daughter alive. The very fact that she alone was spared out of that massacre proves that for some reason she is safe with her captors. Moore tells me he has with him the best trailers and scouts on the frontier: that is all important. Every hour gained now is worth more than we can estimate."

"We have with the scouts two soldiers of your old Florida command."

"Who are they?"

"A giant they call 'Pike,' and Bob Stearns."

"Yes, I recollect them well. The giant is the most stolidly brave soldier I ever knew. Stearns was only a boy then, but plucky and bright. I should think he would have made an excellent scout."

"He is one of the best on the frontier. He would have been chief of scouts long ago, but for his one fault. I trust he will overcome that. He is devotedly attached to my little daughter, whose life he once saved. He brought us the news of the attack at Castalar's."

"I should like to see and question him."

"If you will ride forward with me, Major. He is there in front."

"An instant. Colonel, may I serve with the scouts? I can possibly be useful with them: some of my old Florida men are in the corps."

"Certainly; where you choose. Say, Beall, suppose you take command of a squadron when our troops come up? I will give you Moore's company, the scouts, and our Osage allies. You understand Indians, and Moore will show you, if we overtake those scoundrels, how the 1st Dragoons can fight."

"No, give Moore the squadron; but if you like I will be glad to take command of the scouts of his party."

"Very well, if you prefer that"; and the colonel rode with Captain Moore, whilst Beall and Leszinksky passed on rapidly to the head of the column.

Some distance in front were our soldiers and Black Beaver; with them was Oscar, whose tearful entreaties to come, his master could not resist. The last argument had been, "She was sorry fur me *that time*, an' she's all I've got lef'." Bob's cheeriness and bright spirits had vanished. He was almost as silent as the taciturn Pike. An occasional question from Oscar and answer from Black Beaver made the sole conversation of the party. As the two officers rode up Leszinksky said:—

"Stearns, here is your old Captain of the 2d, Major Beall. He has accepted the command of the scouts and my detachment for this expedition"; and Leszinksky rode on, questioning Black Beaver, whilst Bob saluted his old captain.

"I'm mighty glad you're with us, sir; leastways I would be, so be and I could be glad of anything onct more. You see, Capt'n,—beg pardon, sir, Major I oughter a-said—this accident to the leftenant's little one is part my fault, and if anybody can holp us get her outen the hands of them cussed redskins, I know it's you, sir. I ain't forgot that scout after Waxchadjo; and how, whenever we went with *you* after the Seminolies, down thar in the Big Cypress, we always got 'em. But, Major, these Pawnees is wuss 'an the Seminolies."

"How is that, Stearns?"

"They ain't so gentlemanlike. Now, Osceola was a gentleman,—the real quality,—and so is Coacoochee. I saw him last week. But these Pawnees has larnt the wust parts of a white man from them low-down, white-livered traders as is sent amongst 'em, besides bein' the meanest kind o' Injins. The most of thar fightin' is killin' settlers and stealin' hosses. They goes in for plunder. Now, the Seminolies is genu*ine* warriors. You remember, sir, when we found the bodies of the dead after they whipped Major Dade, thar wah n't a ring or a watch or a purse even took from 'em. They fit like gentlemen. I must say our dragoons themselves would n't a-done as well by the killed. We're most apt to fall 'ar to all the property that's left."

"You say you saw Coacoochee last week?"

"Yes, sir; I was over thar at the Seminolie village with Capt'n Moore, and he sent me and Black Beaver to the Washita to invest*egate* the doin's of a party of young Seminolie braves and them nigger Injins who fit agin us in Florida. The people in the village stuck to it they was out on a hunt down by the Washita; but Black Beaver and me follered thar trail nigh a week, and if it wah n't a war party I'm a blamed poor judge o' Injins."

"Do you think these marauders are on the way to join them?"

"Yes, sir; it 'pears to me most like that, though they've never been friends with the Seminolies before.

But this here fuss that's a comin' with Mexico will show before it's done what kind o' neighbors we've got out here on the plains. These border Injins 'll quit fightin' one another any time to lift a 'Merican scalp. You see, sir, they're mad 'cause the Government keeps a movin' them. So be and I was a Injin, I would n't like it nuther. 'Pears like them treaties was all travellin' *contracts*."

"How did Coacoochee look?"

"Not much like that time I seen him in San Augustine. That time he rode through the place with on'y five warriors, jest at sundown, and the garrison was so stunned like that they never moved till he was out in the Pines. I s'pose it was his way to tell ole King Philip to take heart and be a man. You must remember it, sir."

"Yes; I was one of the stunned garrison," laughed the major.

"Well, you must say, sir, he did it grand like."

"Yes, like a knight-errant. Next to Osceola he was the most splendid warrior I ever saw."

Then the major cross-questioned Bob as to the affair at Castalar's, getting minute details of what seemed unimportant facts, which, before this exhaustive examination, had been apparently of little value to the sagacious frontiersman, but which, when reckoned up by his old commander, gave new light to this sinister tragedy.

The major's brief was not yet made out when Leszinksky rode back to meet them, with a new arrival, — Tisson. He had cautiously followed the trail from Castalar Valley to the Kiamesha, where they had been joined by detached bands; and from there until he was sure their flight was directed across the headwaters of the Boggy to the Washita, and so by the Comanche trail to the fastnesses of the Witchita Mountains. Having determined their course, Tisson hastened by the most direct route to meet the party he knew would come from Fort Gibson, his hardy little pony having made quite one hundred miles in fifteen hours.

The command now halted, Colonel Kearny sending back to hasten the march of the troops immediately following, and leaving orders for the rear-guard, with the supply train, to cross the North and South Canadian just above their junction, and then go up the hills on the south branch to the mouth of Little River, where they were to encamp and await orders. Express riders were also sent to Forts Towson and Washita to direct the movement of the military and the volunteers whom the hue and cry of the massacre would already have brought together.

In two hours two more companies of the 1st, together with a party of about fifty Osage Indians, who had arrived at the fort the day previous with game and other articles of barter, and who had gladly volunteered to fight Pawnees, halted at the temporary camp. It was now daylight, and after a hurried breakfast the troops were again in motion, Colonel Kearny and the last arrivals going almost directly southward until they should strike the trail of the Pawnees where Tisson had left it; while Captain Moore's company and "Beall's Scouts"—as they were already christened—were to strike across to the Seminole village on the South Canadian, and then join the main body at the headwaters of the Boggy, at a point known as the Willow Cove.

The movement of Colonel Kearny's command, until their arrival at the given rendezvous, was somewhat delayed by the broken trail, which had separated at several points,—the usual Indian stratagem to delay pursuit,—and then resumed again, to break and disperse after short halts. The colonel reached Willow Cove before sundown on the twenty-sixth, and found Captain Moore, who had arrived an hour before, arranging his camp with the prudence of an officer who knows he is in the enemy's vicinage. Major Beall and the scouts had just started over to the headwaters of the Blue River to examine the indications and see if any of the band of Pawnees had come so far northward. This Captain Moore told the colonel, and also of their stop at the village of Coacoochee, who, as he said, had received them in a cool, haughty manner.

"Did you offer any reward for information?" the colonel asked.

"Yes; Leszinksky insisted I should, and Beall also advised that I should make a personal appeal to the chief, who, he said, was always a generous, magnanimous fellow. He preferred I should do this, as Coacoochee might not listen to any appeal from him. It seems the widow of Waxehadjo is living in Coacoochee's lodge. She is his sister, and is insane from the shock of her loss. The dragoons killed two of her children at the time of Waxehadjo's capture, and the two others died on their way from Florida. Then, too, the chief has married the daughter of Osceola. So the family influence would not have been favorable to an entreaty from Beall. I thought Leszinksky would not be sufficiently cool in manner when speaking of his child's danger, so Beall kept him apart while I talked to the chief. He could or would promise nothing. Said his young men were 'off on a hunt,' and that if the Pawnees were on the war-path he knew nothing of it; that they were enemies of the Seminoles. If they crossed into his country he should repel them; in that event, if he recaptured the child, he would return her without ransom. He neither warred against nor sold children. This was said with a disdainful look toward Beall, whom it was evident he recognized, for he went into his lodge, and, although he gave us the supplies we asked, he declined payment or gifts. If we have a brush with the Mexicans I should not be surprised if the Seminoles all go on a hunt the other side of the Witchita Mountains."

"Damn them, let them go! They had better be there than near the settlements, itching to take scalps enough to avenge old scores. The Government had better have finished the 'exterminating' it commenced in Florida than have forced their removal. It will be the same cry until they are driven into the Pacific. There is n't a gentleman in the army who is n't ashamed of the whole damned business. I'm willing enough to fight them when my blood's up with some such outrage as this last, but I *am* tired of being a frontier policeman, always yelling 'Move on!' to some red rascal. Why, what the devil is up now? Here come Beall and Leszinksky, riding as though 'all hell had broke loose.'"[1]

[1] Paradise Lost, Book IV., line 918.

CHAPTER XXI.

*In worst extremes, and on the perilous edge
Of battle.*
MILTON.

AT the head of the little ravine the ascent was easy to a broad, gravelled plateau which divided the sand-hills, making a wide and firm highway that curved through and then around the base of the ridge, suddenly ending in a grove of cottonwood that bordered the South Canadian. The entrance into the little ravine from the prairie at the head of the Blue River, and the exit of this natural turnpike into the secluded wood, made a secret pass known only to a few Indian hunters and two white men. Fortunately for Lo-loch-to-hoo-la, it was unknown to the Pawnees and the Ottoes who were with them on the war-path. They had given up the pursuit more willingly because they believed he would be hemmed in among the sand-hills, where he would finally be forced to sacrifice his captive to the exigencies of the situation. The distance from the camp of the Pawnees to the head of the ravine was about six miles, the road on the plateau to the cottonwood-grove possibly two more. Emperor had made it in less than half an hour.

Rue had wakened with the plunging leap that took them into the ravine. For the moment she struggled with her bonds, but the network around the blankets held firmly. The regular motion of Emperor's grand stride again lulled her to sleep. Lo-loch-to-hoo-la was left free to watch his pursuers and his wound.

The jaded ponies soon lagged in the rear, and a mile

from the head of the ravine the last of the Pawnees turned back. The chief's wound bled profusely; but during the race he had managed to wrap it closely with a strip hastily cut from his blanket. Two hours more, and darkness would overtake him. He must at least put the Canadian between himself and the party he had left. But then this pass that he had so fortunately stumbled upon might be known to the white men he knew were following them. He was in danger of meeting enemies at every step. This blind trail through the cottonwood-grove led eastward: from this direction the "Long-knives" would come. He rode slowly to the edge of the wood, keeping beneath the shelter of the trees. There the buffalo which had escaped from the chase were resting in the grassy slope that swept eastward; he had passed stragglers and wounded animals constantly since leaving the ravine. The herd in front out there seemed uneasy, yet they did not look in his direction. No, they too were looking eastward. There! down there in the coming twilight there was a line creeping onward, every instant growing more distinct. Yes! they were soldiers. The red reflection from the western sky glinted along the burnished guns and sabres. Doubt was not possible: they knew the pass. His people would be taken in the toils, attacked on all sides — for the warrior instinctively read the tactics of his enemies — without warning. Feasting in fancied security, his people would be an easy prey. He must go back. The splendid stallion he rode had not yet been put to the top of his speed. There was time. But then the sleeping *chincha*. At that very moment the little rosy hand touched his own. She stirred uneasily in her sleep; a long, deep sigh told the prisoner's dream. He would not take her to those who were thirsting for her life. Yet he could not desert his tribe when the foe was about to strike. He had no time now to take her to the shelter he had intended to seek. He would hide her in the wood down by the river-side, and return after he had warned his people. If he should *not* return — if he should be killed! The stern warrior shuddered as he thought of *that*,—of the child alone, starving in the wood.

Only half decided, he turned Emperor, and rode rapidly into the dense thicket by the river, the horse's hoofs sinking silently into the moss. Suddenly he came into an opening where three Indians sat upon a fallen log. They sprang to their feet and drew their weapons, when one of them recognized him. Fearlessly he advanced, and asked in the Comanche language, "Are the chiefs with Senaco friends of the Indians, or slaves of the Long-knives?" And he looked inquiringly at the two Seminoles, whose *totem* he had instantly recognized.

The younger of the Seminoles, whose eye and color betrayed the anger the query had excited, looked instinctively to the elder for permission to reply. The wily Comanche, anxious to prevent any difficulty between his Pawnee ally and his late interlocutors, said:—

"My brother has heard of the deeds of the great chief of the Seminoles. The warriors of the pale-faces were gathered in Florida as ten to one, when Coacoochee fought them in the Everglades. Lo-loch-to-hoo-la has seen the chiefs of his own people bury the hatchet when their wounded warriors were prisoners, and their women and children were surrounded by angry enemies whose brothers' scalps hung from the lodge-poles of the Pawnees."

Lo-loch-to-hoo-la, since the first brief glance of recognition, had never once turned to the Comanche; but whilst listening to the speaker had looked fixedly in the eyes of the Seminole chief, as if to read not only the answer to his spoken question, but to the thought in his heart. He dismounted, carelessly holding the bridle over his arm.

Face to face were two of the most marked and distinct types of the North American Indian,—the warlike chief of a powerful tribe who had once roamed at will over the trackless plains from the Mississippi to the Rocky Mountains, and the gentler and more chivalric warrior of the Florida savannas.

Lo-loch-to-hoo-la was dressed in the full panoply of a Pawnee warrior. His head was shaved after the fashion of his tribe, leaving only the scalp-lock, ornamented with a beautiful crest of deer's hair. His moccasins and leggings were of tanned skins, gartered with broad bands of wampum. Over his shoulders a heavy silver clasp held together one of the exquisitely made blankets of the Navajos, so highly prized by the Indians of the plains, to which a sinister effect was given by a fringe of scalps. Around his brawny throat was a necklace of grizzly bears' claws, whilst his wrists were ornamented with a number of silver and wampum bracelets. The dress and bearing of the chief agreed in their savage grandeur. Even the scar that gashed the cheek and nose added to his martial appearance, as did also the vermilion tint that lit the dark bronze visage.

Coacoochee was about forty years of age, a little above the medium height. Eyes dark, full, and expressive gave a singular charm to the sad but mournfully sweet countenance. His perfectly symmetrical figure was clad in a simple hunting-dress of tanned deer-skins; its sole ornaments a broad belt, embroidered with the pearls once so common a possession of the Florida Indians, and a curiously wrought breastpiece that hung from a wampum band around his throat. The only weapons carried by the Seminole chief were a rifle and a simple hunting-knife in its silver scabbard, thrust carelessly in the girdle about his waist. Yet with all this simplicity there was a natural grandeur, a magnificence in the presence of the man, that instantly impressed the beholder with the idea of his kingly rank. To these natural advantages of person add the magnetic quality of a voice clear and soft as the low notes of a silver flute. When with fluent speech and graceful, rapid gesture he urged an argument, or deigned to persuade, the effect upon the people of his race, always so sensitive to the peerless charm of oratory, seemed magical.

The Seminole chief advanced a few steps; and then,

folding his arms across his breast, repeated the name he had heard from the Comanche, emphasizing it with a soft note of inquiry, — " Lo-loch-to-hoo-la?"

The barbaric Pawnee thrilled from head to foot at the mere sound of his name; then, instinctively tutored to the etiquette of royal presence, gave a mute gesture of assent.

Coacoochee continued: "Five summers ago the daughter of Osceola was a prisoner in a village far to the northwest. Coacoochee had been called to a council of his people in Mexico; and the cry of the last child of the great chief who had fought with him on the savannas could not be heard across the Sierras. The medicine-men of the Pawnees doomed her to die. They were on the war-path against the white man, and the heart of a virgin must be offered to the Spirit of Battle. The fagots were piled in the middle of the wide prairie, where all the Pawnees were assembled.[1] The young maiden of the Seminoles was bound to the stake, a torch was lit to fire the fagots, when a gallant war-chief rushed forward to the pile, leading two horses, the swiftest in the tribe. He cut the bands that confined the prisoner, lifted her to one of the horses, mounted the other, and before his surprised people knew release was attempted, they had cleared the ring and were in the path of safety. Two days he rode with her southward. Osceola himself could not have cared for his daughter more tenderly. Then he left her on the trail of her people with provisions for her journey. Unstained and pure she was decreed to the fire of sacrifice: unstained and pure she was restored to her tribe. She is in the lodge of Coacoochee, — the wife of his bosom, the delight of his eyes. The preserver of the child of Osceola, the chief with the big heart and the strong arm, is the brother of Osceola's friend. The Seminoles and the Pawnees are enemies, but the life of Coacoochee is ready to answer any need of Lo-loch-to-hoo-la."

[1] This story of a Pawnee chief is told in Thatcher's "History of the North American Indians."

The listening Pawnee flushed with gratified pride until his face glowed like flame-lit bronze. He trembled at praise as he had never trembled at danger. For a moment he was silent. Then a short, imperious cry from the child, who had wakened and was again struggling with the resistant net-work, recalled him to recollection of her, and also of the danger of his tribe. With a harsh, guttural tone that feeling had deepened, he said, " Lo-loch-to-hoo-la's heart is glad. The words of the great chief are sweet to his ear as the sound of running water in the forest. But the path of his people is even now beset with danger. From the edge of the wood he has seen the soldiers of the pale-faced chief. They know the pass through the hills to the camp of the Pawnees, there, where my people are resting, not thinking that the Long-knives have so soon found and followed their trail. Lo-loch-to-hoo-la must go to his warriors; but he has here a little captive he saved from the tomahawks of his people. They have asked of him her life. But the prisoner of Lo-loch-to-hoo-la is his own. The deadly plague of the white man has made his lodge desolate. There is not a child of his blood alive. The Great Spirit has opened his heart to the brave little eaglet he found upon the war-path. See! she is the color of the pale-face, but her spirit is that of the red man."

Hastily releasing the child from her blankets, he held her toward the Seminole chief, saying, " Coacoochee cannot lie; his tongue is not forked. My brother will take this little child to the daughter of Osceola. He will say to her, ' Lo-loch-to-hoo-la gives you the child of his heart while he is upon the war-path with his people. If he falls in the coming battle, his spirit will not go to the happy hunting ground until it passes the lodge of Coacoochee. The sight of Ning-ah-shaw-na-quit-a[1] in the arms of the wife of the Seminole chief will make him glad as he crosses the dark water before reaching the land of the Great Spirit.' "

He took from his shoulders the magnificent Navajo

---

[1] Ning-ah-shaw-na-qui-ta, *Brave Little Heart.*

blanket, and, doubling it about the child, fastened it with the heavy clasp. Even then he remembered that it had seemed to please her. Coacoochee held out his arms for the child: she turned away from him to Lo-loch-to-hoo-la, with the pretty, nestling movement of a young bird. The Pawnee's heart grew heavy with the pang of parting. A moment he hesitated, then resolutely gave her to the Seminole chief. Her lips quivered; a little, moaning, tired sob seemed to come from a breaking heart; but she caught the sound of Coacoochee's voice as he talked with the three Indians, and its charm held her. When the sound ceased and she looked for Lo-loch-to-hoo-la he was gone.

CHAPTER XXII.

He is come to ope
The purple testament of bleeding war.
SHAKSPEARE.

MAJOR BEALL'S report to Colonel Kearny was soon made. He had discovered the camp of the Pawnees, who were so unconscious of the nearness of their pursuers that they had neglected their usual precaution of outlying guards. They had all collected at the camp-fires, the smoke from which could easily be seen, forming a hazy curtain against the red light of the setting sun. He had left Stearns and Black Beaver with the Osages to watch and instantly report any movement to Colonel Kearny. There was a pass through a little ravine at the head of the Pawnee's camp, known to Stearns and Pike; so he had brought Pike and the rest of his little party to venture the attack through this pass in the rear of the Pawnees, should Colonel Kearny conclude to attack at once.

At the council of officers nearly all were for immediate attack; but there was one puzzling objection. If the Indians were surprised, or so worsted in an encounter that their escape seemed doubtful, the fate of the little prisoner would be instant death. Another point: was the force large enough to surround the enemy successfully? A weak line could be easily broken, and separate detachments overpowered in detail. But there *was* a chance of complete surprise: then the odds would be certainly on the side of the dragoons. At this moment an express rider came with news of a strong detachment on the way to join them that night. Every man in the

Red River settlement who could bear arms was out with the military from Fort Washita, to avenge the murder of their neighbors; more troops were coming to-morrow from Fort Towson. The question of numbers was settled. The little prisoner was the vulnerable spot in their arrangements. Leszinksky, who until now had quietly kept his place with the junior officers, approached the colonel.

"Well, Leszinksky, say what you would suggest. I shall be glad if you can assist us here. I tell you frankly that this is one of the most trying questions I have ever been called to decide. From Beall's report, we can catch these rascals at such a disadvantage that a stinging punishment can be inflicted; — but then the baby? A victory over these skulking Pawnees would never repay her loss. Major Beall's plan, to surround them to-night and parley with them in the morning, will possibly be best. But then there is a chance they may slip through our fingers. In that case they get off scot free, after all these horrible butcheries through the country; and we shall not even regain the captive, for whose release we shall have sacrificed almost the certainty of their complete discomfiture. I favor whipping them first and parleying afterwards; but if you can suggest anything you would like, it will have great weight with us all."

"I have only one thing to say, Colonel. If the chances seem to you equal, that they will murder my little daughter in event of defeat, or escape with her to the Comanche country if we fail to attack them, — then I beg of you, sir, to order an instant advance. Only give Major Beall an hour's start through the pass, and let me and those of my comrades who came here as volunteers, go with him. I shall beg of them to shoot at any Indian who is seen trying to escape with my child, if the bullet goes straight to her heart. I had rather she was safe in heaven than given over to the tender mercies of the marauders who have committed the outrages just reported to you."

There was a steady light in the clear eyes, and a ring in

the voice of the speaker, that went straight to the hearts of the brave men who surrounded him. There was no longer hesitation or doubt. Instant preparation for attack was ordered. The party to the pass to go at once; and to Major Beall's scouts, and the young officers who had volunteered, was added Captain Moore's company, which could be spared from the command, now that the reinforcing party was only ten miles distant; and the news of the coming fight would bring them in time to count for something in the battle.

An hour's start was given to Beall to get through the hills to the bank of the South Canadian. From there, their route was direct and uninterrupted to the head of the ravine. Pike led the way. Bob Stearns or Black Beaver, in his place, would have found some indication of the traveller who had so lately come and gone through the cottonwood, but Pike stolidly went on to the pass. He had no orders to look for trails; and without orders the giant never worried his slow-working faculties. Beall, who rode just behind Pike, was talking to Moore, Leszinksky, and Carson; so neither of them observed the print of Emperor's shoes in the mossy bank at the edge of the wood. To the men who followed, a horse-shoe more or less was nothing, though the track of an unshod pony would have caught their attention.

As the dragoons passed through the wood skirting south, there to the north, where the jutting bank of the river made a tiny bay, surrounded by bending trees, where from bough to bough vines had intertwined and crossed until a close screen hid it securely from any chance passers, the two Seminoles and the Comanche resumed the conference Lo-loch-to-hoo-la had interrupted.

A canoe was fastened to the shore. In it sat Baby Rue, securely muffled in the chief's blanket, gravely eating the last of Lo-loch-to-hoo-la's luncheon, whilst her eyes wandered from the Indians on the bank to the broad silver clasp that the slipping folds of the blanket had shifted from its place on her breast to her lap. Suddenly the measured tramp of the dragoons' horses,

11

as they struck the rocky highway that led round the base of the hills, was heard; there was the clank of scabbards as the column closed. The little child dropped the bright ornament that had pleased her, and a cry of "Papa! Papa!" rang over the river. Her struggle swayed the light canoe, and as it swung round sideways to the shore, the breeze from the south lifted the tangled curtain of vines, and through the arches of the slender trees the troop could be seen clearly, out in the open by the hills. Again she called, "Papa! Papa!" half frantic with delight at the sight of the familiar figures of mounted dragoons. But the breeze that had given them to view carried the cry of the child down the river, where it was heard only by the water-fowl as they gathered their young to their nests in the cane.

. . . .

The dragoons had closed up at a fast trot, and were soon over the two miles to the head of the ravine. As they crossed the last ridge before their descent from the line of the sand-hills, Lo-loch-to-hoo-la reached the point where a sudden turn of the creek formed the angular opening into the hills. Hidden by the darkness that was gathering in the hollows, he could see against the sky-line the troop crossing the ridge. A moment more and he had turned the point of the hills and entered the open prairie. In the lingering twilight he saw the ponies grazing by the little stream. He rode up the ridge, so lately the scene of his passage at arms with Non-je-ning-go, and plainly in view were the camp-fires, where all were assembled for the feast. He crossed the hollows, and, dismounting, climbed the next ridge, cautiously crawling when near the top.

Yes, there were the advance scouts of the pale-faces. Not twenty yards below him an Osage was lying on the ground, watching the scene at the fire. He had been so intently interested there that he had not seen the chief ride into the hollow. On the rolling ridge still further eastward, there was a little group gathered, and towards them a man was running rapidly, in a stooped position. The chief could tell it was a scout, possibly one who had been nearest the unconscious revellers. He was safe from the group over there; but what to do with the watcher so near him, who could see him pass to the fires, and who would at once suspect he carried news of the coming foe? That problem was quickly solved. He waited until the man across on the far ridge had reached his comrades, and then, knowing they would be for a moment absorbed by the story being told, he drew his bow and carefully adjusted the arrow. There must be no need of another, — no intimation given to those far-away watchers that their comrade had gone to another questioning than theirs. The left arm of the chief was stiff and painful from his wound, but the stoicism of the Indian was regardless of pain. Though the tingling and tortured nerves quivered for an instant, the bow was clasped steadily and the arrow sent home, — home to the citadel of a life. It entered the brain of the Osage just behind the ear. Not a cry, not a movement, told that death had come in the flight of an arrow. But Lo-loch-to-hoo-la knew. He could now go to his tribe unseen. The hunters were about them: they must be instantly ready or they would be taken in the toils.

CHAPTER XXIII.

A STILL, small voice comes through the wild,
Like a father consoling his fretful child,
Which banishes bitterness, wrath, and fear,
Saying, "Man is distant, but God is near!"

AN hour after the departure of Moore's squadron the officers and men of Colonel Kearny's command were in the saddle and moving cautiously toward the Indian camp. Twice they were met by messengers. The first reported the Indians' preparation for the feast and their apparent unconsciousness of danger; the second brought better news. Stearns and two of the Osages had captured the only guard between the command and the Indian camp. He was perched on the summit of a sand-hill, eagerly watching some fracas in the valley, when the crust gave way, and he slid into the midst of the little party, who had just decided that, as they could not capture, they must in some noiseless way dispatch him. They had him gagged and tied before he had recovered from the astonishment of his slide into their hands.

When within two miles of the camp, Colonel Kearny halted, and sent forward an Osage scout, who soon returned, with Bob Stearns. His report was: —

"Well, Colonel, I don't see how we can holp cleanin' 'em out this time. They are sarcumvented and signed over, and 'bout as good as delivered up, though I must say it ain't so much the dragoons as will a-done it as themselves. Thar's somethin' that ain't natcral 'bout it somewhar. I've been a-fightin' Injins from Florida to here, and it's the fust time I've saw 'em play such cards as these. Why, it's a plumb leadin' of a jack up to a ace, — a-stoppin' thar to hunt buffaler without mindin' one bit who's a-huntin' them. It's been a-botherin' me mightily. Thar must be somethin' the matter with the chiefs. Black Beaver says Lo-loch-to-hoo-la's a tip-top warrior; but he's got a high and mighty sort of a way that wins Injins to hate him. It's jus' that; and I'm powerful 'fraid it's 'bout the little capt'n they've quarrelled. You see, Colonel, from all the repo'tes we've got, they ain't took nary another prisoner, — they jus' went in for scalps; an' that ar*guys* that they ain't a-goin' back to the villages, but down thar with the Comanches in Mexico, and they don't want to be bothered with no prisoners. You see this, 'bout who's got the baby in charge, is a puzzler. It's a cur'us thing for a chief to do on the war-path; yet I ain't never knowed Tisson wrong when he was tellin' jus' what he seen himself. Now, if so be and Lo-loch-to-hoo-la has took a notion she sha'n't be killed, — which is jus' the on'y idee I can come at, — then it's purty apt to raise a rumpus with the other chiefs; and, if they've got the warriors thar way o' thinkin' then the big chief'll have to take a back seat at the council. That's the on'y way I can 'count for thar lettin' us get the bulge on them like this."

"How many Indians do you think are in the party?"

"Nigh onto three hundred, sir."

"There must be more than three hundred. Why, they struck nearly every settler from Castalar's to the Red River. The Chickasaws will not be troubled to send in any more notices to quit."

"No, sir; and, whatever they pretend, *they* ain't a-goin' to be sorry much. But it's a new move for the Pawnees to do thar constable work. You are mighty right 'bout thar havin' been more Pawnees than these over on the Kiamesha; but thar's some of t'em gone on with the horses they stole."

"What! the horses are not here with them?"

"No, sir; on'y the ones they're ridin'; and they've tired them out with the hunt to-day."

"Could you get anything out of that fellow you caught?"

"Nothin' but grunts, sir. I didn't dar' loose his tongue till I got him most over here, and then he was sullen like, and would n't talk."

"I think Beall told me it was prairie south of their camp. Will it be possible to send a detachment to head off their escape in that direction?"

"Yes, sir, if they goes 'bout a mile south of here fust. Then they can cross the little creek that runs through the prairie down thar, as it cuts through the big hollow they've camped in, and you'll have them sarcumnavi-*gated*. If they knows of the pass up thar, — which I don't much think they do, — they'll jus' run direckly into Major Beall's weepons. Them as don't like bein' shot 'll have a mighty good chance of bein' finished with the dragoons' sabres. Then, too, the wind's on our side, — and that's 'bout the best al*ly* we could a-had. A Injin's hearin' 's good as a dog's or a mule's. If the wind's a-blowin' thar way, you can't count on gettin' mighty close up before they know it."

"How is the road through the pass? Can the dragoons ride rapidly?"

"Yes, sir; it's main good; the creek's low, and the sandy ridges is most hard-baked with this clar, breezy weather. You mought ride all the way through to that cottonwood-grove on a gallop. The dragoons 'll be out on the prairie in a half hour more, I'm thinkin', sir."

"Send me the most reliable guide you have for Captain Allen's detachment. He must cross the creek down there at once. As soon as they are at the creek I will advance. Go back to your men, and do not fail to watch if the Indians discover this movement of Allen. If they give the least sign of fright, let me know at once."

Stearns saluted, and was gone. The command halted some ten minutes longer; then the order was given to advance quickly. They were within two hundred yards of the ridge beyond which the scouts were, when Stearns came running to the head of the column.

"Colonel, thar has been some movement down thar at the camp whilst I was over yonder with you. I can't jus' make out what yet; but thar's a scout up thar on the ridge a-watchin', and I've sent Black Beaver to him. Here's Black Beaver now."

The Indian came close, and then said in a low tone, "Osage scout no good. Pawnee got um scalp. May be so Pawnee all gone."

"Could you see the camp?" asked the colonel hurriedly.

"Fire down thar all by heself."

"Then how do you know they are gone? If they are warned of the presence of the enemy, they will not stay near the fire. That would be to seek death."

"Injun he don't know nothing. Injun big fool; white man mighty smart, — he know heap. Maybe so he take one little walk, he see he no see Pawnee."

To cover the impertinence of his sarcastic red friend, Bob said hastily, "If they've killed the scout, they must a-been warned. Some on 'em has chased the buffaler up thar and seen the dragoons. If them Injins has lit out through the prairie, they'll make it mighty hot for Capt'n Allen. Major Beall must be purty close here by now."

The colonel ordered an instant advance. At the top of the ridge the "Charge" was sounded. In a moment it was re-echoed from the head of the prairie, and down from the south by the creek. Beall and Allen were ready. With cheers and yells of triumph, the dragoons fired, and then rode thunderingly at the dark spots on the prairie that, unmoved by the shot or the tramp of the squadrons, still waited. A few moments, and horses were snorting and men swearing, as they stumbled over the carcasses of the buffalo left from the day's hunt.

It was plain the Indians had escaped. Not a moving object upon the star-lit plain gave hope of the capture of a solitary straggler. Pawnees and ponies had disappeared like the "phantasms of a dream."

The colonel, Beall, and Allen drew rein at the campfire. Coming from opposite points, they gazed at each other in blank surprise, until the imp of farce that lies hid beneath the robe of tragedy stamped each broadening visage with such a strange commingling of amazement, anger, and mirth that the dumb silence was at length broken by peals of laughter. Beall's hearty, loud bass and Allen's nervously hysterical falsetto were doubled and redoubled in volume, as the colonel rolled out a volley of oaths, with a running accompaniment of cackles and snorts that would have made the fortune of an *opera bouffe* actor.

How the Indians had discovered the presence of their pursuers, and then contrived to elude them, was a mystery that puzzled even Beall and Bob Stearns. The latter was as completely miserable as possible for so sanguine a temperament. To his grief and remorse at the loss of the child was added the crestfallen feeling of a baffled official. Installed by Beall as chief of scouts, he had made a most promising beginning of the affair in hand. He had told of the pass known only to himself and Pike; he had the entire directing of the guides; and he and his lieutenant, Black Beaver, had been near enough to the camp of the enemy to be sure that — until the unfortunate hour they had, in the blindness of confident success, trusted the watch to that ill-starred Osage — there was not a movement of the savages that betrayed the slightest alarm or uneasiness. Anxious to repair his blunder and save his tottering reputation, Stearns called Black Beaver, who, confident in the opinion he had given the colonel, had disdained any movement toward the prairie, and getting torches they went to where the dead Osage was lying, on the crest of the ledge to the east.

Just below in the hollow was the little clump of cottonwood under which Lo-loch-to-hoo-la and his captive had spent the entire afternoon before the flight up the ravine. Their search soon determined several important facts. Rue was alive and in the care of the "Big Chief," who had evidently rested there for some time with the child. After the most careful and minute examination of every foot of ground under and around the cottonwood, they sought the temporary headquarters of the officers, who were straggling in from their useless gallop in the darkness of a cloudy and moonless night.

Carson and Leszinksky were the last to return. There was a quick movement in the group of officers, to make place for the late comers. For the first time since the night when the story of his child's capture was told him, Leszinksky seemed hopeless and despondent. The clear eyes had lost their light; his face had a haggard, anguished expression; there were lines in it that told of a quick transition from youth to age. His step dragged, his movements were uncertain, all elasticity was gone. The blaze of sullen anger in Carson's face was far less painful. It was apparent that he suffered; but then, too, it was apparent that there was capacity to take punishment. One might have been the Sorrowful Knight whom affection brought to the lists of Templestowe; the other was a boxer, sturdily set in the ring to give and take heavy blows.

The colonel was of right the host at that modest spread. He made place instantly, and called, "Come here by me, Leszinksky. You must try our rude fare, and then get what sleep you can before our early start. We will be off as soon as it is light enough to get the bearings and the trail. They will not slip through our fingers again. Crowd in, there, Carson; you must be hungry after the long ride."

Leszinksky took his cup of black coffee and drank it, without apparent knowledge of what he did. He had fallen into absent thought, — his wife, his child, the little broken home, — when a hand touched him on the shoulder.

"Marse Stan, thar's good news, sir. Black Beaver and Marse Bob Stearns is out heah a-waitin' fur you all to get yo' supper; but I would come to let you know, sir, they's foun' little Miss Rue's tracks, sir, up heah in the holler, an' they's sho she's alive an' well, sir."

For an instant the young officer trembled all over. He was ghastly pale. Moore, who sat beside him on the ground, took out his ever-ready flask, and insisted on his taking it instantly. There was a general uprising, and the colonel's voice rang out sharply.

"Stearns, come here at once! What have you found?"

The soldier's voice, as he answered, had in it vibrating, joyful tones of triumph that carried conviction and hope with every word.

"I went up thar on the ridge, sir, with Black Beaver to whar the Osage was killed to see, if so be and I could, how they come to find him. Thar was a arrer shot clean through his head, and fastened in his hand whar his face was a-leanin' on it. It's a oncommon long, heavy arrer, and Black Beaver says it's the Big Chief shot it. That, sir, made me more careful like not to spile any tracks or Injin signs that mought be round thar. We commenced at the dead Osage, and struck out the way the arrer come, holdin' our torches close to the ground. Furder up the ridge, close to the sand-hills whar the hollow ends, we found whar the Injin that shot the Osage had crep'. He must of already knowed we was most onto 'em, for he had crawled up outen the slant at the top o' the hollow mighty cautious. He rested thar a spell, watchin' us. It was easy to see whar his elbows dug in the sand thar. Then he seen the Osage, who was a-lookin' down at the camp-fires. The Big Chief — for I know it was him — crawled down over a gulley till he got behind some bushes of prickly pars: here he tried his arrers. He threw away this one, sir; you see the head's loose." (And the arrow was passed round the circle.) "Then he found one to please him, and he shot. It couldn't a-been blind dark, so I know it must a-been 'bout the time Black Beaver come back from lower down the ridge, jus' before I met you, sir. So you see they had purty nigh a hour's start on us. Arter he shot the Osage, the Big Chief crep' down the hollow agin till he got jus' below the ridge whar the Osage was a-lyin', and then he went up for his scalp. Trackin' him, we come to a little clump of scrubby cottonwood, up thar by a damp place, — a sort o' blind spring, — and thar the track was plain. On the edge of the cottonwood, a horse had been tied, — a shod horse, with small, thoroughbred feet, but it wah n't no Injin pony. We went back to see whar the horse-tracks come from; and we follered them in the sand over the ridge and the prairie, goin' toward the pass, and thar we lost the trail in the marks of dragoons' horses. So we come back agin to the cottonwood, and commenced to look under the bushes, whar I found them little tracks in the edge of the damp place."

Here he turned to Black Beaver, who held carefully on his folded blanket, for the officers to examine, about a foot square of damp, sandy earth, in which was the distinct mould of one little stockinged foot and one wee moccasin. As Leszinksky stooped and kissed the print of his child's foot in the sand, mist came to eyes unused to tears. Around back of the officers, men were grouped, looking and listening. He spoke to them: —

"If there is a soldier here who will walk back to Fort Gibson, and carry carefully and unbroken this token of my child to her mother, I will give him a hundred dollars. It is a small sum for such a service, but you know that I am not rich enough to make it larger."

"And I will give another," said Carson eagerly.

"And I," "And I," the chorus was swelling when the colonel called, —

"And if any of you undertakes the job, and fails to deliver it in the perfect condition it's in now, I will give him nine-and-thirty lashes, and the guard-house for a week."

A beardless, handsome boy came from the ranks. "I will go without any reward, and take your punishment, Colonel, if I fail. It is little to do for an officer who saved me in a hand-to-hand fight with two Indians, in that scrimmage we had on the Arkansas, when my horse was shot and my arm broken. I ain't forgot, Lieutenant, how you lifted me up right from under the tomahawk and brought me out. And I never can forget that Mrs. Leszinksky took me herself in the ambulance out to Bouie's Hill, when I had the fever, and the doctor said I'd die in the hospital, and had me tended as kindly as she could one of her own. I'll be only too glad to go. You'll let me, won't you, Colonel?"

"Yes, and give you all I promised if you fail," growled the colonel, as he blew his nose like a trumpet and turned to Bob Stearns. "Well, what else? I see you have not told all your story yet."

"No, Colonel, not all. I found this little piece of the baby's dress on a prickly-par' bush that was close by whar the chief had put her on his blanket."

"How do you know he did that?" asked Leszinksky.

"Why, sir, to a Injin trailer it was plain as writin'. Thar was the mark o' the blanket, and the baby on it, on the little patch of runnin' vines that grew in that sandy, light kind o' ground; and I found a piece o' bread and a beef-bone thar; and over nigh by the blanket the chief had been settin', leanin' agin a little rise in the ground; he was turned toward the camp-fire, watchin', I reckon. His horse was a-grazin' in the young bushes and the few tufts o' buffaler-grass that's thar. So you see, for some reason, he wah n't sociable like with the chiefs and warriors. Thar wah n't another track close up thar, though thar was some a-goin' up and down the hollow not fur off."

"Then you think the child is not only alive and well, but well cared for?"

"I'm sho' of it, Leftenant. For some reason, sir, — that's what I can't make out, — the Big Chief's took to her for good. Thar was some bright leaves and hollyberries and little pebbles all shook together, whar the blanket was picked up, that he must a-give her to play with. So you see it's for kindness to her, and not for spite, he's saved her life. I'm sho' of it, and so's Black Beaver. Ask him."

The general attention was turned to the Indian.

"Pappoose all good safe. May be so Lo-loch-to-hoo-la take um home to em wife. May be so that woman he no got any. May be so he lose um,—he cry all ee time. See heap womans that a way. Maybe so Lo-loch-to-hoo-la got nodder one wife—that one wife he got plenty pappoose. He make that nodder one woman got no pappoose heap mad. He tell Lo-loch-to-hoo-la ketch um one. Now chief ketch um one no 'fraid Injun — no 'fraid nowhere. Chief heap glad — much like this a one. Won't let Pawnee kill um, won't let nodder one hurt um."

All the officers now walked up to the cottonwood clump, Stearns, Black Beaver, and Oscar in front with torches, and many of the men bringing up the rear with a fresh supply ready to light; Beall and Leszinksky next to the torch-bearers. The second examination confirmed belief in the scout's theory of the protection and care given the child. The mark of the spread blanket, the food, the gathered playthings, the remoteness from the crowd at the fire, told of a care that was kindly and watchful. Emperor's tracks were recognized by a man in Captain Moore's company who had shod him. Everybody began to be hopeful of the child's rescue.

At a council of the officers that night, Leszinksky made a request that was strongly supported by Major Beall,—that the command should camp where they now were, and await the reinforcements and supply train, which could be ordered on at once, while Leszinksky and a small party should push on rapidly to the Washita with a flag of truce, and, if possible, see the chief who had his child and arrange for her ransom.

After some discussion the colonel consented, only insisting the escort should be strong enough to inspire the Indians with respect.

CHAPTER XXIV.

Yea, truth faileth; and he that departeth from evil maketh himself a prey. — Isaiah.

WITH the first gray glimmer of dawn Captain Moore's company, Lieutenant Carson with twenty picked men from Allen's, and "Beall's Scouts," started for the crossing of the Washita. In advance of the squadron a white flag was carried; and the telegraphic smoke, rising from the highest points ahead, told plainly their movements were being observed and signalled.

About noon, a large party of horsemen showed themselves several miles distant. From the glistening of the lances, which blazed as they turned them in the sun, the first conclusion of the officer was that they were Mexican cavalry, who had been apprised of the approach of the Americans, and had advanced to contest it. An examination with field-glasses at nearer quarters proved them to be a war-party of Comanches. Suddenly they disappeared over the hill, and soon reappeared on another summit farther off and slightly different in direction. The squadron again advanced toward them with like result. The command was halted.

Major Beall and Leszinksky, with Carson as flag-bearer, rode forward and signalled the Indians to approach; when one of the warriors, carrying a white buffalo-skin on the point of his lance, came dashing across the prairie until he met Carson, who was slightly in advance with the flag. The Comanche rode a small but powerful silver-gray horse; the prominent eyes, sharp nose, high nostrils, small feet, and delicate legs proving him a wild horse of the plains, sprung from the mixed Arab and Andalusian stock introduced by the Spaniards at the time of the invasion of Mexico. The rider looked Carson steadily in the face, then, leaning his lance against the flag, whirled his horse in a wonderfully executed series of demi-vaults, reining and spurring the spirited steed as he came prancing and leaping along, tacking to right and left like a ship beating against the breeze, to where Beall and Leszinksky waited. He held out his hand, which Beall instantly grasped. Seeing his friendly reception, the rest of the party advanced under "full whip." After a general hand-shake, all dismounted, and the pipe was lit and passed around.

Major Beall and a Comanche who could speak Spanish being the interpreters, the object of the expedition was fully explained, — "to ransom the little daughter of an officer there present." Then the major, in a florid address, sketched skilfully what would be the material gratitude of the officer and his comrades to any brave chief of the Comanches who would see the captor of the child, known to be now in their country, and arrange the terms of ransom.

For a short time after the interpreter had finished the translation, the Comanches were silent. Then the warrior, who had first advanced to meet the flag, addressed the Indians in a few short, emphasized sentences, to which they gave ready assent. He now turned to Beall, and, to the surprise of that officer, addressed him in excellent Spanish. He said: —

"We have listened to the words of the chief of the Long-knives. They are good words: the hearts of the Comanches are touched with the pain of the chief who has lost from his lodge the child whose presence made pleasant the faces of his friends. They will do what they can to make his heart glad, — to turn this trouble away from his people. But the Comanches have not been upon the war-path; they did not cross the Washita until their young men told of the coming of a great war-party of the pale-faces. Over there" — and he pointed in the direction of Colonel Kearny's encampment — "the Great Chief is gathering his warriors. If he only seeks a little child who has been stolen by the Pawnees, why are the Long-knives from the forts on the Arkansas and the Red River all turning into the trail that leads to the Comanche villages?"

It needed all the major's *aplomb* to answer this naturally and without the hesitation that would have been seen instantly by the wily Comanche. Long experience and a little native impudence served him at need. He explained that straggling parties of Pawnees had been reported as scattered from the Washita to the Kiamesha, raiding through the country of the Chickasaws, the allies of the Great Father, murdering the white settlers who were not immediately under the protection of the guns of the fort, and driving off all their cattle. For this the garrisons had all been at once alert and out in pursuit. Here came the best touch of the major's diplomacy, reserved as the concluding and convincing phrase: "The Great Chief had hastened on to the headwaters of the Blue River to intercept the Pawnees at the pass, and after the failure to capture them there, sent out runners to arrest the advance of all other parties to the Comanche country, until the bearers of the flag of truce should make the request which the Great Chief was there to enforce, if need be. That although he desired above all things to preserve a friendly relationship with the Comanches, he would be compelled to cross the Washita and search the entire country, if the little prisoner was not at once forthcoming."

This speech told on his audience: first the promise of reward and ransom, then the threat to come to the villages. They were not ready for such visitors. Later, when their Mexican allies, who were now some distance south of the Red River watching Taylor's forces, should not be far off; when the league with all the disaffected border-tribes should be perfected; when Senaco, that shrewd diplomatist, should have won the great war-chief of the Seminoles to new effort against the foe he had fought so long, — then the soldiers of the pale-faces might come. For then their villages would be deserted; their women and children safe the other side of the Witchita Mountains, beyond the salt plains, in the fertile valleys of the Pecos, where winter brings no hardship or suffering. For the present, they must temporize; must yield to the necessities of the time, and make what they could out of the advantages offered. The major's interlocutor, His-oo-san-ches, began: —

"The chief has spoken like a brave man. He is not afraid of the truth. The Comanches will talk with Lo-loch-to-hoo-la. To-morrow, when the sun rises, His-oo-san-ches will be here with the answer of the Big Chief of the Pawnees. The Great Chief and the warriors must come no farther. The Pawnees have eyes — they would see the war party far off. They would then go to the north of the Comanche country, and the little prisoner would be lost to her people."

The arrangement was soon perfected. Captain Moore encamped on a little hill with a creek hard by, where they could have the advantage of water, grazing, and wood; yet sufficiently elevated to watch the plain across which the Indians must come. Dispatches were sent to Colonel Kearny, begging him not to advance until after the coming conference.

At the rising of the sun, His-oo-san-ches and his party were seen coming across the prairie. There was the greatest possible excitement in the command when Black Beaver, looking at the Indians, who were now close at hand, exclaimed, in a startled manner unusual to his race, "See Lo-loch-to-hoo-la!"

"Where? where?" asked a dozen voices.

"There — that a one — heap big. Got Mexican blanket — Mexican sombrero. No show Pawnee shaved head — no ride 'Merican horse. Think white man heap fool — no got somebody here tell um."

Carson and Stearns, with the same impulse, hastily examined and re-capped their pistols. There was a general movement as if to have weapons in readiness, — a touch of sabre-hilts, an uncovering of holsters. Even Beall and Moore gave quick glances at each other as they shook themselves in their saddles, with the cavalry instinct that sounds the perfectness of trappings. There was an instantaneous resolve in every mind that, come what would, the child-stealer should be their prisoner, — at least until his captive was given up. Captain Moore only uttered the thought in every mind when the order was quietly spoken, " Look out there, all of you: we may have a fight here any moment. Buford, take ten picked men and watch every movement of that damned Pawnee. *He is not to go back*, no matter how this conference ends. We'll have a prisoner to add to the ransom offered for the child. If the Comanches resist, seize the chiefs; we will hold them as hostages until she is given up."

Leszinksky, who had ridden a little to one side, and then down the hill toward the Comanches, had not observed the preparation or heard the order. A soldier, he detested diplomacy; a gentleman, he abhorred deceit and chicanery. He was distrustful of the shifts of Beall's strategy, and tired of circumlocution. He had thus far held his peace in the conference where his dearest interests were being discussed. Not only his child, but his wife's life hung in the balance. Longer delay, the agony of suspense and apprehension, added to the already delicate state of Margaret's health, would almost of a certainty result fatally. He thought of the doctor's look of warning that evening before the news came of his child's capture, and then of the mother's wild cries of anguish — the last sounds he had heard from the voice that made the heart-music of his home. He was still the lover of his wife. The beauty, the delicacy, the womanliness of her character, so gilded her daily life that the halo of romance was preserved. She was as sovereignly the queen of his thoughts and fancies as Margaret Cartaret had been. To this adoring, respectful worship was the added quality of tenderest affection, of a perfectly reciprocal confidence and trust. *This* lover had not merely plucked a sweet flower, to toss it carelessly aside when faded: he had transplanted an immortal blossom into the garden of his life. Every unfolding leaf had been the revelation of a new beauty. There were no littlenesses in the character of the woman he loved, no conceits of pride, no petty jealousies. She assumed her place in his life and his home, as part of himself. His friends were her friends; his comrades were always sure of her welcome,— a welcome so cordial, yet so simple in manner, that it left them free from any artificiality of compliment. Her rare and perfect tact accomplished something more difficult: it left her husband free with his friends. She did what is so hard to the ordinary woman, — she kept out of the way; yet her presence was always desired, because it was never obtruded. The house had the *insouciant* charm of bachelor's quarters, with the added attraction of the near presence of a graceful, accomplished woman. What wonder that men, smarting from the petty tyrannies of the sex that rules through weakness and complaint, canonized her!

Thinking of this peerless wife, grieving with her grief even more than his own, Leszinksky determined to try the heart of the savage who had spared his child. There must be love in it, for she had entered at that portal. There must be a brave, unreckoning generosity, for it was evident his protecting care had cost him the supremacy so dear to a chief. How thankful he felt that the imperious habit of study, the enthusiasm of the student of philology, had led him to examine closely the different Indian dialects, and that the providence mortals call chance had given him a competent teacher of the Pawnee language the winter they were in Laramie, the winter his child was born, when, evening after evening, a cheery, helpful, companionable French priest taught him the harsh gutturals that Margaret's voice softened to melody, and that must now be used to win the freedom of her child.

These thoughts had made him totally unobservant of Moore's arrangement to capture the chief. He only watched for the first glance of the man who held in his hands the liberty of Baby Rucheil, the life of Margaret. The Comanches halted as he reached the party.

From the officers on the hill came a warning "Gardez vous!" in Beall's voice. His-oo-san-ches commenced the customary hand-shaking. Leszinksky made the custom serve his need. He shook hands down the line until he reached the Pawnee, and then, turning his horse without care of who followed, rode beside the chief, who from the first regarded him with watchful curiosity. There were quick glances of surprise from Comanche to Comanche as Leszinksky addressed the chief in the Pawnee tongue, which not a Comanche present understood.

"From the kindness Lo-loch-to-hoo-la has shown my daughter, I know he has the heart of a father. He will let his heart speak. I will only ask him one question,— a question I would answer instantly were I the guardian of the chief's child, as he is of mine. Is she well?"

For an instant the Pawnee started as Leszinksky repeated his name, then he only grew more impassive. The white man should not think it was through fear he had sought disguise. At the last words there was a quick look at the speaker. The fiery black eyes sought to penetrate the very depths of the clear gray orbs that met his gaze so fearlessly. They were the eyes of the little *chincha;* the lights were not so bright and changeful in expression, but more steady and constant. "If I were the guardian of the chief's child, as he is of mine": the words pierced the defences of pride, or, rather, they wakened a grander pride,— the pride that finds reward in the confidence it compels, the trust it brings. He *must* answer. All the more because it was a difficult thing to do, he must answer truly. Again the thought of the little *chincha* who died on his breast came, this time to claim his sympathy for the father who suffered, as it had claimed his sympathy for the child in the extremity of peril. He *would* answer. But here the mind of the savage passed through a new change,— a phase that lifted him from the last plane of barbarism. He hesitated to answer, *because the answer must give pain.* He was no longer a savage, but a gentleman who had studied "the humanities" in the school of

Nature. The teaching of the great Mother had begun when the uplifted tomahawk had fallen harmlessly before the fearless glance of a little child. The next lesson was an indefinable sense of the beauty of helplessness, caught glimmeringly from the sheen of golden curls and the rosy tips of baby fingers. His first degree had been taken when the life of his captive was laid in the balance, and it outweighed the traditions of race, the supremacy of chieftainship. The teaching was finished in this crowning lesson, the sum and end of human ethics, — the pain in giving pain, the sorrow that is sorrowful through the sorrow of another.

"Ning-ah-shaw-na-quit-a is in the lodge of the friend of Lo-loch-to-hoo-la. The Indian women watch that the fever spirit, who touched her by the river, does not enter. After the going down and rising of another sun the child will be safe."

For a moment both were silent. They had reined up at a little distance from the group of officers and chiefs, who were soon smoking the pipe of peace around a council-fire at the foot of the little eminence. The band of Indian braves was some fifty yards distant, in the direction whence they had come, sitting and lying at ease, holding the lariats of their own and the chiefs' horses. Some of the soldiers were dismounted and in small parties on the side of the hillock, behind and not far from the council-fire; others, mounted, were drawn up in a line on the summit. A small party was riding slowly down the slope away from the fire, but in the direction of the chief and Leszinksky. The chief was watching the approaching horsemen, when Leszinksky spoke : —

"My little daughter is suffering from the separation from her family, from the hardship of the long journey and the change from the life to which she is accustomed. I know the heart of Lo-loch-to-hoo-la has warmed to her. I know the Indian women are kind; but her mother is grieving as for the dead. She is the only child the Great Spirit has given us. The chief has learned to love her in the few days she has been in his care: he can tell what silence there is in the home where she dwelt, what sorrow in the hearts that had only her. He has heard from His-oo-san-ches what ransom is offered. If there is aught else I can give, it will be given freely to the warrior who saved my child. For the love he has given her, for the kindly care he has taken, no reward would be too great."

Leszinksky had blundered. His anxiety for the suffering child made him think only of her illness and the discomforts to which she was subjected. He had not trusted his first judgment of the brave, generous heart of the savage. He had gone back to the dicta of the frontier, to the logic of the Indian trader. He had struck the right key with the first question; but he lost the true sound that answered him, and the harmony was broken. The mistake was fatal. Had he stopped with the picture of the empty home and the sorrowing mother, there would have been hope. Even then the savage would have found it hard to break the oath he had sworn to himself, — the oath to keep the child, come what might. Now, when her father made her recovery a question of payment, he could refuse. The pale-faces were all traders, and in their bartering the red man always lost. Step by step they had come upon him; acre by acre they had taken his land. Treaties were written as they willed, with specious clauses by which they held the Indians bound so the Great Father might divide their hunting-grounds at his pleasure. They had been decoyed with invitations to councils, and then held as prisoners. Coacoochee was truthful and brave. Only at the setting of yesterday's sun, in the new lodge the Seminole had built beyond the Washita, they talked of the history of the red race; of the treachery of the white man; of the death of Osceola in the prison where the brave spirit could only break its bonds by bursting from the clinging hold of the body that bore the bloody impress of fetters. Tecumseh was right. The only hope of the Indian, who was vanishing before the white man like snow before the sun, was a confederation of all the tribes. He himself had talked with the brother of the great warrior, the prophet of the Shawanos, when he was journeying from nation to nation among the Indians of the Northwest trying to unite them against the common destroyer. He remembered how his heart burned at the story of the wrongs endured by the Shawanos, who had been driven foot by foot from the great ocean where the sun rises to the base of the Rocky Mountains. Tecumseh was dead; but Coacoochee was left to unite the tribes, — to lead them to battle, if the Seminole would only rouse himself from the burden of his griefs.

True, the Comanches were crawling snakes that the warriors of the Pawnees had despised; but then they could sting the enemy. Here he thought of his distrust of His-oo-san-ches, and, looking toward the council-fire, he saw the Comanche in close talk with the white men; whilst there — why were those horsemen there? Why had they stopped near by? Coacoochee was right in this also. It was a rash and foolish thing in him to come with the Comanches. They had always hated the Pawnees; and he himself even now carried Comanche scalps at his girdle. He had come through love for the child. He would keep her; but he had thought to learn the heart of her father by watching him unseen whilst His-oo-san-ches spoke of his child. His own heart had opened to the chief with the truthful tongue and the honest eyes. He had felt the pain he must give, and almost — no, he would not have broken his oath. Now, his way was plain. He could speak, not through the lying Comanche, but man to man with the chief who had thought to buy this new delight that had come to his life.

These were some of the thoughts of the chief, as he sat silently in his saddle for several minutes after Leszinksky had spoken. Then, suddenly reining his horse around to confront his listener, he said: —

"Lo-loch-to-hoo-la has not come to take ransom for the little *chincha* who has nestled in his breast, but to hear the words His-oo-san-ches was to say to the chief of the Long-knives. The Comanche is a crawling snake;

his tongue is forked. Lo-loch-to-hoo-la feared he would take the gifts of the chiefs, and not say that Lo-loch-to-hoo-la would not sell the child who has made his heart glad. She is brave and fearless; she has eaten the bread of the Indian, and slept by his fire. All the treasure of the Great Father of the white men cannot buy Ning-ah-shaw-na-qui-ta." [1]

Too late! Leszinksky felt he had lost his opportunity. He must content himself with hope for some new occasion to persuade the warrior before this conference ended. He would try to win the chief's trust, his friendship. He would urge nothing. He would be honest and frank, and trust the better feeling of the man he had not understood. He had always believed an Indian could be truthful and just; now he began to see he could have the finer instincts of a gentleman. Dismounting, he held out his hand: the chief also dismounted.

"Will not Lo-loch-to-hoo-la be the friend of Leszinksky?"

The Pawnee grasped the extended hand. The two men regarded each other intently. The chief, still holding Leszinksky's hand, said in a low tone: —

"Lo-loch-to-hoo-la believes that Leszinksky," — he made an effort to get the name, — "the father of Ning-ah-shaw-na-qui-ta, is a brave warrior; that his tongue speaks the words in his heart. But his people are creeping panthers; and their flag of peace is a lie. Even now their horsemen are coming to close the path of the Pawnee. The Comanches have sold Lo-loch-to-hoo-la at the council-fire while he was here talking to his friend."

The accent of these deep-toned sentences was a master-piece of wild oratory. It taught and convinced. The young officer knew, before he turned to look, that the charge was true, that an act of treachery was about to be attempted. For the first time in all Stanislaus Leszinksky's life the spirit of the imperious voyvode possessed him.

[1] Brave little heart.

"Stand back, men! Halt there! Buford, why are you coming here?"

The answer was given rapidly, that the Indian might not catch the meaning: —

"It was the captain's order. We're to arrest the chief at all hazards."

They still approached, riding slowly and cautiously, not to scare their prey.

"Halt, I say!"

The clear voice rang out imperiously. Buford hesitated. The men obeyed the senior officer, and halted.

"Buford, this is a mistake; you have misunderstood. What! arrest a brave enemy who has come under the invitation of that flag of truce?" and he pointed to the fluttering folds that waved at the summit of the hill.

"I am not to blame, Lieutenant. It was the captain's order, given as you rode forward to meet the chief."

Carson came galloping down the hill. Leszinksky turned quickly to Lo-loch-to-hoo-la, who stood apparently unaffected by the excitement about him, though certainly conscious of his danger.

"Will Lo-loch-to-hoo-la trust his friend?"

A quick grasp of the extended hand and a confident flash in the dark eyes was all the answer.

"Then mount my horse. It is the fleetest on the plains. Leszinksky wishes to exchange with Lo-loch-to-hoo-la."

The chief vaulted into the saddle, and waited as carelessly as if they were alone there on the prairie. As Leszinksky mounted the pony, Carson called out: —

"Look out, Stan! Buford is going to capture the damned red-skin. We will have the chiefs as soon as he is surrounded. Why the hell did you let him mount Sultan? We will have to kill him now to take him, and we wanted all the prisoners we could get."

Again the men advanced, at a motion from Buford. Leszinksky looked to the hill. There was no mistaking the waiting attitude of the officers. There was the flash of a sabre in the sunlight, and again the imperious call: —

"Halt! By the God that made me, you shall not stain me with this dishonor. The chief who spared the life of my child is here as an envoy. That flag is his protection and my justification in killing the first man who advances."

A voice at his side said: " Lo-loch-to-hoo-la has seen the heart of Leszinksky; he will not forget!"

There was the rush of a flying steed; then the click of muskets. Leszinksky threw himself between Buford's squad and the fugitive. There were shots from the hill, and a struggle about the Comanche chiefs; but out there on the rolling prairie Lo-loch-ta-hoo-la rode unharmed away from his pursuers.

PART VI.

THE CONFLICT.

The necessity of war, which among human actions is the most lawless, hath some kind of affinity with the necessity of law.
                                                        Sir W. Raleigh.

PART VI.

THE CONFLICT.

CHAPTER XXV.

We looked for peace, but no good came : and for a time of health, and behold, trouble ! — JEREMIAH.

THAT evening Colonel Kearny, with three companies of the 1st Dragoons, reinforced by a detachment of the 2d, two companies of infantry from the forts on the Red River, and a mounted company of volunteers, arrived at Captain Moore's encampment. Whatever may have been thought by the senior officers of the justice or right of the arrest of the chiefs who had trusted to the sacred character of the flag of truce, the expedience of their arrest was not questioned. The only regret expressed was that Lo-loch-to-hoo-la had escaped ; and but for the fact that Leszinksky was the person most interested in his capture, that young officer would have been severely reprimanded for his interference with the execution of an order.

The few Indians who had been captured with the chiefs (the larger body, having been some distance from the council, had escaped) were released at nightfall, their arms and horses returned, and messages sent to the Comanches and Kiowas to the effect that the invasion of their country was only made to capture the band of Pawnees. That in case they were given up, and their prisoner returned uninjured, the Comanche chiefs would be released immediately, and valuable gifts added to the ransom originally offered for the child. If, however, the Pawnees, who were known to be in

their camp, were suffered to escape and carry with them
the little prisoner, then the chiefs would be held in close
confinement at the fort until their punishment should be
decided by the Great Father at Washington. Moreover, their villages should be destroyed and their
country laid waste, if they did not at once, and without
subterfuge or delay, assist in bringing to justice the
perpetrators of the murders on the Kiamesha.

That night, at the council of officers, it was decided
to leave the supply train at this point, as it was admirably adapted for a temporary station. The position of
the little knoll, which commanded an extended view of
the prairie, and which could be easily defended with
hastily constructed earthworks; the creek, with its
patches of cottonwood; the buffalo-grass in the prairie,
— all contributed to the security and convenience of the
hastily improvised fort.

In pursuance of this plan, all the wagons, except
those absolutely needed to accompany the command,
were parked at the foot of the hill, near the creek, and
the little howitzer, which it was decided to leave, was
put in position on the eminence. All being arranged, a
detachment of fifty men (thirty dismounted dragoons,
whose horses had given out, and twenty from one of
the infantry companies) besides the teamsters, who
were frontiersmen, and could be relied on as a fighting
force in an emergency, were left under the command of
Leszinksky.

It was the only mark of disapprobation given to his
resistance to orders, but one he felt more as a personal
misfortune than a reproof. He, not having heard the
strong terms in which Captain Moore had denounced his
blank blanked Quixotism, nor the equally pious manner
in which the bold dragoon begged he might not be
permitted to come to another council where he would
have occasion or opportunity to repeat such blank
blanked folly, could not altogether understand why the
empty honor of this command was given him, whilst
his comrades passed on in the pursuit, the success or
failure of which was to re-create or wreck his happiness.

The reader has not seen my hero as I have desired to paint him, if he does not already understand that the governing characteristic of Stanislaus Leszinksky was a single-thoughted sense of duty, which ruled every act of his life, and to which the strongest affections of his life were subjected.

To such a character any conflict of duties is painful. To the conscientious young officer even the appearance of insubordination was a thing to be regretted, but not avoided, if obedience was made to mean violation of the rights of another. Acquitted to his conscience of any wrong-doing in his resistance to wrong, the soldier now yielded prompt and uncomplaining obedience to an order that gave exquisite pain to the heart of the father. There was a longing look in his eyes, as he watched the line of horsemen wind around the hazy slopes and vanish in the distance, that gave "trouble in his mind" to the usually unobservant Pike, who had been left with the reserve through the accident of a lame horse. It was seldom the taciturn giant broke his Trappist-like silence, but now, moved by the spirit, he said: —

"It ar' a pitty, Lootinent, we could n't a-gone. I don't know nothin' much but Injuns and thar pints, and a man orter foller the bizness he knows. It's purty apt to be one thing or t' other with the reg'*ment* this lick. I've trouble in my mind."

"You think they will have a fight with the Comanches?"

"I ain't nary doubt o' that. What's a-troublin' me is who's a gwine to do the runnin'. It won't be the Comanches, I'm a thinkin': and if it's the reg'*ment* thar won't half on 'em git back this side the Washitaw. *Thar* best holt's fitin'. It don't do to turn tail to a Injun or a grizzly. You 're sho' to git clawed if you do."

"We must do what we can here, Pike, to make this camp secure and strong, and then watch the river vigilantly. It is the only way we can assist our friends. Do you think the teamsters can be relied on if all our force is needed?"

"Yes, most on 'em: they ar' a sprightly lot, and won't dodge fi'tin', though they'll be main hard to rein and mighty apt to kick in the traces if they ar' let to feel thar oats. If you'll 'low me to say, sir, the best thing is to set 'em at work; and thar's some a-doin' hyar that mought be better. I've trouble in my mind."

The giant shook his head in a doubting manner, and then, as if to stir the reluctant brain to action, took off the wide-brimmed hat worn by the scouts, and rubbed his forehead until it glowed in crimson streaks beneath the tangle of his curling yellow hair.

"What's the trouble about the work, Pike?"

"Why, you see, Lootinent, that ar' young infantry officer who's a buildin' them arthworks up thar" — and he pointed to the summit, where the soldiers were at work — "ain't got no idee o' Injuns and thar durned deceivin' ways. He'll do better when he gits the West Pint kinks out from under his scalp-lock, — that is, if he's got any scalp left at that time, — but now he do n't know hide or taller o' Injuns. Not as he's to blame: sometimes it's a gift, but most ways it's larnt from the fool's schule the Bible tells on. Now, Lootinent, I jus' put it to you, who has seen some Injuns and larnt some schulin' on the plains: Whar ar' you gwine to put the hosses, and how you gwine to git water if the Comanches think o' cuttin in hyar and grabbin' up all the pervishuns and ammunishun? That prairie is good grazin', and that creek's got water anuff to run a mill, but it don't run up into them arthworks."

Leszinksky had listened, first with half amusement and then surprise at the newly-blown orator, whose zeal had so warmed him that the perspiration was rolling in streams down his face, and dripping from his tawny beard.

"Why, Pike, you seem to think there are Comanches enough around us to eat up the colonel's force and swallow us for a dessert."

"When Black Beaver and Starns and me was a-dodgin' through hyar last year, sir, we laid by close to thar villages thar in the Whitchiter Mountains, when they was havin' thar games and hoss-races. Thar was more 'an four thousand warriors, of Comanches and Kiowas, and sence they've made peace with the Pawnee-Picts and Wacos — and they all ar' the splendidest Injuns on the plains. I saw a Kiowa, nigh onto seven feet high, run down a buffaler and kill it with his knife. And them Comanches is the finest riders in the world — they might a-been bawn on hossback, so to speak. Why, they hang like, by thar toe-nails, right under thar hosses' bellies, and shoot thar arrers like a Kaintuck hunter, takin' his case a standin', would his rifle. And all them Seminolies, and niggers, and runegade Creeks ain't out a-huntin' fur nothin'. T' other day, at the Seminolie town, I tole Starns they was a gittin' ready to move. I could *feel* it, sir, when I saw Coacoochee look round quick like, all the time the cap'n was a-talkin' to him. I would n't be tuck back a bit, sir, in my 'pinyun, if thar was more 'an three thousand Injuns of all them nations over thar in the timber t'other side the Washitaw."

"Why did you not tell Major Beall what you thought of the Seminole chief?"

"Cos, sir, I allus lets Starns do the talkin'. He likes it and I don't. I would n't a-said so much now, sir, but fur the trouble in my mind; and I saw you wah n't peart like, yourself."

"Stearns said nothing of any preparation at Coacoochee's village, neither did Black Beaver. I wish you had spoken, then, to me or the major."

"I could n't a-done it, and Starns thar. I'm used to have him do the talkin'. He and Black Beaver nuther saw nothin' themselves. They could on'y a-tole you I felt it. You see, sir, they've larnt thar schulin' and I ain't. I was allus so slow like, I never could a-got this Injun bizness into my head, if it had n't been thar. It's a gift from the Lord. He gives it to all the dumb things, and the creeturs o' the woods and the plains. It's bawn in 'em. The wolf-cub hides from the hunter, and the fawn can tell whar he comes. I allus knowed the woods and its folks. The trees and the vines and the grass, even the little posies, hidin' under the leaves, tells me who's been about. I couldn't a-larnt it. It's a gift." And he looked reverently up to the sky, then far out over the prairie, and fell into his usual silent, waiting manner.

It was the first time Leszinksky had ever heard him talk except in monosyllables, so the effect was greater: it was as if one of the dumb animals to whom he likened himself had spoken. It did the young officer good, in that it roused him out of himself. He left the musing giant and sprang up the little hillock. The soldiers, who were digging in the earth, looked up with merry, twinkling eyes, as they saw his astonished glance turn from angle to angle of the miniature bastions, and finally rest upon the rosy face of the handsome stripling who was superintending the work, and who now stepped up to his senior with such evident consciousness of meritorious desert in his expectant face that Leszinksky had much ado to keep back the smile that would have gone direct to the heart of the boy who was bashfully waiting for praise.

"I see, Hancock, you have not forgotten the teaching of Mahan; but if we fight at all here, we have to fight an enemy whose tactics have taught us that with them the simplest defence is the best. We may be ordered away from here at any moment, and this elaborate work would be lost. It will be better if you merely order the men to throw up a breastwork. You will not need to stay to superintend: leave your sergeant to do that, and come with me, please, to the wagons, where Buford is waiting. I wish to consult with you."

The last sentence saved the wounded feelings it was meant to spare, and the boy, hastily giving the order, followed his new commander to the wagons.

Pike was called, and in a very few moments the really bright young subaltern was learning a lesson that assisted in forming the base of a reputation which in after days rung through the world when gallant deeds were being chronicled.

Before night their defences were complete. From the slope of the hill to the creek, a distance of about fifteen yards, the wagons were parked in two lines, inclosing sufficient space to corral the horses at night; and at the outer edge of this space the wheels of the wagons were bedded in slight earthworks. Below the wagon-beds, and protected by those little mounds, the riflemen could be at ease. Here were the quarters of the detachment of dragoons, and the teamsters, who were organized into a corps of sharp-shooters, with officers elected from their ranks. By acclamation the dismounted scout was chosen captain, which honor the giant accepted without a speech of thanks; but the gravely earnest manner in which he went about his duty proved he thought this was not likely to be child's play.

Whilst this was going on in the camp they had left, Colonel Kearny's command had crossed the Washita just above the mouth of Wild Horse Creek, going due west to the Witchita group. From the Washita River to the Witchita Mountains the country is an inimitably beautiful rolling prairie, broken into occasional knolls and billowy ridges, with here and there clusters of timber and shrubs that give a lovely effect to the landscape, which ends in a magnificent background of conical peaks, rising abruptly from the level surface, on which huge blocks of granite exhibit brilliant and varied shades of crimson, yellow, purple, and green. From the foot of almost every cone issues a limpid stream, pure and cool as a fairy well. The woods are vocal with the songs of the thrush and mocking-bird; even in winter, which is full of warm, bright, sunshiny days, the air is laden with the odour of wild sweet-violets, whilst athwart the deep blue of the sky drift light, fleecy clouds that etherealize and soften the tints they catch and reflect from the glittering masses of colored granite.

This special twenty-ninth of December was one of the brightest of the beautiful days of that enchanting climate. The troops were in high feather from the easy capture of the five chiefs, who rode sullenly in the centre of their escort, turning, from time to time, watchful eyes to the distant ridges from which the envoys who were to bring them release must come. The 1st Dragoons were marching in beautiful order, forming, with the mounted volunteers and the two companies of infantry who brought up the rear with about a dozen army-wagons, a train nearly a mile in length. There were occasional stops to cut a passage for the wagons through the closely interlocked plum-trees that spread over hundreds of acres, sometimes so successfully disputing the path that the train would be forced to go round long distances. In and through these orchards were patches of wild currant and raspberry bushes, and in sandy spots the brilliant leaves of the prickly-pear caught in a network the late-blossoming running rose-vines that half hid the dangerous coil of some huge snake that had not yet sought its winter quarters.

Colonel Kearny had instructed the Indians released after the arrest of the chiefs to send a deputation to the eastern point of the Witchita Mountains with the answer of the Comanches and Kiowas. The train had made a leisurely march to give the time needed. The belief was general among the officers that the Pawnees would either be given up or sent instantly out of the country; but in the latter case no one doubted that the little daughter of Leszinksky would be detained by the Comanches, and exchanged for the captive chiefs. The only malcontents with that belief were the mounted volunteers, whose families or neighbors had been among the victims of the late massacre, and who could illy be propitiated, by the release of one prisoner, into willingness to let the perpetrators of outrages they were in arms to avenge go free. Their voice was still for war.

At sundown, two days after crossing the Washita, Colonel Kearny arrived at the given rendezvous, but as yet not an Indian had they seen, though the very silence and solitariness of the far-stretching plains which at this season were usually the grazing grounds of hundreds of herds of buffalo and wild horses, were the most indubitable proof of their recent presence. The command camped for the night, still trusting to the coming of the envoys the following day. The pickets were carefully posted, a cordon of sentries surrounded the camp, and a guard was placed about the captive chiefs. Just before dawn an alarm shot from the outpost, and the startling cry of "Indians!" quickly brought the command under arms. The fusillade which opened immediately and the defiant ring of the wild war-whoop were the answer of the Comanches to Colonel Kearny's demand for the marauders and their prisoner. The reports from the outposts were, "Indians by the hundred advancing to surround the camp."

The first shot had wakened every sleeper, and, in less time than the telling takes, brought them into line, armed and equipped for battle. At the first onset the Americans suffered a heavy loss. The horses of two companies, and the mules belonging to the wagons, were stampeded. Trusting to security from attack given by the presence of the chiefs held as hostages, the horses had been loosely hobbled, and left to graze at the foot of the peak near a little stream. The teamsters and herders hastened to secure them, but it was too late: the Comanches were among them, driving them to the open plain, while effectually screening themselves from sight by lying at length along their horses' sides; whence an occasional arrow, sped by a strong, sinewy arm, struck and stung to death some hapless herder as he gazed in astonishment at the strange spectacle of his own horses driven by riderless steeds that swept by him in the dim light.

Captain Moore's depleted little company had picketed their horses near by those of Beall's Scouts. Almost at the sound of that first ringing shot from the outpost, the two "fighting Bens" were afoot. They mounted in hot haste and reported to the colonel, who sent Moore to the outposts and Beall to increase the guard around the chiefs.

The *beau sabreur* was one of the few who had anticipated evil, and so was ready when the warning shot wakened him.

Apprehensions never weighed a feather with Moore when a superior officer was about, to take the responsibility from his broad shoulders; so he was sleeping the sleep that comes with carelessness of care: but with the instinct of a soldier he grasped his weapons and sprang to the horse that was being saddled near by. Bareheaded, coatless, with his naked feet thrust in his stirrups, he led his men to meet the flying picket-guard. They were none too soon: the pursuers were pressing at their heels. The attack was being made from every quarter of the compass. Indians were swarming on the dimly-lit plain. A party of about two hundred splendidly-mounted warriors had taken advantage of a little ravine, to pass a sentry who was watching the masses in the distance, moving like shadows in that indistinct light. At the stumbling of a horse he turned quickly, and was tomahawked as he fired his musket. Moore heard the sentry's last warning, and came up with his little band of dragoons. From the ravine there was a rush of dusky horsemen, then a quick trampling of iron hoofs, a sharp rattle of musketry, a whizzing of arrows and rifle-balls, exultant war-whoop and defiant cheers, a clash of sabres leaving their scabbards, and then a hand-to-hand conflict, with a frightful chorus of groans and yells and oaths, and, to increase the din, the almost human cries of horses in the frenzy of pain or the agony of death.

Outnumbered and hard pressed, the little squadron gave way; step by step they were forced backward, but their faces were to the foe. Never had the mettle of the men been so tried, never had it rung so true. The indomitable courage, the obstinate pluck, of the Anglo-Saxon was opposed to a savage foe, who fought bravely and well.

Moore, who had led the advance, was in the very thick of the fight. Thus far they had saved their wounded; the dead they were compelled to leave. A junior officer, fighting by his leader, fell from his saddle, mortally wounded, but living. With fiendish yells the Indians pressed forward. He looked imploringly to Moore, who, reckless of himself, stooped to lift him to his horse.

"No, Captain; I am dying. Only, for God's sake, shoot me, so I shall not fall into their hands alive."

Moore looked up, as a soldier, who had given his life to protect his officer for this one moment, fell dead. There was no hope. Behind them, the infernal noise of battle proved that none could come to their aid. He himself was bleeding from a dozen wounds. With one desperate effort he cleaved the head of the Indian who was swinging his tomahawk for its flight; and then the last load in his pistol went straight through the brain of the young officer, who smiled his thanks as the muzzle touched his temple. Half-blinded by the blood that streamed from a cut on his head, Moore fought on: it was all he could do, for now his only thought was a constant echo of that pitiful prayer, "not to fall into the enemy's hands alive."

On the opposite side of the camp the rifles of the volunteers were doing deadly work. The splendid marksmen of the frontier were glutting their vengeance with lives. An empty saddle or a horse motionless on the plain counted for every bullet fed to those murderous weapons.

Three times the Indians charged within ten feet of where the volunteers lay, slightly protected by a little swell the waters had washed there ages ago. Three times they had been driven back by those cool fighters, who had waited until every shot was a certainty. Yet here and there bloody gaps in the line of defence told of the wounded, of the sufferers carried hastily behind the wagons, where the surgeon and his assistants — those premeditated sarcasms of war — awaited the work wrought for them out of healthful human bodies. There was no slack now: from where the infantry fought, from Colonel Kearny's dismounted dragoons, from every quarter of the camp, men came bearing burdens, — burdens dripping a deadly dew of crimson life-drops.

The gray dawn paled and faded into misty whiteness, dying of sorrow and shame for the story of suffering and sin it must carry to the Great Unseen. The new day blushed at its birth that it must bear the burden of this barbarity, the blame of this blasphemy against the bond of human brotherhood. The chirping of the birds ere they left their nests, the twittering prelude of their thankful chorus, was hushed; their songs were silenced, as they swept swift-winged from the sounds and sights of slaughter.

From a bath of blood uprose a flaming sun; and as if he had lit anew the torch of battle, the struggle raged afresh. The spirit of Cain was a-field. Anger, Hate, Murder — the fabled Furies — had crept, not from the nether world, but from the covered recesses of human hearts, and cried, "Kill!"

The broadening light clearly revealed to Colonel Kearny the perilous position of Captain Moore and his handful of men. He instantly ordered to their relief a detachment from Eustis's, under Carson, together with Burgwin's company, whose horses had not been lost by the stampede. It was time. A sergeant and eleven men were all that were left of the detachment that had ridden to the outposts; and these were fighting with the stubbornness of despair around the bold dragoon, who was lying crushed and helpless where he had fallen from the horse that was shot under him, not twenty paces distant from the young officer, whose mutilated and trampled corpse was an almost unrecognizable thing of horror. Moore was alive and conscious, though the life-blood was running in crimson streams from a dozen gaping wounds.

Reckless of the approaching reinforcement, the Indians pressed closer around the little circle, apparently determined to finish their work at any cost. Burgwin's greatest disadvantage was having to risk the lives of the beleaguered party if he fired at their antagonists. Speed and their sabres were the only trust of the rescuers; so

> "Into the jaws of Death,
> Into the mouth of Hell,"

rode the dragoons.

Hate could not have done so well as the unselfish friendship that led the way inside of that doomed circle, where brave men despaired of life until the clash of their comrades' steel rang out the story of soldierly devotion.

At the same instant Burgwin and Carson dismounted beside the fallen officer. He was lifted as tenderly as might be to a horse in front of a trooper; and with one bold charge through circling foes, they reached the camp.

In obedience to Colonel Kearny's command, Major Beall had hastened to the infantry quarters at the base of the peak where the captive Comanches were guarded. He was too late; the chiefs had escaped. Warned by some signal of the intended attack, they had managed to cut their bonds, though constantly watched by the guard around the camp-fire.

At the moment the first shot was fired at the outpost, there came from the apparently inaccessible side of the mountain-peak a shower of arrows. Before the dazed infantrymen recovered from the confusion into which they were thrown, a body of horsemen swept past their fire, — rescuing the captive chiefs, and leaving in their trail a line of mangled and scalped corpses, yet quivering and warm when Captain Alexander found them. The guard, a lieutenant and twenty men, belonged to his company. Only two soldiers had escaped the slaughter: they had gone for fuel, and were returning as the Indians charged. One ran to the captain's tent, and then to the scouts' near by, to give the alarm; the other barely escaped the tomahawk of the chief who led the attacking party, and who had reined in his horse — a powerful gray stallion — to defend their retreat while the late captives were being mounted. Captain Alexander was questioning this soldier when Beall arrived. The description of the chief convinced Beall it was Lo-loch-to-hoo-la.

It was no longer possible to doubt the existence of an offensive and defensive alliance of the Indians of the plains, when such apparently irreconcilable enemies as the Comanches and the Pawnees were on the war-path together. Had Major Beall still doubted, the prisoners — a Comanche, two Pawnees, and a Witchita Indian — soon brought in would have dispelled the doubt.

The scouts had reached the fire in time to give the Indian horsemen a parting volley, and then, without waiting for orders, climbed the abrupt and rugged side of the conical peak at the base of which the command was encamped. Over and around huge masses of coarse, soft, flesh-colored granite that stood out in broken and jagged crags; up the acclivities to where stunted cedars grew on stony ledges; behind rough edges and broken points of lofty cliffs, — they chased the flying archers, whose weapons at close quarters were useless.

Through the din of rattling musketry and whizzing rifle-balls in the camp, of Indian war-whoops, and hoarse cries of command from the circled dragoons on the plains, Beall and Alexander could hear the sharp crack of the revolvers and the shouts of triumph from the dizzy heights where those unequalled mountaineers and marksmen pursued the routed enemy. Their work was short, bloody, and decisive. They returned, bringing one dead and two wounded scouts, and four prisoners.

They had other trophies besides the captured savages, — horrible, barbaric trophies of their mountain-chase; gory scalp-locks, wild offerings of stern grief, funereal flowers of black and crimson, the mourning of vengeance, gathered by hands hastily unclinched from the grasp of stained weapons to lay at the feet of the dead infantrymen. Civilization had stifled her creeds on the altar of Barbarism. War, the *Imperator*, who checks the growth of the godlike, whose mailed hand arrests and whose triumphs brutalize ages and peoples, had again trampled under foot the pitying, peace-loving tenets of the gentle Nazarene.

CHAPTER XXVI.

> HE is as full of valor as of kindness;
> Princely in both.
> SHAKSPEARE.

THE evening Colonel Kearny's command crossed the Washita, Leszinksky's preparations for defence were complete. Everybody had worked with a will. At sundown the horses and mules were corralled in the space between the wagons, at the base of the little knoll. Supper was over. The two young subalterns were pitching quoits, and around them was gathered a group of lookers-on. Others of the soldiers, including Pike's newly-organized volunteers, were sitting around the dying embers, where a young negro was picking a banjo he had contrived to hide in one of the wagons, despite the vigilance of the train-master.

Leszinksky was sitting alone on the gun-carriage when Pike came up the little hillock with some buffalo-rugs which, with much solemn shaking and grave deliberation that involved repeated change, he finally settled to his satisfaction in a pallet near the slight earthworks. Then the cause of all this care was made manifest.

"You better lay down hyah, Lootinent, and git a nap, sir. I hearn you put them young gentlemen on the fust watch, and so I knowed you was a gwine to take the last half, the Injun time, yo'self, sir. Oscar ain't hyar to take care on you, so I jus' made free to git these things o' yourn and bring 'em up hyar. You ain't slep' much sence we left Bouie's Hill. Now that's weakenin', and a mighty poor way to do if thar's gwine to be fi'tin' hyar. You see, sir, it's most apt to be slow work they'll give us. We ar' too well fixed to be scooped and swallered in thar fust rush, so we may have a long spell of it."

"You seem sure they will attack us," said the young officer as he smiled his thanks and took possession of the pallet, while the giant, with his usual slow separation of action and word, took the vacated seat on the gun-carriage before answering.

"I ain't nary doubt of it, sir. You see them smokes over thar behind that ridge to the northeast?"

"Yes; I have been watching them."

"Well, they mean *biz*ness. They ar' nigh onto right behind us. And out yonder beyont the Washitaw is a little thin line that sometimes breaks into balloon swells. You've got to look close, sir, or you mought n't notice. It hardly shows agin the hazy sunset; but it'll tell them Injuns behind us that thar's Injuns betwixt us and the reg'*ment*. And now off thar to the south whar the little creek turns back to git to the Washitaw, thar's another lot o' broken puffs just a gwine up. Thar won't be no lack o' Injuns hyar 'fore to-morrow, sir."

"I think you are right, Pike: they will probably attack us in the early dawn. Well, we are ready."

"Yes, Lootinent, we couldn't a-got fixed no better 'an we ar'. Every empty place in them wagons and betwixt 'em is packed with the grass the boys has cut. It'll stop bullets and arrers from the hosses, and feed 'em too. And we've burnt all the grass near by the camp, so they can't burn us out. We've a plenty of pervishuns and ammunishun and water, and a set o' fellers that I don't think'll flinch; and this time we've got, nigher 'an usual, right on our side."

"Then you do not think, Pike, we always have the right on our side?"

"Not allus, Lootinent. We've been a fi'tin' Injuns most ever sence I jined the army. We've been allus a-tellin 'em to go from somewhar, and a-pushin' 'em to make 'em go. I didn't see it so much at fust, cos I wahn't a-lookin' at it that way. In the Black Hawk

War I on'y seen what they done to us. They was a-killin' settlers and a-burnin' houses, and we did n't stop to ask whose land it was; nor how Injuns had been killed and cheated. The army was sent thar fur vengeance — and we tuck it. They did n't call it that, but that 's what it was. I sometimes think, sir, the vengeance t' other way 'll come yit. In the Seminole War, the day I was one o' the guard of honor — that was what they miscalled it, sir — when our general asked 'em all into a council, and then had us seize 'em and tie 'em, I larnt thar was two sides mought be looked at. And the side the Injuns saw that day wah n't one I 'd like to be anserable fur up thar."

Pike bared his head as he looked up to the blue sky. Leszinksky moved uneasily. The blunt soldier had roughly touched a hurt. Leszinksky had begun to see as through a glass darkly that the savage was not wholly responsible for the savagery of the border. In the last few days *the young officer had found two sides to the question.* This ward of the nation had been taught by the example of the nation to break faith. It was in Leszinksky's blood to value courage, to believe that in its higher expression it could only coexist with truth. Coacoochee and Lo-loch-to-hoo-la were new illustrations in his Indian study. Major Beall's histories of the fights in the Everglades were given with the coloring of the partisan, but even that coloring brought noble figures from the background of swamp and hummock. In the major's chronicles, Coacoochee was a patriot and Osceola a hero. No way of telling their story could mar that noble epic, — the unwritten Iliad of the Seminoles and Mickasuckies. To this Leszinksky was adding his own late experience. The savage who had captured his child, had, to save her, risked life and relinquished chieftainship. There was a hot flush of shame, a bitter scorn for his own lack of judgment, when he thought of his offer of payment to the man he had misunderstood and insulted, because he belonged to the contemned tribe of a wronged race. He was glad when Pike broke the course of his thought.

"Lootinent, will this gun"— and he touched the howitzer — " fling a shell as fur as that clump o' trees over yonder whar the creek turns round and runs into that deep gulley to the Washitaw?"

"Yes, easily."

"Then I wish you'd aim it exact, sir, fur thar 'fore it gits dark. I'm a thinkin' it's right thar the Injuns'll crawl up. It's the nighest they can git to us without bein' seen, and it's most like whar they'll crowd."

The gun was soon sighted and ready to carry its salute. Buford had called to know if anything was wrong, but being negatived had gone on with his game. The soldiers had stopped their stories and the banjo was hushed. Leszinksky was sitting on his buffalo-rugs, but his anxious look over the prairie told of wandering thought, when the banjo, touched by a more skilful hand, rung out the jolly chorus of a drinking song. For a little while Pike unconsciously whistled the refrain; then, stopping suddenly, asked, —

"Lootinent, what's the reason the devil's got all the best tunes?"

"I do not think he has, Pike."

"Did you hear that last, sir? Why 'twas just full o' laughs and hot blood-spurts that sets your fingers tinglin' fur a bottle, and makes your throat hot and dry like. I would n't a-liked Starns to hearn it if thar was a sutler or a trader in miles of him. That's the devil's music, sir: it jus' puts all the good to sleep and sets every sin on watch for a chance. You can't get shet of it nuther, — it rings like into your veins. I'm fond o' tunes, and they allus seem to stay in my ears whether I will or no."

An order from Buford sent the men to the creek to fill the water-barrels, and the banjo was again hushed. Pike, who was sitting on the ground, his arms on the little rise, and his bearded face in his great brown hands, seemed possessed by the melody, softly humming it and then breaking into a whistling trill of its catches, when suddenly the evening air was filled with the noble measure of that grand old hymn, "How firm a foundation, ye saints of the Lord."

Leszinksky sung the hymn to the close. The men below had finished their evening work and were silently listening, as also were the young subalterns who were sitting at the foot of the little hillock. For a few moments after the singer ceased, all were silent; then there was a murmur of voices below them, and in the gloaming Pike raised a tear-stained face to Leszinksky.

"Thar's a verse or two, Lootinent, I'd like to larn so be and I can. If you'd just say 'em to me a time or two tell I git the words like. I ain't willin' to let 'em go. I don't think I *could* let 'em go, but I want to be clar that I've got 'em right. I hearn my mammy sing that a long time ago. She died when I was on'y a little chap, and I had forgot. But now most like I can git some of it. If you'll just commence "Fear not"—that's whar I'd like to begin."

He asked with the confidence of a little child. (Surely, of such is the kingdom of heaven.) Leszinksky repeated slowly and distinctly these verses:—

> "Fear not, I am with thee, oh, be not dismayed!
> I, I am thy God, and will still give thee aid;
> I'll strengthen thee, help thee, and cause thee to stand,
> Upheld by my righteous, omnipotent hand.
>
> "When through the deep waters I call thee to go
> The rivers of woe shall not thee overflow;
> For I will be with thee, thy troubles to bless,
> And sanctify to thee thy deepest distress.
>
> "When through fiery trials thy pathway shall lie,
> My grace all-sufficient shall be thy supply;
> The flame shall not hurt thee: I only design
> Thy dross to consume, and thy gold to refine."

Pike had interrupted only to turn his teacher back when he thought the lesson sufficiently long. He slowly repeated the verses with Leszinksky; then the repetition was aided by the setting of the words in the tune, again and again repeated until memory was caught and tied by the magic of melody. The musical gift of the pupil was so true it reproduced even the enunciation and intonation of the tutor; and Leszinksky fell asleep to the low diapason of a matchless bass, singing in a sort of awe-stricken undertone of wondering reverence: —

"Fear not, I am with thee, oh, be not dismayed!
I, I am thy God, and will still give thee aid."

. . . .

Contrary to their expectation, the morning dawned peacefully. The little camp wakened merry and hopeful. The talk was of the regiment, — of how long it would take Colonel Kearny to reach the proposed council-ground, and what were likely to be the terms of the child's ransom. Even Leszinksky was hopeful; he could not help trusting to the promise he felt was implied in those last words of Lo-loch-to-hoo-la. Pike alone seemed not to share the general cheeriness. He had relapsed into his usual silent manner; only in place of the far-away, dreamy look in the blue eyes, there was evident and constant watchfulness. The men were about to hobble the horses and turn them out on the prairie, when their recently elected chief spoke a few words to his second in command, and the method was changed: the animals were picketed near the creek.

Seeing the change, Leszinksky called from the top of the knoll, "I see, Pike, you are yet distrustful of our neighbors."

The giant came slowly up the little eminence, looking backward occasionally. When he reached the young officer he touched his shoulder, and, with a sweep of his great arm, describing a circle, he said, "Yes, Lootinent, I am. Look around thar. At daylight this mornin' thar signals was a gwine from every side on us. I thought, sir, you must a-seen 'em."

"May it not be a notification of the council?"

"Now I put it to your own sense o' Injuns, Lootinent, — fur you *has* larnt somethin' on the plains, — to your own sense. Who is thar about hyar to notify? This land belongs — leastwise till the Government takes it agin — to the Chickasaws and Choctaws, and they don't dar' live on it fur fear o' the wild tribes. So it stands to reason them smokes ain't thar fur *them*.

Now I put it to you — ain't they Comanche signals? Mebby they ar' tellin' the Pawnees to go, but I don't think that's it. To me it 'pears most like it's to show each other how many on 'em's about hyar and when to hit us."

Without waiting further question, Pike, suddenly roused from his constitutional slowness, hastened down the hillside to the creek; and, after a moment's inspection of the bank, called in stentor tones to his men to bring spades and axes. Then he shouted this explanation to Leszinksky : —

"Keep a good lookout up thar, Lootinent, — you and them young gentlemen: watch every side, sir, and let us have all the men down hyar, sir. They're all wanted. We've got to dam this creek mighty quick or we won't have no water hyar long: the Injuns has dammed it up thar whar it cuts through the ridge, or else turned it. Mebby they larnt some o' our young lootinent's ingineerin'." And a quiet smile that sparkled in the clear eyes showed that when the giant was roused out of his heaviness by the pressure of danger, there was a grain of humor somewhere stirred in the slow-moving brain.

In a few hours the dam was finished, and to economize the water in the holes below it, they steeped in them dry grasses newly cut from the prairie, and then packed the wet mass over that in and around the wagons: thus burning arrows shot by the savages, and animals that might have to do for some time without water, were provided for. The rippling stream, now quietly widening into a silent pond above the camp, was soon an empty bed, with here and there a few small, still pools. Leszinksky and the two young subalterns had kept a close watch from the top of the knoll. There was an indistinct movement beneath the clump of trees that Pike had distrusted, and a powerful field-glass revealed the presence of Indians, who were evidently watching the camp. Pike was called to the council on the hillock. Leszinksky gave him the glass, asking, —

"Who are they, and what are they doing there?"

After several trials, the giant, getting the focus, looked

long and steadily, then, handing the glass back in his usual deliberate way, said, —

"They ar' Comanches mostly, but there ar' some Pawnees. They ar' all in thar war-paint, and they ar' waitin' to begin thar deviltry. They must count by hundreds round us, Lootinent, or they would n't a-risked our seein' em, or a-tuck daylight fur the damming of the creek up thar."

"Do you think they will attack us at once?"

"No, sir: they think most like that they 've got the game in thar hands and kin wait; and then I can't jus' make out what they ar' a-waitin' fur, unless its some chief that ain't thar yet. It can't be fur the reg'*ment* to git furder away: if 't was that, they would n't a-showed themselves."

"What do you think would be the effect if we sent a flag of truce, to propose a ' talk '?"

"In my 'pinyun it would be the very wust thing you could do, sir. They purty much don't believe in them kind o' flags. It 's like a *i*nvite to a council: it 's the spider a-axin' the fly. That flag up thar, sir," pointing to the national flag that waved over the earthworks, " is the best thing fur now. They know what it says, — that if they begin a fight when *it 's thar* we ain't a gwine to let it come down till we 've done all men could do to help it. But look, sir! They ain't a gwine to wait fur no *i*nvite. You see them lines a-movin' over the ridges? We 'll have all we can do in less 'an no time."

Pike hurried back to the teamsters, and in a few moments the horses were within the inclosure, and the wagons that made the gateway pulled into place. The infantrymen and the dismounted dragoons were behind the earthworks on the little knoll where Leszinksky and his aids watched the advancing horsemen. From between the wagons the clouded barrels of Mississippi rifles were held by marksmen who had learned the one great economy of the frontier, — never to waste a shot. For nearly an hour, a distant and uninterested spectator would have thought the wide prairie the practice-ground of the Comanche cavalry, as the long line of horsemen debouched upon the plain, and formed into files that commenced slowly to surround the camp. But each revolution of the circle narrowed the diameter and increased the speed, until the Indian line was whirling in a furious gallop within easy rifle-shot of the encircled knoll.

Then the waiting, patient temper of the young commander of the post was shown. He gave low-spoken directions to the subalterns beside him, and called, —

"Pike! Do not let your men fire a shot until I give the order, unless the Indians should suddenly charge — then resist to the death. We will not begin this fight, neither will we lose it. We know now that the regiment over there across the Washita is surrounded by enemies. The camp and its supplies must be held at any and all cost. The lives of our comrades may depend on our holding it. I trust you, Pike, and I trust the men to obey the order."

"You can do it, Lootinent. We'll wait and we'll hold our groun'. I'm easy in my mind 'bout the right this time, sir. Thar ain't no doubt 'bout what *we*'ll do it, sir. They ar' a fitin' over thar most like, but it's fur the life of a little child; and we'll hold a place of re*fuge* fur 'em hyar, so be and they're wusted. We ar' clar in the right this time, and we'll hold it, won't we, boys?"

The answer came in a shout, —

"Yes, by God!" and that answer lost its apparent irreverence when the young leader called out, —

"You have sworn an oath to the Lord. Let us look to him for strength to keep it." And the rapt face that looked heavenward had a confident, appealing look that was reflected in the faces of the men around him.

Two cycles had passed since the prayer of the Palatine was the inspiration that led his vengeful cohorts to the destruction of the Janissaries — two cycles, and another Leszinksky in silent speech thus appealed to the God of battles : —

"Father, aid us, that we may stand fast and quit us like men; that we may be constant and prudent and merciful, looking always to thee who alone can give us the victory."

The amen to this prayer was the ringing war-whoop of the savages as their circle swept nearer, sending arrows and rifle-shot over the knoll and through the wagons.

The cry of a horse in the death-agony was the first note in the overture of battle; then Buford's dragoons and the infantrymen added volley after volley, — a full crescendo, through which the trilling whiz of the rifles could be heard. Hard by the little howitzer stood Leszinksky, watching the field, yet turning from time to time a quick glance to the young infantry officer, who, calmly as if on parade at "the Point," was sending shell after shell to the clump of trees where the wavering rush of the scattered Indians proved there were wounded and dead to be carried off.

All day long the smoke and sound of battle filled the air. Many a volley was wasted as the soldiers on the knoll fired at the galloping line, where, from under their horses' necks, the Comanches sent arrows that struck above the earthworks and whistled through the canvas covering of the wagons; rarely a shot was lost that sped from the rifles of the men below.

Blackened with smoke and grimed with powder, all day long the boy officer stood by his gun; jacket off and hat thrown aside, the fair, full throat and round arms bared, the damp brown hair brushed hastily back by a hand that left powder-stains, and eyes ablaze with the fire of battle. At noon Leszinksky had offered to relieve him.

"O, no! Please, Lieutenant, let me stay, sir. This is a splendid little gun, and I like the work. Am I firing too fast?"

"There is no fault, Hancock. It is not that. You have been as steady and cool as a veteran; but you need rest and food."

"O, no, sir; I could not eat. It's my first trial, sir, — my vigil of battle: I must win my spurs fasting. The breath of powder kills hunger, except the hunger for honor. But, Lieutenant, it is a horror to think of the lives that go out with the flash of my gun."

"Ah, my dear young comrade, you think of that? Keep the thought, let it be a fear in your heart; it is the only fear a brave man may keep, — the fear for his enemy, regret for the blood he must spill. That fear, side by side with obedience to duty, and the Christian may be a soldier."

As the boy looked up at his young commander a soft light came into the clear eyes; he held out his hand.

"Thank you, Lieutenant. I understand now what a soldier may be. All day I have tried not to think of my mother. *She* is a Christian, and I feared to think of her. You see, my blood was hot at first and I was glad when a shot told; then as I cooled I saw the results, — lives were ended: and the thought of my mother was a pain. I see now, sir, that duty need not banish pity. I thank you for that; and I thank you for calling me comrade. It is so much to me to have you say that! I have felt so alone out here in this new way of living, I have so missed home people. You see, at 'the Point,' my classmates were like brothers."

"I will always call you comrade. With me, comrade means brother: I have no other."

The extended hand was clasped in a close grasp while they yet talked, and at the close the pledge of brotherhood was spoken with a look and a silent pressure of the hand. Then Leszinksky turned to watch the enemy, and the work of the boy went on. The shells sped swiftly and surely to every point where for a moment the enemy gathered; but the young face had now a quiet, sweet expression that told of a new and deep experience. The instinct of feeling was being submitted to the judgment of reason.

Twice the Indians charged up the side of the knoll opposite, and out of range of the rifles they had learned to dread; they charged in force, though the thinning circle still swept threateningly around the camp. Twice Buford drove them back with heavy loss: at close quarters the musketry volleys counted. At the second charge the howitzer was trained down the slope, and a raking fire of grape forced back the attacking party, who for the first time left their dead where they fell, — a disaster that to the Indian is defeat. They made no effort to charge again, but suddenly drew back. At sundown there was no longer an Indian to be seen, except the corpses near the knoll; before the twilight closed, these were buried.

Of Leszinksky's command, only three were slightly wounded; they had not lost a man. Surely the God of battles had listened to that prayer. At nightfall, when all was hushed, a clear, fresh tenor joined the baritone of Leszinksky and the bass of Pike, —

"Fear not, I am with thee, oh, be not dismayed!"

CHAPTER XXVII.

> Her angel's face
> As the great eye of heaven shyned bright,
> And made a sunshine in the shady place.
>
>   Spenser.

WHEN Burgwin and Carson reached the camp, Moore was dead; yet there was a thrill of bittersweet in each brave heart as they looked upon the bloody corpse of the bold dragoon. He had died a soldier's death, — died in the arms of the comrades who had perilled life to come to his aid, and at every step backward had faced death to save his lifeless body from outrage.

At the council where Colonel Kearny gathered his officers, some few fiery advisers urged the advance of the command to the Indian villages. This course the prudent thought of the majority overruled. The escape of the Comanche chiefs in that desperately bold rush of Lo-loch-to-hoo-la lost Colonel Kearny his advantage in the matter of the child's ransom. In her interest, further advance must be postponed. A truce must now be proposed that would include the Pawnee chief as one of the contracting powers. It was evident that any demand for his surrender would be useless. Never in the history of Comanche warfare had the tribes been so successfully led, so admirably handled. It was the unanimous opinion of the officers present, all old Indian fighters, that in the entire history of the border they had never before had opposed to them such masterly generalship. Every scout and frontiersman was questioned. The questioning was rich in reward: here a bold stroke, there a bit of color, with faint shadings taken from Osage chroniclers; and as the romance of the great Pawnee was pictured, general acclaim named him the leader of the Indians, the Tecumseh of the Southwest. Only Beall dissented: the story of the Pawnee warrior, and the Seminole girl saved from the burning stake, suggested to the astute major the idea of an alliance to which the Pawnee brought indomitable courage and ability to execute, but which courage and ability were subordinate to warlike genius of a higher order than any that had been schooled on the plains. Where all said "Lo-loch-to-hoo-la," as the picture of the past was rapidly sketched, Beall saw behind the chief the dim outline of Coacoochee. Trusting to Beall's judgment, it was now an object of the greatest importance to Colonel Kearny to have positive knowledge of the position and designs of the Seminoles now in the Comanche country. Thus far not a Seminole had been seen in the ranks of the allied Indians.

The necessity to know what to expect from the Seminoles that were between the command and Fort Gibson, together with the losses he had sustained and the pressing need to provide for his numerous wounded, decided Colonel Kearny to force his way back to the camp east of the Washita, where he would be in a better condition to think of reprisal or offer peace.

Surrounded by the circling lines of at least two thousand enemies, the dangerous retreat began. The two companies whose horses had not been lost in the stampede were dismounted, and the animals harnessed to the wagons (now filled with a sinister load of wounded and dead), which were formed in a double line in the centre of the marching column. Between the wagons, on the few spare horses, were mounted the slightly wounded. In front of the column a twelve-pound gun, from time to time, swept their pathway with grape, while the little howitzer in the rear sent flying shells at every gathering group of Indians that ventured within range. Outside the wagons marched Cady and Alexander's companies of the 6th Infantry, and the four companies of dismounted dragoons under Johnston, Allen, Eustis, and Burgwin; to the last was added the little remnant that had escaped death when Moore fell.

The scouts and mounted volunteers were engaged in almost constant skirmish along the line, which the enemy was continually trying to break.

The slow movement of the environed command across the succession of rolling prairies so delayed their retreat that it was three days before they reached the Cross Timbers. Colonel Kearny had decided to wait there for reinforcements, before attempting with his crippled and depleted force the dangerous road through the thick undergrowth, which would afford such perfect concealment to an ambuscade.

From the camp the first evening after the retreat began, under shelter of the closing twilight, Tisson and Black Beaver had crept through the circle of surrounding foes with dispatches to Forts Washita and Towson. At Beall's suggestion Colonel Kearny had left Bob Stearns, Oscar, and the captured Witchita, who, in exchange for his liberty and a large promised reward, was to guide the scout to a Seminole encampment which he knew to be concealed in the mountains, where he said Coacoochee and Lo-loch-to-hoo-la had gone the day before the attack.

Bob and his little party were to hide in the rocky shelter of the peak where the Witchita had been captured, until after the departure of the command and its accompanying foes. Their after-movements were to be determined by their success in finding the Seminole camp.

At the second night's halt, about one o'clock in the morning, the Indians charged in force, making an effort to stampede the few remaining animals, now of such vital importance in the transportation of the wounded and the two field-pieces. Beall, Burgwin, and Carson were in the colonel's tent, where Carson was receiving his instructions, he having volunteered to go through to Fort Gibson for reinforcements, when the din of the party who were trying to frighten the corralled horses, rang through the camp. Lieutenant Anderson of the artillery, who had charge of the twelve-pounder and the little howitzer, was on watch. He had kept slow-matches burning in the linstocks, and the answer to the war-whoop was the harsh, bitter whistle of hurtling grape-shot that went tearing through the dense growth of diminutive shin-oak, from which the acorns rattled like pattering hail as the little stems were mown down in clean swaths on the low, rugged range of sand-ridges across the creek where the command was encamped. The flash of the guns brought into momentary but startling distinctness the moving masses on the ridges and the plain. Again the twelve-pounder raked the sand-ridges, while the howitzer sent shell after shell into every group revealed by the flash of the cannon. By the time the officers were out the camp was fully aroused; every soldier alert and ready, every volunteer waiting to sight the enemy. Not a moment too soon! The Indians charged to within fifty yards of the cannon, when Anderson sent its murderous contents into their rushing advance, causing such havoc and confusion that when the little howitzer followed suit with its bursting balls of fire, Mike O'Dowd, who was with the squad serving the guns, called out, —

"Arrah, but it's yourself is me darlint, me little jewel of a how-its-sure! Divil a need of a fiddler when you're about to tache thim red divils the dandy stheps of a jig. Kape it up, mavourneen! Let's see how they'll stand another slap of your hot little fist!"

There was a shout of laughter, — a new prelude to the hoarse note of the cannon, but its mirth had better effect than answering cheer of battle. The startled savages, thinking it the presage of some new, some terrible weapon of destruction, fled in confusion. Carson, ready for his dangerous venture, was standing with the group of officers near the guns. Again Colonel Kearny repeated his instructions, and then, turning to the young artillerist: —

"Anderson, shell that sink in the ridge there to the north, where the growth of dwarf-oak is thickest. Drive the Indians out; then cease firing until Carson has had time to cross the sand-ridges. After that he must take his chance."

His parting advice to Carson was:—

"Make directly for the Cross Timbers. The Osage will soon strike a trail that will lead to the Washita. Keep in the Timbers until you reach the Canadian. Light no fires, and do not risk a shot unless it's an absolute question of life. Remember you will be in the route of wandering Seminoles near the Canadian, and it is just possible they are allies of the hostiles. Stop at the pass at the head of Blue River and send the Osage with these dispatches to Leszinksky. Wait twelve hours for his return; an Indian runner can easily make the distance in that time. If he fails to return you will know that Leszinksky is surrounded. The more need for you to push on to the fort. Be prudent and wary, and I hope you will get back safe. Now be off as soon as Anderson sends another shot."

A general farewell, and Beall put in Carson's hand a pair of derringers, saying, "Don't fall into those devils' hands alive. Keep to the woods when you can, and do not trust any Seminole you may meet on the way. Good-by!"

Carson and the Osage were over the creek as the last shell burst, and soon gained the ridges, which they crossed rapidly. In the last little hollow they crawled through the dwarf-oak, between parties of Indians they could hear talking on either side, and came out in a thicket of post-oak and black-jack that bordered the heavy timber up the dividing ridge between Wild Horse and Rush Creeks.

Mindful of Colonel Kearny's advice, Carson and his guide followed the divide due east to the Cross Timbers, where they soon found an apparently unfrequented trail leading directly north. By noon they had reached Rush Creek. After an hour's rest they crossed the divide between Rush Creek and the Washita, which for some distance ran in almost parallel lines. Arrived at the Washita, they had proof of the late presence of passers that way, in a freshly-cut tree that bridged the deep, muddy river, where its miry banks were highest. The Osage carefully examined the footprints upon the bank, and, motioning Carson to wait, he crossed lightly over the felled tree. Not a leaf or broken twig escaped his scrutiny. After a short inspection of the opposite bank he returned, and again examined the footprints that led westward along the south bank of the river. Carson followed until they came to a broad trail coming up the bank, where horse-tracks were easily seen.

After going down to the water, the Osage returned to where Carson waited, and, holding up both hands, rapidly opening and shutting the fingers to denote twenty, said "Seminoles." And then, with the index finger upheld, "Pawnee Big Chief bring little pale-face pappoose this away," pointing to the tree-bridge and then up the trail westward. "See him track other side. Pawnee walk over tree way." Then holding out five fingers, "Seminoles walk over. Other Seminoles swim horse here. No let little pappoose get wet."

Carson turned, and rapidly followed the Indian, who again crossed the slight bridge. On the north side he pointed to the print of the child's feet going to a drooping holly, the red berries of which had evidently been the attraction. The broken leaves and scattered berries on the ground were also carefully lifted by the Indian, and when Carson asked, "Can you tell when they crossed here?" he readily answered, holding up seven fingers, "So many day. Horse all go that away," pointing up the river. "Big Chief carry little pappoose this away."

"How do you know it was the Big Chief?"

Without a word the Indian pointed to the unequal steps of long, slender moccasined feet in the sandy soil of the shelving ridge above the north bank, and then limped to show Carson the gait of the walker.

Convinced that the Big Chief had passed with Rue, the next thing of importance was to learn at what time they had passed. To this question the replies of the Indian were again minute and exact, although given in disjointed words, illustrated by such slight things as broken leaves, bent twigs, and trampled blades of grass. It was made evident to Carson that the tree had been felled and the party had crossed seven days before, which was the morning after the first heavy frost of this late season.

They followed the trail in the opposite direction from that which the Seminoles had come until dark, and then, sheltered under the close undergrowth, awaited the coming morning to pursue their route, which was in the direction they were to take, and which Carson was anxious to follow that he might gain all possible knowledge of Rue and her present custodians. The next morning they pushed on rapidly until they reached a sheltered little woodland glade on the north slope of the divide of the Washita and the Canadian, where they found a few deserted lodges, which had evidently been the recent habitation of a small party of Seminoles. There had been women here with the child. In one of the lodges they found a torn little moccasin that Carson instantly recognized as the mate of the one Tisson had picked up in the wood near Castalar's. From the lodges the path led to the Canadian, and a less experienced trailer than the Osage could easily have told that from there the women had gone back to the Seminole villages north of the river. At the river more indubitable proof was found in a canoe pulled out on the sand, and the print of two others that had here pushed out from the bank. Mindful of his instructions, Carson pursued his route on the south bank, keeping when possible the trailers' path near the sand-hills, until near sunset they reached the cottonwood grove, at the outlet of the pass from the head of Blue River. After an hour's rest the Osage started through the pass with the dispatches to Leszinksky and a hastily written note from Carson, telling of the discoveries at the crossing of the Washita and in the deserted lodges.

Carson watched the Osage climb the ridge until he disappeared in the entrance to the pass. Then he entered the grove at the southwest, where nine days before he had come through with Beall, Moore, and Leszinksky. Thinking of the bold dragoon, of his death, of the comrade over in the little camp on the prairie, who might even now be fighting with his handful of men as heavy odds as the regiment had faced in that morning battle which cost so dear, and in the retreat, where step by step their path had been disputed by a countless horde of stalwart savages, Carson had unconsciously left the trail made by the dragoons, and turned into a narrow opening that wound through the trees to the river.

Here he was startingly brought from the past to the present. In the little cove before described, a canoe was fastened to the root of a tree by long slender stems of willow, so hastily twisted together that the leaves had not been stripped from the pliant cord. A look told Carson that the boughs were freshly broken. Already learned in the woodcraft of the trailer, he saw where light steps of small moccasined feet had left a faint impress upon the moss about the tree, and its slowly uprising tendrils told how recent had been the pressure which had bent them downward. Fully aroused, he cautiously and noiselessly followed the footprints, which led to the left of the opening that had brought them to the river. A few minutes' walk and he stopped behind the thick curtain of a tangled grape-vine just at the edge of the little glade where Lo-loch-to-hoo-la had interrupted the conference of Sénaco and the Seminole chief.

Hearing voices, Carson left the path and carefully crept upon a fallen tree which the vine had caught in its meshes, until, in the close boughs of the tree and the drooping runners of the interlacing creeper, he reached a leafy balcony which sheltered him from sight, while giving him a point of observation that commanded the glade. Not ten paces from his hiding-place, seated upon a log, was an Indian woman, whose skeleton figure, parchment-looking skin of lustreless brown, and fantastic dress gave a weird, witch-like effect, increased by the wandering glance of small, fiery eyes, and the constant motion of long, bony fingers, that kept twisting and untwisting over and through each other the yellowish-white hair that hung in scant, thready locks to her waist. The log upon which she was seated was the broken segment of a trunk that had been cast there, torn and splintered by some fierce storm. The bare and matted roots were twisted into a curving elbow, upon which the woman leaned, resting there one scrawny arm as she still threaded the thin tresses through the twitching fingers that never for an instant ceased their tremulous movements.

The log lay at an angle that turned slightly outward from Carson's right, thus giving only a suggestive profile of the woman seated on the outer side of the log, whose body, from the waist down, was entirely concealed by the matted curving roots next to Carson, and by the log itself.

But this position of the woman brought into full view of the hidden watcher a figure that knelt at her feet, — a young girl, whose wonderful beauty was thrown into striking relief by the startling contrast presented by her companion. The slender, exquisitely moulded arms, bare nearly to the shoulders, were clasped about the woman. The small, shapely head was thrown back, its crowning glory of dusky tresses, bound with a fillet of wampum broidered with pearls and tiny, delicately tinted shells, had taken a warm, rich color from the reflection of sunset clouds that were piled above the western horizon in purple and flame-lit rifts. The uplifted oval face, the perfect curves of the slightly aquiline nose, the bow-shaped arc of the scarlet lips through which flashed the ivory whiteness of the small teeth, the pure outlines of cheek and throat, the delicately rounded swell of the perfect bust, — all these, added to the glowing richness of complexion, gave the effect of a Psyche in fire-gilt. Psyche or Diana, the statuesque picture held Carson spell-bound through the charm of perfect beauty. Then, as the low murmur of the fresh young voice captured another sense, the charm was complete.

Carson had loved Margaret as a boy loves the woman

who brings into actual breathing existence the ideal of his imagination, the goddess waiting to be born, the armed and panoplied Minerva who is perfected in the central cell of every masculine brain. He had so loved her that she could never lose her place in his life. She had saved him from the grossness of passion. Through her and because of her he had a profound reverence for what is highest in womanhood. The love sacrificed to friendship had failed in fruition; it had not failed in its higher purpose, — in the supreme good that comes of *loss*. Pain and sorrow are the gateways of angel visitors; tears blind us to their presence, vain complaints lose us the sound of voices that would fain console and uplift.

A more dangerous archer than Comanche or Pawnee had found Carson in this woodland glade. Through the leafy covert of the wild grape-vine Love had pierced him to the heart. The tumultuous Hour was about to strike that banishes the past into far-away cycles, that has neither knowledge nor care for the future, — the Hour that lives through the delighted senses in a magical present, lost even to the heart-throbs that count its golden seconds, — the Hour that was born in Paradise at Eve's creation. A weeping angel caught it from the hands of Time the Devourer, and dropped it through the golden bars, so that every child of the banished pair might meet the lost wanderer, and for that brief space hear counted the silvery chimes that ring through the sixty minutes of Heaven's lost Hour.

The Hour of Paradise is chased by the serpent. When powerless to beguile, he raises his threatening crest to terrify, — unseen when he comes to tempt; visible and repulsive in the presence of the pure.

Through the musical murmur of the young girl's liquid voice Carson heard the warning rattle of the deadly crotalus. Pulling aside an obstructing vine, he saw, in a bed of yellow and brown leaves behind the log, the coiled folds of an enormous snake; its yellowish-brown length marked with dark blotches would have been undistinguishable among the leaves but for the upraised scaly head and the ear-piercing rattle that for the second time sounded the fatal battle-cry.

The girl sprang to her feet, catching in her slender arms the resistant woman. With a supreme effort of her lithe, agile force, she threw her burden aside, and turned to face the coming danger. As the springing reptile straightened his muscular folds, there was a sharp report, and he lay broken and wounded upon the log, yet still trying in the wrath of the death-agony to strike his envenomed fangs into the prey almost within reach. Carson had hastily followed the shot of his derringer. Breaking a bough as he sprang from the tree, the rattlesnake was soon dispatched. The woman had fallen in a sitting posture upon the ground, and, without apparent consciousness of what was passing, commenced plucking from the low bushes the bright leaves, vainly trying to twist them in the threads of her flowing hair. The girl stood motionless as a statue, the only evidence of life the soft, glancing light of the dewy eyes that watched, as if in a dream, every movement of this protector, who seemed to have dropped from the sky at the moment of need.

The colonel's warning against firing a shot, Beall's caution not to trust any Seminole he might meet in the way, were treasured in Carson's memory, as words pregnant with wisdom, up to the very instant there was occasion to put them in practice. Alack! alack! In the logic of youth, the glance of a soft, dark eye, the sheen of a maiden's tresses, are more potent argument than the gathered and sententious precepts of every graybeard who has

"Dipped his nose in the Gascon wine"

since its first vintage ran in ruddy drops through the twinkling feet of laughing girls.

Hat in hand, Carson stood smiling and blushing before the maiden, dumb through ignorance of a language in which to address her; but the clear light of the blue eyes flashed to the very depths of those soft, dark orbs, and came glancing back, as if twin stars had stooped from the radiant path of a summer's night to see themselves reflected in the shadowy, changeful depths of silent pools.

There was a swaying, wavy motion of the slender figure; long, curling lashes drooped over the tender eyes, where tears slowly gathered and fell. The shapely head bent, and the clasped palms gave touching expression of grateful and submissive waiting. Then soul gathered its impalpable elements into sound, and a sigh, — a low, tremulous, faint sigh, — stole through the scarlet lips to the tympanum of the listener's ear.

I do not know what you would have done in Carson's place, O fastidious reader; but I know what I should have done; and, because he was a manly fellow, it is just what Carson did. Madame, you need not blush, neither should any old, smirking sinner grin. I was not there to listen, and then betray the sweet secret of youth. Ah, madame! ah, monsieur! not for them, not for them, need even the angels fear! Where Purity and Honesty meet, Love may come; but — the serpent lies dead at their feet.

CHAPTER XXVIII.

> Bosomed in yon green hills alone, —
> A secret nook in a pleasant land.
> Emerson.

TO the north of a towering peak in the Witchita chain, now known as Mount Scott, is one of the loveliest valleys of that romantic and picturesque region. Caught in between three broken mountains that encircle it to the west, north, and east, and a spur of the range that curves around its southern border, it is secure from the fierce winds of the plains and the tempestuous "northers" that sweep the western prairies.

The swift current of a brawling brook enters the valley from a gorge in the dip between the summits of the two highest cones to the northwest. High up the broken ridges it tumbles and foams over masses of loose rock, then rushes wildly down a continuous succession of rapids, over shelving stretches of upland meadows, until it reaches a little lakelet at the head of the valley.

Its surface dimples and breaks into tiny waves as it swells from shore to shore, sending with each pulsation a fresh current into the swift stream that flows from it in gentle curves a distance of seven miles to the extreme southeastern boundary of the valley, where it finds outlet through the rocky defile of a narrow cañon, or ravine, rent through the inclosing spur. Here the perpendicular walls, three hundred feet high, form a columnar structure of porphyritic trap, occasionally studded with dwarf cedars, which take root, and draw their meagre sustenance from the scanty decomposition of the broken flutings that traverse the face of the escarpment.

On the northeast corner of the wall, where the creek enters the cañon, the columnar trap has broken off at an angle which exposes to view veins of cellular or spongy quartz, filled with liquid naphtha, having a strong, resinous odour. Above the rocky plateau made by the falling *débris*, a hot spring issues from the cleft angle. The steaming water has washed for itself a basin, the overflow from which is lost in the pebbly bank. On the south of the creek, commencing three miles above, and continuing to its entrance into the cañon, is a broad and level piece of bottom-land, covered with a dense growth of wild-rice and rich grasses. The vegetation is less rank up the gentle and easy slopes, though the gama-grass extends up the south ascent from the valley to the very verge of the acclivity, where broken, frowning ridges shut out all view save the towering peak which pierces the distant and blue horizon.

The little sylvan landscape thus inclosed has a charming variety of scene, — mountain, woodland, glade, and brook bring it beauty. From the wild-rice field up to the head of the valley, around the north and east shore of the fairy lakelet, and below the broad plateau of the upland, is a thick wood of oak, walnut, overcup, pecan, and hackberry, with a fringe of cottonwood and willow near the brook-side. Here and there a shady glade shelters the delicate sensitive-plant; or the self-woven tangle of the wild passion-flower curls over and around some gnarled old stump, where, beneath the mosses, the sweetest of wood-violets hide. At the head of the lakelet a wide and extended plateau, a hundred feet above the level of the water, commands a view of the entire valley to its narrow entrance through the cañon. Above this, in gradual steppes, hang the upland meadows, kept fresh and green through the dryest summer by the spray of the falling brook. Sheltered and circled to the west and north by the lofty ridge that binds, in one continuous chain, the truncated cones of the three mountains, even the uplands show patches of tender green, long after autumn has browned and dried the tall grasses; while the heart of the valley gleams like an emerald, when, for a day, winter has set it in a pearly circlet of snow.

In January of '44 the Seminoles of Coacoochee's tribe settled twenty families of their negro allies in this valley, preparatory to a final removal of the remainder. For some time the chief had determined to quit the reservation where the United States held his people (not so expressed in the treaty it forced upon them) as tenants at will. The officious care and supervisory control it affected were as intolerable to the proud spirit of King Philip's son as the chains he had worn in San Augustine. In exile, with only a broken portion of the warlike band that had for so many years upheld the falling sovereignty of his father, he determined to use the exile's last privilege and choose a home. In this search he had twice visited the warlike nations of the plains and the sierras, and the Mexican Indians of the pueblos. The wild savagery of the free nations repelled him, while the tame submission of the Pueblos was only a shade less humiliating than the enforced dependence of his people upon the enemy who had banished them from the Everglades.

With the prophetic instinct of experienced intelligence, and the foresight of the great warrior who reads in every movement the intentions of his foe, the chief was sure of the coming conflict between the United States and Mexico. The game of the Everglades was to be played on a larger scale and with a different race. The nation that had *pacificated* Florida by the extermination and expulsion of her native tribes was now about to *pacificate* Mexico by the absorption of all her territory east of the Rio Grande, and such mining property as might be useful in the future of the Great Republic. The taint in the blood had come through centuries. The robber instinct that had levied tribute upon the Jew, and even upon the weaker Gentile, during the dark ages, broke out afresh in the full light of the nineteenth century. The commercial spirit of the time intensified this instinct. Looking for the friendless, it found the Indian. Greed of private gain upheld the national greed of conquest. The trader cried aloud for the subjugation of the savage, the extermination of the warriors, confiscation of the land, and *indemnities:* the last was not a salve to conscience, but a chance for individual gain.

The nation heeded the voice of the trader. Honor, good faith, pledges, truces, and treaties, and even the flaming rhetoric of the "Declaration of Rights," were unhesitatingly bartered for millions of broad acres. To quiet a few brave, honest souls, who cried "Shame!" the indemnities were voted *and paid*, — paid through agents who cheated the savage out of the greater part of the miserable pittance the Government doled out. The trader got the remainder. Why should he not? *His cupidity had devised indemnities.*

The Anglo-Saxon found the red man of North America hospitable, honest, brave, generous, and sober: if, after three centuries of Christian contact and example, he is wily, treacherous, cruel, a thief and a drunkard, whose is the fault? To prove it is not altogether his, we will go on with this history.

In the fall of '43, a hunting party of Seminoles, following up an affluent of Cache Creek to its source, penetrated the close undergrowth of a densely-timbered bottom to where the clear water of a beautiful cascade rushed through a narrow ravine, high up the mountain side, over a ridge, in a fall of some two hundred feet upon several immense granite boulders. These rocks divided the current into two separate branches, that wandered apart in mazy turns until the narrowed bottom-land again brought them together five miles below, just before their junction with the Cache. After long and tiresome search, the hunters found a point of ascent around the cascade, winding in zigzag lines to the mouth of the cañon, with an entrance through low, broken walls, and where a practicable path was found beside the stream the source of which they traced to the lakelet in the valley.

These first discoverers of hidden loveliness found the treasure they sought in captures made from a populous community of beavers, that, until then, had built dams at their own good pleasure, living honest, laborious lives in their submerged dwellings, far from the wiles of the trapper.

The hunters' report and a visit of inspection to the valley determined Coacoochee to make it the fastness of his people and their persecuted friends until the settlement of the border disputes between the United States and Mexico should leave the way open to the new Florida he had found, shut in like this by a mountain chain, beside a fresh lagūna near the gulf that washed the shores of his lost home. The secret of this valley was known only to his people. Imitating the enemy, who had taught him something of engineering in the battles of the Big Cypress and in the defences of his prison at San Augustine, with the assistance of the hunters and such of the negroes as they could trust, he cut a narrow causeway, that gradually descended in a curving slope around and down the side of the southeastern ridge, from the mouth of the cañon, above the cascade, for a distance of four miles. Then it emerged from the dense undergrowth at the base of the chain, into a rocky glen at the head of a small branch, and in its pebbly bed the trail followed the descending water to where it joined two larger brooks. The united streams ran through a defile, where the track would be lost in the broad trail of the buffalo that here crossed to their grazing ground south of the Canadian.

To make the entrance to the valley more secure, the path the hunters had found around the cascade was obstructed by loosening huge masses of rock, the fall of which left a bare and inaccessible precipice. This completed the security of the fastness; for although the ascent within the valley to its southern boundary was gentle and rolling, it ended in outhanging, beetling cliffs, at least five hundred feet above the bottom-land below the cascade. The outer sides of the three great mountains that completed the circular boundary were bare masses of broken granite, thrown loosely together. Rising abruptly eight hundred feet high from a naked prairie, detached from the surrounding peaks, their dangerous ascent made them secure from venture of hunter or wandering traveller.

Defended in winter by the great height of its northern boundary, cooled in summer by the breezes that swept over the southern ridge, the salubrious and mild climate determined Coacoochee to settle in the valley a portion of his tribe and his hunted allies. As before stated, in January of '44, there were already there twenty Seminole and negro families, with substantial lodges of logs erected on the plateau at the head of the lake. Sheep, cattle, and ponies grazed the rich pasturage: the following summer the enormous yield of corn proved the fertility of the soil. The natural meadows, with their diversity of luxuriant grasses, would of themselves have subsisted all the cattle and horses belonging to the tribes.

Pike was right in his intuitive judgment. The morning Major Beall and Leszinksky arrived at the Seminole reservation Coacoochee *was* preparing for the removal of his family. The messenger of Senaco was then in his lodge. The Comanche had met the hunting-party of Seminoles on the Washita; and having learned from the scouts of the movement westward of the lodges, — he believed on their way to Mexico, where it was known Coacoochee intended to go, — he determined to invite the chief to a council with the allied Comanches and Kiowas, and if possible induce the renowned warrior of the eastern tribes to join in their newly-made league. To this end the interview on the Canadian that Lo-loch-to-hoo-la interrupted had been arranged.

There was much to tempt the great Seminole in the offer made by Senaco. If the border tribes could be united under a fearless and experienced leader, armed with the weapons of civilization, with cannon and Mexican artillerists, the dream of Tecumseh might yet be realized. If they could drive the Americans back to the Mississippi, and make that their line of defence, the

Seminoles could pay themselves for their lost savannas out of the reconquered territory that had once been the heritage of the peoples of his race. Distrust of the Comanches, — those Ishmaelites of the plains, — and of the courage and constancy of the Mexican government, made the chief hesitate. He had known some of the Mexican leaders. At Santa Fé he had seen the governor of New Mexico, — the blustering and cowardly Armijo, — and had heard from the Indians of the pueblos the story of his infamies. When with the Apaches, he had met Salezar, the lieutenant of Armijo, who was delivering to the Indians the guns Armijo had sold them, though he knew they were to be used in robbing his own countrymen. Such allies could not be trusted if the league should be broken, or should encounter reverses.

The appearance of Lo-loch-to-hoo-la was at the most opportune moment for the furtherance of Senaco's designs. Coacooche knew the Pawnee chief to be fearless, courageous, and true. If the border tribes could number many such allies in their confederation, the result might be a constant and united resistance to the aggressors, who he knew would not easily relinquish the sovereignty of half the continent. The wily Comanche, who had at first read refusal in the manner of the Seminole, now saw the chief's hesitation, his doubt. From that moment Lo-loch-to-hoo-la was an influence to be counted, an ally to be assisted. Except for that recognition by the river, the Pawnees would have been surrendered, and the child, whom Senaco supposed he could at any time retake, would have been delivered to her father. That meeting in the cottonwood grove changed the currents of many lives.

The day after the attack upon the encampment, about four o'clock in the afternoon, Bob Stearns and Oscar, accompanied by the Witchita Indian who had been captured in the skirmish on the cliffs, and who claimed to have been forced to guide the Pawnees and Comanches up the peak-side, arrived at the rocky dell at the head of the little stream through which the Seminole trail led to the valley of the three mountains.

For some time Bob and the Indian had been talking earnestly in the Comanche dialect, which is the court language of the southwestern plains. As they rested at the spring, while the Indian commenced his hound-like search for the hidden trail, Oscar asked, —

"What did he say, Marse Bob?"

"He says the path round the ridge, up to that valley in the three mountains whar the Seminolies is, begins somewhar in the undergrowth 'bout here. I'll look presently myself, when I get a little rested. Now, the pint that sticks is, I don't half believe in that Injin, no how. He belongs to the stealinest, lyinest tribe to be found anywhar between old Missoury and the Rockies. The red-faced great-gran'son of Judas 'Scariot is jus' as apt to sell us to the Seminolies as he was to sell them to Colonel Kearny. I've knowed a heap o' Injins; but I never knowed any but the meanest that'ld turn tail on the war-path, and go back on thar own color. Now, if Black Beaver and Tisson had n't a-had to go back to the forts for help, I'd a-jus' left this cummelion cuss tied up with Major Beall till we four could a-come up here and tuck our chances o' findin' the valley. Now, last night, down thar by the Witchiter village, when I was a-goin' through the Pawnee camp, if you had n't a-had your hand on that Injin's slippery hide thar, the chances is the Pawnees would a-had my har, and the turkey-buzzards the pickin's by now."

"Dunno, Marse Bob, what he mought a done, but I tuck mighty good keer to do jis' what you tole me, sir. I jes' grab hold on him thar in the bushes an' I never let go a minit till I heerd you say 'Oscar.' I reckon I hel' him powerful tight. He grunted a heap, an' talked sometimes sort o' squeezed out like, but I jes' kep' on, sayin', 'Hole still! I'll let you go soon as Marse Bob says so, but if he don't come 'fore mornin' I'll squeeze you worser 'an that.' So he hel' still, cos he sort o' understood the motion, 'cept that he kep' gruntin' 'Umph! umph!'" At the recollection, the childlike negro nature rolled out a merry laugh, that grew uproarious as the Indian bounded to his feet and looked at him in stupid amazement.

Bob, who had joined in with a quiet chuckle, hastily checked himself, and said, —

"If that Injin knows you was a-laughin' at him, it ain't a-goin' to be healthy for us about here. He'd a-got over a knock-down sooner. The meaner they ar', the more revengin'er they ar'. If he knows — and I think it's most like — he'll find some nasty sly way o' gittin' even. Now you see I would n't keer a damn about his temper an it wah n't for little Miss Rue: she *must* be up here with the Seminolies. Lo-loch-to-hoo-la ain't down thar in the Pawnee camp, and the Witchiter says the Big Chief rode through thar village with Coacoochee and the baby two days before they fit us: he says they are mighty good friends. So be and Coacoochee is up here in the mountains, it's most like they would be together: they're much of a whatness for pride and hatin' pale-faces. They're the kind as would be *consortin'*. The Seminolie chief never did any better fightin' over thar in the Big Cypress Swamps than that rush of Lo-loch-to-hoo-la the other mornin' when he cut in through our camp and carried off them Comanche chiefs. You see it was a pint o' honor with him, 'cause they was arrested when we went for him and did n't get him, all along of our leftenant's squeamishness 'bout not foolin' a Injin. It ar' a strange fact about a heathen savage, out here whar thar ain't no civilization, nor penitensharies, nor churches, but so be and he's anything at all of a warrior, he'll do the hardest kind of stand-up fightin' for anybody as has got in a muss on his account, or that he's friends with or kin to. Now thar's Black Beaver: he'd jus' be cut up and fried into hash, hide and taller, for Pike or me. All them old Seminolie warriors was like that. Why, every last one o' them come in and stuck thar heads in the noose, so to speak, when we had Coacoochee and threatened to hang him. The dragoons 'll fight like hell when any o' thars is in a hole. By God! You saw how they was cut to pieces tryin' to save Capt'n Moore." Here Bob gulped down his grief in half-smothered oaths, and then, taking a fresh quid of tobacco, continued, —

"They'll fight like men for a comrade, but they don't do no more 'n a real Injin warrior will. I saw Waxehadjo the day he was killed; he stopped and fit us to let his squaw and her young ones get safe to the hummocks, across a big log in the lagoon. When some of 'Ours' who'd got grudges shot two o' the pappooses, a Injin boy — he could n't a-been more 'n sixteen or tharabouts — run out o' the hummocks and swum toward the log whar the squaw was screechin' over the dead young uns. He got the livin' babies safe to the thickets and come back to help the woman with the others; he made her go before him, so 's to be between her and our fellers, who 'd been shootin' steady at 'em all the time. Damn poor shootin', not to hit till then; sort o' buck ager — they was narvous, so nigh the game. At last the boy was hit and fell backward into the water. Waxehadjo had swum the lagoon as the woman and the boy started with the limp little bodies: he had got safe under the droopin' moss of the live-oaks. The minit the boy fell he was in agin, and with two or three desprit stretches — he was a powerful long-stroke swimmer — he got the boy and was carryin' him out when a volley from the dragoons fairly riddled 'em both. We got Waxehadjo's body; it had nigh onto twenty bullets through it. I remember Major Beall a-sayin', 'What a handsome red devil he was!' Well, you see that's one o' the things Coacoochee ain't forgot: his sister was Waxehadjo's squaw. I saw him scowl at Major Beall, who stood off one side with our leftenant when Capt'n Moore was talkin' to the chief."

They were both silent a moment when Oscar began, —

"Poor Marse Cap'n! poor Marse Cap'n Mo'! It don't seem nateral, nohow, to think o' him dead, an' the sun a-shinin', an' the 'ar a-blowin', an' the birds a-singin' all the same. He was so much alive — so mighty much. Such a dancin', bright look in his eyes when a laugh struck 'em on its way out! So big and strong and good, — always a-helpin' somebody! He'd take anybody's troubles up, and carry 'em like they was feathers — that's what he would take from anybody; but he'd give of his best. Always a-givin'! An' now he's done give his life fur little Miss Rue — fur little Miss Rue, an' he didn't save her — an' she did love him so!"

The faithful fellow hid his face and sobbed aloud.

"Hush, Oscar!" exclaimed Bob, springing to his feet. "S-t-o-p-it! How the hell am I to stand all the strain that's a-comin' and you goin' on like a orderly callin' the roll o' the missin' and the dead? And not a canteen o' whiskey to be got, so be and we was bit by a whole den o' rattlers. To make me a-wantin' liquor, and me swore off! Why the devil do you keep me a-rememberin' every misfortunit thing that has come up? Ain't we goin' right now for the little capt'n? And as for Capt'n Moore" — he took off his hat, and then, as if to make excuse to himself for uncovering, wiped his forehead and continued, "the capt'n's gone to a better world 'an this, and he fit his way thar like a soldier!"

And with his characteristic distaste for thinking of or lingering over troubles, Bob walked over to where the Indian was carefully lifting the low boughs of a drooping willow, at the very instant a rush was made from a dozen leafy coverts; and before he had time to grasp the pistols in his belt, he was a captive. Oscar, his eyes still clouded with the tears Bob's oaths had checked, sprang to his feet and knocked down two Indians who tried to seize him, then, with his hastily drawn knife uplifted, stood like some dusky Hercules whose grand pose of defiant rage brought to sight the power of every swelling muscle. At the instant Bob was captured a tomahawk had whirled past him and cleaved the skull of the Witchita. With the quick instinct of the frontiersman, Bob realized that the attacking party did not intend to kill him; he also saw, from the waiting attitude of the warriors who fell back before Oscar's threatening knife, that they were held at bay, not through fear, but in obedience to some superior, to whom they were evidently trusting for orders. A quick glance back to the willow beneath which the Witchita had fallen, and he saw Coacoochee standing with folded arms beside Lo-loch-to-hoo-la, who touched the dead Indian contemptuously, as with an impatient movement he caught his bloody tomahawk and buried it to the hilt in the damp moss, saying in the Comanche dialect,—

"The dog that my brother found hurt and starving in the forest has scented his trail to show it to an enemy. The outlaw from his tribe, who was sheltered by the Seminoles, has sold the secret of the valley to the palefaces. He should not have died by the hand of a warrior: he should have gone to the Great Spirit marked by the scourging of the squaws."

As the chief stooped to regain his weapon, Bob again looked at Oscar. What he saw made him shout, "Don't, Oscar! don't rush on 'em! They don't want to kill us; but you'll make 'em kill us both, if you cut one on 'em. I'm a capt-*y-ve* and I don't want to be brained jus' now when we've got a chance to hear news o' the little capt'n. They ain't done no hurt to us; they've on'y tomahawked that lyin' redskin, and, from what I jus' hearn the Big Chief say, they sarved him right. Hold on! don't you see it's the Big Chief here as has got the baby?"

The negro looked at Bob, and then a fierce light came into his eyes. He made a bounding, panther-like spring and stood face to face with Lo-loch-to-hoo-la, as he said, in the thick utterances of intensest passion, "You've got my marster's little child, an' if you don't promise me right heah to give her up, I'll drive this knife straight through you. The Lord's put you in my han', an' if I die for it, I'll do it."

"Oscar! Oscar!" again shouted Bob. "You ar' throwin' away every chance to get the baby. You'll kill the Big Chief and we'll both be tomahawked. Don't you know he's her best friend? You're jus' playing hell with what the Lord's put into your hand. You cussed jackass, you're foolin' away her life and ourn. Why, he kept them murderin' Pawnees from finishin' her."

Another voice — a voice with a soft vibrating ring,

speaking in that sweet southern English that lends to its flexible force the charm of Latin vowels — was heard: "Are you here in search of your master's child?"

Oscar turned at the sound; his hand dropped to his side and his eyes lost their fierce fire as he met the magnetic look in the soft, dark eyes of Coacoochee.

PART VII.

COACOOCHEE.

Lord of himself, though not of lands;
And having nothing, yet hath all.
                              Sir Henry Wotton.

PART VII.

COACOOCHEE.

CHAPTER XXIX.

> I am Sir Oracle,
> And when I ope my lips, let no dog bark.
> — SHAKSPEARE.

AT the moment the Seminole Chief spoke to Oscar, Bob, finding himself released by his captors, laid his hand lightly on the negro's shoulder, who stood dumb and motionless, held by a power he had not skill to analyze or understand. The clear intelligence that dominated him with its magnetic force, looked into and through the passionate, childlike nature; and finding there rage and hate, held, as in a leash, those hounds of the soul, controlled, if not subdued, by the power of the tamer. With a quick glance, that included Bob in the conversation, the chief, without waiting Oscar's answer, continued: "My young men have constantly watched the two warriors that came with the Witchita dog to the mountains. Otulke," and he pointed to the young Seminole who had been with him in the glade when Lo-loch-to-hoo-la interrupted their conference with Senaco, "the brother of Coacoochee, followed the brave white warrior through the camp of the Pawnees, where he risked death at every step in his search for the child of his chief. Coacoochee, himself, waited in the darkness of the forest, near the faithful black man who held the Witchita hound by the throat while his friend was in the path of danger. The heart of the black man is loyal and brave. It is no idle word, no boast of the braggart who rests by the lodge-fire, when he says he is ready to give his life for the child of his master."

The voice ceased, and there was a look of waiting for question in the face of the chief. Bob cleared his throat nervously, trying to find something to say; but the ordinarily loquacious spokesman was scarcely up to the occasion. The single-thoughted and simple-hearted negro had less consciousness of his own personality. His one idea was the child, his one feeling unswerving devotion to the search. He had looked into the eyes of Coacoochee, and to the perfect fearlessness of self-abnegation was the added quality of appealing trust, as he said, —

"I want to find little Miss Rue. Whar is she, sir?"

The chief looked at Lo-loch-to-hoo-la, who answered with a glance of assent to the silent question. Again Coacoochee addressed the negro: —

"She is with the wife of Coacoochee, at the Seminole camp in the mountains."

"I want to go thar, sir. Thar's whar we was a-goin' when you cut in on us heah. The Witchita said she was with you all; an' when we did n't fine that murderin' devel thar, last night" — and he raised his clinched fist to designate Lo-loch-to-hoo-la — "down with the Pawnees, we just knowed the Injun was right, and she was up thar. I must see her, sir. Thar ain't no time to lose. 'Pears as if I could hear Miss Marg'ret — that's her mother, sir — callin' me over the hills an' rivers, to bring her chile befoe the grief of it kills her. An' my marster — that's her father, sir — he's thar the other side o' the Washter a-waitin' fur news of her, — *waitin'*, an' he knows Oscar's started to fine her. The Lord's led me; an' now I've foun' the way, nothin' could n't hole me back. I must start this minute to your house."

"The lodge of Coacoochee is open to the black warrior with the true heart. If he will stay with the Seminoles he will find freedom. He can walk through the forest and under the sunlight *a man*. The warriors of his race were the allies of the Seminoles, in the hummocks and the Everglades. When the great chief of the Long-knives sent his warriors with the Creek hunters to catch slaves, when the women and children were torn from their villages in the territory of King Philip, where for generations they had lived peacefully under the shields of the Seminoles and Mickasuckies, then Coacoochee swore by the Great Spirit that the son of King Philip would never bury the hatchet until the slave-hunters were driven from his land, and his black friends could rest in peace under the shade of the live-oaks that bent over their lodges. The grass of the Everglades that was reddened with the blood of the Seminoles, the leaves of the hummock that have concealed the warriors of Coacoochee, the cypress of the swamps that have heard the bay of the bloodhounds when the white man followed the trail of the escaping slave, can tell how that oath was kept. When amnesty was offered to their allies, the little remnant of the people of King Philip left alive after the seven years' war surrendered; when the slave-hunters had been turned from the path of the black man, the Florida Indians were willing to make peace. The great chief of the Cherokees was sent to pledge the faith of the government of the white man to the perpetual protection of the Seminoles and their allies, if they would remove to the lands west of the mighty river. The Cherokee chief was truthful and honest. When the Seminoles were homeless, he sheltered them; when their allies were claimed by the slave-hunters, he raised his voice and called to the war-chiefs at Fort Gibson against the lying officials of a perjured government. To-day Coacoochee is looking toward the war-path; he is calling his tried warriors and young braves to the mountains. The pledge made through the great Cherokee is broken. There are slave-hunters in the Creek country, and the sleep of Coacoochee has been disturbed by the cries of captured women and children. If my brother will come to the fastness in the mountains, to the lodges of the people of his race, Coacoochee will break his chains, and he shall dwell near the child he seeks."

The intonation of these sentences was a master-piece of persuasive eloquence. The commanding, kingly bearing, the earnest, protecting manner, carried every word straight to the listener's heart. Oscar had heard the story of the Everglades, told by brave men who had fought for a cause they did not scruple to denounce, in the freedom of talk where comrades were gathered. His master had not said much. King Stan was never a denunciatory talker; but, from his interest as a listener, from the kindling of the clear eyes and the expressive quiver of the mobile mouth, Oscar could easily translate his feeling. It was a face he had studied since they were children together: he had watched its changes to anticipate command, he had learned it well. It was a mixed knowledge, — some such thing as might result if the sagacity of the Newfoundland were added to the deep affectionateness of an unlettered clansman, whose reasoning follows, but never precedes,-the decisions of his chief. Oscar also knew that slave-traders were in the territory, come for the black Indians (as they were called), who, though of slave extraction, had been free for three or four generations. The opinions of the officers in the garrison had not been hid under a bushel. He had heard Captain Ben's deep oaths; and the doctor's quiet sarcasm had not entirely failed in getting lodgment in his understanding. He knew that wrongs were being permitted, if not committed, by the Government. Moreover, the clannishness of color in a measure identified him with these exiles. He had seen the few in the fort, who had been rescued by the military from the traders, who were waiting the decision of the Supreme Court. He had felt a thrill of fierce delight in their stubborn resistance to captivity, and in their wild, untamed defiance of the curious crowd of camp-followers who clustered about their quarters.

Brought up under other training than that of Mount Hope, or by any other master than King Stan, Oscar would have been the most intractable of slaves, the most resolute of revolutionists. His sense of justice, and the unshrinking self-devotion of his character, would have made him the stubborn defender of the helpless and the oppressed of his people. As it was, the insidious appeal of Coacoochee, for the moment, carried him out of his present self, into that other self which lies buried under the "what might have been,"—an effect not uncommon to oratory; else how could we explain the phenomena of the repeated relapses of converts?

By this time Bob had found his voice, and was ready to take the burden of conversation upon himself; moreover, he did not altogether relish the prominence the Seminole chief seemed disposed to give Oscar. For an Indian and a negro to prolong a conversation that utterly ignored the only white man present was a state of affairs he was neither willing to consider or accept. Determined to bring Oscar to a sense of his inferiority, and Coacoochee to a realization of the supremacy of the Caucasian, he commenced: "I don't think, chief, this black boy can get the rights of all that 'bout them Florida al*lies* o' your'n in his head. Not that I ain't free to say thar's been a durned 'sight o' rascality in the doin's of them nigger-traders, fust and last. They've started the same game here, in the Creek country, they tried down thar at New Orl-ee-ns; whar they played hard to disgruntle old General Gaines into givin' up them black prisoners o' war that was in the barrack at Fort Pike. But they did n't know the kind o' man the old general was. He had fit them black Injuns when they was with you, in that fight on the Withlacooche. He knowed they was real warriors; and when he got the drop on 'em he war n't the man to give 'em up to such skunks as took to hunten' 'em after they'd gi'n in and surrendered. More 'an that, the old general was a man with a heart in him; he'd seen them prisoners when the chiefs and warriors o' thar tribes was brought from Tampa Bay,—them on 'em who had come in after that big fight in the Wahoo Swamp, whar our folks got thar squaws and little ones, and the others who come with you the time you brung Louis Pacheco to send him out here. Well, the general seen 'em meet,—the old men who'd fit and starved in the swamps and hummocks, a-cryin' fur happy, with thar squaws and young uns; and the young braves laughin' like gals, with thar mothers and sisters: he *seen it*, and he *felt it* like a brave man would: an' he'd a-fought like *they* did fur thar homes in the hummock sooner 'an give 'em to the nigger-traders who had come fur 'em with a order from them thievin' Creeks in Georgia. I was thar at Fort Pike, and I seen the commandin' officers turn back that trader Collins, and the New Orleens sheriff and his posse, with the biggest fleas in thar ears, when they axed him to deliver up the prisoners; and I was one o' the men who come on to Fort Gibson with Leftenant Reynolds, when he brought the emmy-grants up the Mississippi, whar Collins tried his law-steal ag'in at Vicksburg; and the leftenant would n't give up his prisoners; and at Little Rock they called on the State to get 'em, when Governor Roane said p'int-blank he 'was n't in the nigger-catchin' business, and nuther was the State o' Arkansaw.' Ino and Louis Pacheco come through with us; an' so be and they're any whar about here, I'ud like to see 'em.

"Now *Oscar* don't know nuthin' 'bout them times, and he ain't no right notion o' the difference in thar fix an' his'n. He's always belonged to his master, and he's no more a-hankerin' to leave him than Louis Pacheco would be to leave the Seminolies. But that's nuther here nor thar. You know what we come to the mountains fur, and you seen who we come with. I had n't much 'pinion o' that Witchiter myself; and I'm free to say, I think the Big Chief gi'n him just what he 'arned."

With a deferential nod to the silent Pawnee, Bob closed his politic oration. Its most evident effect was upon Oscar, who was thus recalled from any outside question to the immediate business in hand. His violent outburst of temper at sight of the Indian who had brought such distress upon the family to whom he was devoted had been checked by Coacoochee's look. The address of the chief had changed his mood, and for the time nearly mastered him. But Bob's strategic seizure of the situation had nullified the chief's influence; and

Oscar was now more calmly, but just as persistently, determined to continue his search for the stolen child; to do battle with any, or all, who resisted or delayed her restoration to her home.

Coacoochee had watched the changes of the negro's countenance, and knew that all chance of gaining another adherent was lost.

The problem left for his solution was, how to dispose of the prisoners, who were likely to be an embarrassment to their captors, who were not yet declared enemies of the Americans. To release them without the child would be to invite attack. To retain them might necessitate their prolonged captivity; beside, they would be difficult prisoners to guard. The Seminole chief could, and did, judge them fairly. He understood that they were men of more than ordinary courage and daring, unswerving in purpose, desperately determined; the negro blindly devoted and reckless of consequence, the white man coolly indifferent to danger, yet ready to seize every advantage of defence; as wary as he was resolute.

For a moment the Seminole almost resolved to let them pay the full price of their rash venture, but the trustful look in the negro's face disarmed him. Bob, if alone, would have been in mortal danger: his diplomatic oration would have been his death-warrant; but Bob, as a sort of moral twin of the confiding black man, was entitled to the chief's consideration. So Coacoochee was, in a measure, forced to his final decision, — to separate the men on some plausible pretext, and trust to a temporizing policy until he should be ready to leave the country with his people. Remembering Bob's claim of acquaintanceship, he called, —

"Louis!"

From beneath the willows emerged a medium-sized, intelligent-looking dark mulatto. He had evidently heard the conversation, for, with a quick glance at the chief, he held out his hand to Bob, speaking English with a slight foreign accent.

"I rhemember you verhie well, Mr. Stearns. You

werhe one of our guard. I have not forgotten how kind and obliging you werhe. I do not think you werhe at Fort Gibson, when I was therhe two years ago."

"No," said Bob, shaking hands with some embarrassment, for he saw the mulatto knew of his desertion. "I was out on the plains then with Pike. You must remember Pike?"

"Oh yes; I rhemember I could stand under his arm. Wherhe is he now?"

"Over thar, the other side o' the Washeter with our reserves."

And Bob thought he had made a good point for his own side in intimating they had force enough to detach a reserve. Coacoochee smiled, and then, leaving Bob talking to his newly-found acquaintance, with Oscar as listener, the two chiefs had a short but decisive conference. When it ended, Coacoochee returned to Louis and the men, abruptly, saying to Oscar, —

"If you will promise to wait in the mountain with the little child, without attempting to escape until I can send a messenger to your master, you can go at once to the lodge of Coacoochee."

"Yes, sir, I promise. I'm mighty willin' to wait with Miss Rue, if Marse Stan knows I's with her."

Bob looked at Oscar warningly, but before he could attract the negro's attention, Coacoochee continued, —

"You give me your word as an honest man that you will be quiet and peaceable, — that you will wait without any effort to escape until I release you from your promise?"

Again Bob's nervous cough and clearing of his throat failed to catch the attention of the negro who was earnestly regarding the chief, as he answered, —

"Yes, sir. You can be sho' o' Oscar. If the Lord lets me see Miss Rue, an' I can stay with her while you're a waitin' to hear from her father, it'll be easy fur me to be peaceable an' patient till you tells me I's free to go an' to take the chile; fur nohow I could n't go back without her. So I promise you I won't try to get away with her. I'll wait. I know I can truss you, sir; an' I won't *no way* try to deceive you."

The intonation was so true and honest that the chief was sure the negro would keep faith. Much to his disgust, after Oscar's fall into the trap set, Bob was equally sure. Henceforth he must count Oscar out in his calculation of chances. He had nothing but the almost unerring instinct of the frontiersman and his own pluck to rely upon, in the contest he saw was coming with the Seminole chief, who was saying to Oscar, —

"You can go now, but you must let Louis blindfold you. The pass into the mountains is a secret we cannot give to any but our own people."

"Yes, sir. It'll be slower work — I can't walk so fast. But I ain't afeard — I'm ready fur the blindfold, sir."

"You will not walk. The horses are waiting there in the wood. You will be perfectly safe."

"Yes, sir, I know it. I truss you; an' maybe sometime Oscar'll get a chance to show you *how* he's willin' to thank you fur helpin' him to get to his marster's chile in her trouble."

Then turning to Bob, taking for granted he was the messenger to his master, he added, —

"Good-by, Marse Bob. Tell Marse Stan the baby's safe now. She'll have one of her own folks with her, an' I'll never leave off watchin' of her till she's in her mother's arms. You mus' go on to her mother, Marse Bob, an' say Miss Rue's got me with her; then Miss Marg'ret will feel she's safe. Good-by."

And in his haste he did not see Bob's look of warning. He passed with the mulatto into the copse of willows, and Bob was facing the chief, who had not lost one of his unlucky signals to Oscar.

CHAPTER XXX.

Our acts our angels are, or good or ill.
                                JOHN FLETCHER.

THE sound of Carson's derringer brought other travellers to the glade.

Doctor Randall, who was the advance scout of the first detachment, according to Carson's view of the case, could not have arrived at a more inopportune moment.

The young officer had one arm around the Indian maiden, and was pressing her shapely little hand to his lips, as he caught sight of Randall's smiling visage. The deep color that rushed to Carson's face outblushed his hair, thus destroying the tender harmony of "the symphony in white and red." However, he was too manly a fellow to let his manner reflect even the slightest shade of embarrassment, that might disturb the innocent girl, who unconsciously shrank closer to her protector at sight of this stranger. Releasing her hand, but holding her more firmly by the arm about her waist (believing she did not understand English), Carson said, "How are you, Randall? Meeting you *is* unexpected. I happened here at the most opportune moment."

"I believe you." There was just a shade of mirthful sarcasm in the doctor's voice.

Carson exclaimed impetuously, "Randall, don't be a fool! I never saw the child in my life until a few moments ago, when I shot that snake which would else have bitten her. I was there at the river when I saw indications of recent passers-by, and was led here by the sound of voices. It is always important to know who are your neighbors when in the enemy's country."

"Very important. It is evident you have neglected no precaution. *Au contraire*, you have improved every opportunity. You have captured the enemy and brought her to terms. The conquest has been decisive and rapid,—the old Roman way,—*Veni, vidi, vici*. But as Mrs. Leszinksky is just at the edge of the wood, with an escort, and they are coming this way, don't you think the *child* had better try if she can stand alone?"

The young girl until now had watched the face of her protector. Suddenly she turned, unclasping Carson's arm from about her she faced Randall with a haughty, imperious movement. There was a moment's hesitation, then equally sudden self-control, and she spoke earnestly and rapidly to the woman sitting on the ground. The effect was electric. The woman sprang to her feet and commenced a barbaric wailing chant, waving her arms above her head, then, breaking into moaning sobs, she walked slowly toward the river.

The maiden stood motionless until the chant had ceased, then, without a glance at Randall, she approached Carson, and to the utter surprise of her listeners said, in slightly hesitating, but perfect English, "The young chief has saved from the fangs of the chitta-micco the widow of Waxehadjo and the daughter of Coacoochee. My people do not forget. The lodges of the Seminoles are always open to the preserver of Futtatike and Alaha-chayna.* If he is hungry or tired, he will find rest and food. If he is beset with enemies, Coacoochee will pay with his life the debt of his child."

"What debt does my child owe to a warrior of the pale-faces?"

With majestic mien Coacoochee walked into the middle of the opening, and, standing beside the girl, looked from one to the other of his surprised listeners.

The young maiden caught his hand, exclaiming joyously, "Etautch, Ahi!." †

* Sweet-Orange. † Dear father.

The chief's face softened in expression; and to his question, in their own language, she rapidly gave the history of her encounter. The bright, speaking face, the rapid yet graceful gestures, easily translated her meaning to Randall and Carson; and also to another listener, who was waiting under the trees, unobserved by any but Coacoochee. As Alaha-cháyna ended her relation, she led her father to Carson, and then awaited, with an eager, confident look, the chief's expression of thanks.

The Seminole regarded Carson closely; then, as if content with what he saw, extended his hand, saying, "Coacoochee has owed the pale-faces many debts, but never, until now, gratitude. In the swamps and hummocks and everglades of Florida, he tried to pay what he owed. There are white men now, in the Cherokee country, with whom he has old accounts to settle. But the child of Coacoochee has spoken. Alaha-chayna has pledged the friendship of Coacoochee to the first white man who ever came between Seminole women and danger. The pledge shall be kept. The lodges of the Seminoles are open to the young chief. The heart and hand of Coacoochee will answer his call. If my young brother has anything to ask, let him speak."

Carson took the extended hand; but before he could find words to answer, Margaret walked rapidly from under the deepening shade of the drooping boughs and vines. Taking the young girl's hand in hers, she laid her other hand trustfully and appealingly on the chief's arm, saying, while tears ran down her beautiful pale face, "My brother has saved your child. Will you give me mine?"

"Your child is not my prisoner."

"She has been here in your country, — in these woods. See! I found this at the instant — now, while you were speaking; I found it in the leaves when I stood under that tree."

And she held up a tiny necklace of coral, that Carson instantly recognized as one he had given Rue. Putting it in Carson's hand, she said: "Ask him for my child! My heart is breaking for her. O Rue, my baby;

where are you?" The last words were an agonizing cry.

Alaha-chayna looked appealingly at her father, who stood, cold and unmoved, beside Margaret. The young maiden hesitatingly addressed him. He signed an imperative negative to her request. For an instant she was silent; then, with a quick glance at Carson, who was supporting in his arms the almost fainting mother, she commenced what all those listeners knew to be a passionate entreaty. There was an impatient exclamation from her father. Proudly and reproachfully she regarded him for a moment in silence, then, turning to Margaret: "Alaha-chayna cannot see unmoved the grief of the sister of the brave young chief. If Coacoochee so soon forgets, Alaha-chayna remembers. She will speak, that the heart of the weeping mother may be glad. The little child is in the lodge of the Seminole chief. She is with the wife of Coacoochee, in the mountains. The daughter of Osceola has moaned for a year over the cradle her child left empty, when it was called to the land of the Great Spirit. Ning-ah-shaw-na-quita is safe; for the wife of Coacoochee has taken to her heart the little eaglet Lo-loch-to-hoo-la placed in her care."

In an instant Margaret clasped to her bosom the girl, who warmly returned the embrace, and the two women were weeping in each other's arms.

Carson was so absorbed by sympathy for his first love, and rapidly growing admiration for the second, that he utterly ignored the masculine assistants at this interview.

Fortunately, Randall had not so completely lost his wits. He knew that Chief Ross, of the Cherokees, had been the constant and unfaltering friend of the Seminoles since his unhappy intervention in their affairs in Florida, when he had pledged his honor for the good faith of the Government in their dealings with the Florida tribes, if they would remove to the Indian Territory. The very failure of the Government to redeem its promises, and his, had attached Ross more firmly to the deceived tribes and their much-wronged allies. They had been left homeless and landless on their arrival in the Territory, because they refused to be settled in the country of their bitter foes, the Creeks, which would have subjected the Seminoles to Creek despotism, and their allies to Creek servitude. The representative of the white claimants in Georgia had followed them like a sleuth-hound from Tampa Bay to the inhospitable wilds, where, through the orders of the Government, they were now refused permission to settle, except under conditions that were impossible to this brave though broken people. In this extremity Ross had come to their relief; and they settled as tenants on the Cherokee lands, waiting for the slow and partial justice of the United States to place them, as agreed in the treaty, on a separate reservation.

Thoroughly informed of their history, Randall had instantly determined to back Margaret's appeal by his own entreaty, in the character of friend and medical adviser of the Cherokee chief. He reminded the Seminole that they had met the previous summer at the residence of Chief Ross. Coacoochee courteously admitted the acquaintance, and graciously added that he knew how highly Chief Ross esteemed the doctor, whose services had been so kindly given when a dangerous malarial fever had almost decimated a settlement in the swamp-lands the Cherokees were trying to reclaim. The doctor made a few politic remarks complimentary to his very dear friend, Chief Ross, and then adroitly led the conversation to his present adventure with his patient, who was in failing health, rendered more serious by the great shock of her child's loss. At the allusion the chief looked uneasily toward his daughter and her interlocutors.

Again Randall's diplomacy was quick and effective in effort. He congratulated the chief on his child's escape, and spoke with apparent frankness and heartiness of the great pleasure it was to them all that Carson had been so fortunate as to arrive at the very moment of her danger. Then, when the father's heart was touched by the thought of her risk, Randall spoke of her beauty and sweetness, adding, with the most *naïve* and simple expression of confidence, "Carson's lucky arrival has saved, not only your daughter and sister, but my patient. The reaction caused by the welcome news of her child's safety, and the soothing effect of your daughter's tender sympathy, have given me new hope for the life of which I had almost despaired, when I consented, as a last expedient, to this dangerous expedition. Our fortunate meeting with you has, of course, removed all danger that might have befallen us of chance meeting with hostile bands. Under your protection I know my patient is safe; but to your daughter's ministration I trust for her restoration to health. She was in a delicate condition before this cruel loss, but the shock that I thought for a few days would kill her, brought about such a restless, nervous state that I consented to this journey, knowing the only hope for her reason was constant bodily fatigue, which her anxiety for her child, and her firm belief in the successful result of her search, has enabled her to bear."

For a few moments the chief was silent. He had listened to the last few sentences with downcast eyes, and, when Randall ceased speaking, seemed lost in musing. At length, when he raised his eyes, they met Randall's, which seemed to question him. In a harsh voice, unlike his usual flute-like tones, he said, "You saw here, but now, the sister of Coacoochee, a widow, and childless. The Great Spirit has clouded her understanding, and made her sacred as are the memories of the past. The father of the child you seek killed Waxehadjo. Coacoochee does not hold anger for that death, though the warriors of the pale-faces were a hundred to one. It was the chance of battle, and a brave man does not count his foes. The wife of Waxehadjo, the sister of Coacoochee, was in the hummock with her little ones. Two were mercilessly shot. With two she escaped only to see them die in the pathway of exile. Yet Coacoochee is not deaf to the cry of the wife of the man who murdered the children of his sister. The woman can go with the daughter of Coacoochee to the lodge in the mountains. The Seminoles will see that her path is safe. She can return when she will, but Coacoochee cannot promise that she may bring back the child Lo-loch-to-hoo-la left in his lodge."

The deep tone of the voice had reached the three who were talking together, and held them listeners. Margaret drew near before the chief had ended the first sentence, and waited breathless until he was silent. At the charge against her husband, she flushed in angry amazement. Her king, the keeper of her conscience, do a wrong like that? Her anger lasted through the offer of safe conduct for herself, and deadened the effect of its final clause. Assurance of her child's safety had relieved the mother's heavy heart and aching brain. The charge against her husband angered the loyal and true wife.

"It is false! My husband never ordered or witnessed the murder of little children; he would have been the first to place himself between them and danger. It is cruel and cowardly to make such a charge in his absence."

There was a steady, burning light in the blue eyes that looked into the face of the chief. If her words had ended with the indignant defence of the first sentence it would have been better. But a woman is rarely content with the defensive in any contest. The feminine temper at white heat seems to develop and intensify the latent masculine aggressive quality, which somewhere lies hid in the germ-cells of unused capabilities.

The angry flush in the chief's face that came with the charge in Margaret's last sentence faded to a tawny pallor. But before he could answer, his daughter caught his hand, and, again the sweet voice pleaded for peace and pity.

This gave Randall time to rally from the confusion into which Margaret had thrown him, and regain a hold upon the web of diplomacy, with which he hoped to entangle the chief. In fact, to this able tactician the indignant wife's outbreak was an advantage. Seeing instantly that the chief had mistaken Beall for the husband of Margaret, he counted upon the rectification of the error as a reactionary force that would surely win a partisan all the more zealous because of his recent conversion. With a deprecatory look at Margaret, as if to pray the chief to excuse weakness, he began:—

"I think, Chief, you have mistaken some older officer for Lieutenant Leszinksky, the husband of my patient."

"Leszinksky?" The chief hesitated a moment at the difficult name. "I do not know any Leszinksky." The dark, frowning brow, the flashing eyes, the resolute lines of the expressive mouth, all said how hateful was the name he was now forced to utter. "Captain Beall was the officer in command when my sister's children were murdered."

"That was in Florida?" asked the doctor.

"Yes."

Again Margaret interrupted: "I knew you could not mean my husband. He is the friend of the Indian, as he is always of the oppressed. If you only *knew* him, if you could see him, you *would* know how impossible it would be for him to see a little child suffer harm. He was never in Florida. He came West from Washington. We have lived here ever since our marriage. My little daughter was born at Fort Laramie. The doctor can tell you; he was then with us. He can tell you how we have cared for little children in the Pawnee country. My husband never could have witnessed, without preventing, that cruel deed."

Into the glade came the watcher that Coacoochee knew was waiting in the wood. Regardless of Randall or Carson, or the little escort of three men who were near by under the trees, Lo-loch-to-hoo-la walked into the opening, and stood beside the Seminole chief, to whom he spoke rapidly, and with an excitement of manner unusual to the dignified and silent Pawnee. Coacoochee listened with marked interest; Alaha-chayna with evident delight. At last, as if unable longer to repress her feeling, the young girl turned to Carson and Margaret:—

"Lo-loch-ta-hoo-la does not forget. Three summers ago, when the frozen waters were melting, and the young grass putting out its first leaves, the wife of the Big Chief went to the trading-post at Laramie to beg medicine for her husband, who seemed touched by the spirit of death. Cochosompahatke[1] gave her food and clothing and medicine. She wept with the childless mother, who was afraid her husband was about to follow his little ones to the land of the Great Spirit. Three times the medicine-man" — pointing to Randall — " came to the lodge of Lo-loch-to-hoo-la; he brought gifts from the White Star to the wearied wife, and health to the chief. When the Pawnee woman again sought her friend to speak the words of the grateful Indians, the White Star had gone toward the rising sun with her newly-born daughter. The lodge of Lo-loch-to-hoo-la is desolate; but he will give back to her mother the child he saved from the tomahawks of his tribe."

[1] The White Star.

CHAPTER XXXI.

WHAT! will the line stretch out to the crack of doom?
SHAKSPERE.

THINKING the reader a friend of Bob Stearns (the author frankly confesses the strength of his attachment to that charming ne'er-do-well), we will leave the more distinguished personages of our truthful and simple narrative to care for themselves and each other, while we follow the fortunes of our re-reformed tippler into the Comanche country. The author also confesses to a painful and prolonged wrestling with conscience before he could bring himself to depict fairly the darker side of another character that has taken firm hold of his affection.

The moment the Seminole chief won Oscar's confidence, and his blindly given promise to wait the chief's pleasure, Bob knew his own captivity, and possibly death, was decided. The sagacious frontiersman was not at all deceived by the suave and apparently friendly manner of Coacoochee. Added to the training of the scout who had served his apprenticeship in Florida and was now passed master in the school of the plains, Bob had the instinctive judgment of character, the facility in reading physiognomy, that distinguishes the expert among detectives. As soon as his oration was finished he knew his vaulting ambition had o'er-reached itself. His apologetic manner of sitting down upon the negro and the Indian had not exactly the effect intended. The boomerang of his diplomacy had literally "returned to plague the inventor." In uncovering the stores of his knowledge, he had uncovered the fact of his campaigning in Florida. His vanity relieved, his oratory aired, he looked for results, and as the rosy mists of self-conceit faded, saw himself standing before the chief, a living exclamation-point to accent the end of a bitter past. The self-disgust that fast followed his oratorical exhibition so upset his self-confidence that he blundered into those useless signals to Oscar that had utterly failed to catch the attention of the single-thoughted and trustful negro, — a blunder that was fatal to his freedom, and that would have ended his place in this history with a martyr's crown, very like a fool's-cap, had not the chief fallen into a similar error, and, through contemptuous judgment, undervalued the ability and real courage of the scout.

Bob made no more blunders. The stinging pain of the discovery that he had made an ass of himself, and the collapse that followed his succeeding failure, brought him to his best: vanity was killed, but self-confidence had survived her decapitated twin, and every faculty of mind and sense was alert and active.

The look in Coacoochee's face of ill-concealed hate was followed by a contemptuous smile of amusement at Bob's discomfiture in the matter of warning signals. The smile broadened as the scout's face assumed an expression of perplexed amazement, and with a blank visage he propounded the inquiry, —

"You ain't a-goin' to send me back without Oscar, and without seein' the baby?"

"No: the great warrior of the savannas can rest in the land of the Comanches until the black man hears from his master."

Although the double meaning was plain to Bob, there was not the slightest change in the expression of his features; his eyes were lustreless and staring; there was not a quiver of the partly opened mouth; nothing in the general vacancy to betray the acute, quick intelligence that was even then forming the plan of his campaign.

The scout knew from the manner of Coacoochee that

he had more to dread from the Seminoles than from the Pawnee, the only avowed enemy of the whites then present. Alone and surrounded by foes, that he believed had already determined his death, the indomitable courage of the man never quailed. In thought, he was matching himself against the odds, calling and numbering for action every quality that could aid him in the contest.

In one weakness of Bob's force the odds were terribly against him; for in that weakness his nerves were fighting the enemy's battle. Ever since he had left Bouie's Hill he had been beset by a foe more implacable than Seminole or Pawnee. That heavy debauch at Tisson's had been followed by a shock that for a time paralyzed the nerves of desire.

At first, days of fatigue had been succeeded by a few hours of restful slumber. Then with renewed strength came the craving for re-indulgence, and the clutch of the insensate habit pulled him from sleep. The inexorable retribution of outraged nature had begun.

Since the night attack when the Comanches were rescued, Bob had scarcely closed his eyes. Except for his past experience, that had taught him the futility of faith in such visions, he would have believed real the spectres that, at rapidly lessening intervals, hovered over his path like wandering will-o'-the-wisps.

The imps of alcohol had taken the baby's form. Although Bob was perfectly conscious of the unreality of these apparitions, there was a tinge of superstition in his nature that had already blended in his thought danger to the child with his relapses into drunkenness.

By one of those strange chances that sometimes accompany such delusions, the spectres hitherto had preceded Bob in the path indicated by the Witchita. Here in this rocky glen they seemed continually to wind around and about Bob and the Pawnee chief in the intricate figure of a mazy dance. There was an apparently never-ending line of Baby Rues. Through all his perplexities Bob felt thankful there were so many. *One* would have seemed too real: the multiplied representatives, though more visionary, were less uncanny.

In one way his superstition ruled Bob. He was ready to follow unhesitatingly the leadership that he confidently believed would finally bring him to the real living child. The winding about and around Lo-loch-to-hoo-la confused him. Was the Pawnee chief an ally to be solicited, or an enemy to attack?

Freighted with this doubt, the wandering glance of the scout had unconsciously taken an expression of wistful entreaty, that confirmed Coacoochee in his contemptuous reckoning; but it had a different effect on the more simple and sincere character of the barbaric Pawnee.

Lo-loch-to-hoo-la crossed over to where the Seminole and Bob were standing. Much to the relief of our winsomely dear drunkard, the dancing babies clasped hands around him and Lo-loch-to-hoo-la, making a little dent in the swiftly-revolving wheel at the point where they passed in front of Coacoochee, thus excluding the Seminole from their mystic circle. Their meaning was clear to Bob, and so his mind was at ease.

The reader must not, in his estimate of the scout, to superstition superadd weakness either of the intellect or, save in one deformity, of the moral nature.

The scholarly scoffer of the nineteenth century, who plumes himself upon pure logic and strict conclusions, is not altogether free from the deceptions with which imagination sometimes clothes science. *His* Present is a half-veiled sphinx, who looks over sun-lit wastes of glittering sands; his Future is shadowy with its dim possibilities, its starry expectations; his Past, — well, "there were (wise) men before Agamemnon." What if their wisdom was gathered in narrowed ways and by formless methods? They brought the world into fuller light. Seed-time, ploughing, *then* the harvest: we plant and work that we may reap. Crudeness, growth, fruition, is the Trinity of Time!

While we were musing, Bob grappled the situation. Determined to follow the *rôle* into which he had stumbled, of the vain and confident swaggerer of the camp, with the most ingeniously stupid, the most stupidly honest, air, he addressed Lo-loch-to-hoo-la and the Seminole chief.

"Well, I must say this 's a-playin' it white. I'm powerful tired, Chiefs, o' this sarcumnavigatin' 'round in the Comanche country, and if I can lay off and rest a day or so, while you send in your env-o-y-s, I ain't a-goin' to complain. You see, I've been a-ridin' and a-fightin' now nigh onto a couple o' weeks; and 't ain't no let down if I do stop here fur a few days, and wait fur you to fix up about the baby's ransom; and I don't care if I do tell you that our folks ain't a-goin' to be mean about what they give, nuther. You seen the other day," and he addressed Lo-loch-to-hoo-la, "that her father ain't no crab about givin'; he'll let go of his best when a friend is a-needin' on it. He traded hosses with you, without askin' boot in the swap, when he thought our fellows was a-crowdin' you onfair like. You see, he knowed, fur I told him, that you'd been good to the baby; an' so be any on us fellows can ever do you a good turn out on the plains, why, we ain't likely to forget it. We may sometimes disremember some things; but this here about your standin' the baby's friend ain't one o' them things."

Two pair of keen eyes were watching Bob with different expressions. Glowing through the soft, lustrous darkness of Coacoochee's was a baleful light of flame-like red, angry as the tongue of a viper, while Lo-loch-to-hoo-la's fiery glance had softened in the gathering mist of newly awakened feeling. The Seminole had watched the Pawnee during Bob's second attempt at speech-making. An angry flush told his displeasure with the effect he saw, more truly than did the measured accents now addressed to the Big Chief in the Pawnee tongue.

Through this dialogue Bob stood unmoved, carelessly cutting a fresh quid of tobacco, with an air of listless unconcern that completely deceived Coacoochee as to his linguistic accomplishments. He heard the Pawnee ask that he be permitted to see the baby, and then sent back to her father, with news of the child, and also the horse, that the chief insisted had been lent him to meet the exigency of the time.

Coacoochee listened courteously, but plausibly insisted that, owing to the danger it would be to his hunted allies (the black Indians), he dared not trust a white man with the secret of the fastness; that he could risk Oscar, whose observation and intelligence were less to be feared, and whom he hoped to win through the persuasion of Louis Pacheco and the influence of race.

The Pawnee with evident reluctance gave up the first clause of his request, that Bob should see the child, but urged persistently that he should be sent back with the horse, and a message from Lo-loch-to-hoo-la to "the chief with the honest eyes and true heart, who had saved him from capture." Coacoochee yielded with apparent cordiality, but with one brief glance Bob read the Seminole's face, and knew the concession was meant to deceive.

Ten minutes later Sultan was led into the glen by a Seminole boy. With a frank, kindly look, and a gesture of invitation, Lo-loch-to-hoo-la directed Bob to mount the horse Leszinksky had given the Big Chief in that exchange east of the Washita.

Nothing in all his life had ever required from Bob such a resolute effort of will; for the line of dancing babies were clambering over and around the horse in such pell-mell rushes, such frantic leaps, such reckless tumbles, that every step he made, as he advanced and put his foot in the stirrup, was a danger to some one of this company of juggling sprites. With a last resolute effort, Bob sprang into the saddle, although he could not refrain from a half-uttered cry of dismay as a little golden head flattened under his leg. He caught hastily at the clustering curls; but his hand no sooner went through the airy nothings and touched the saddle than he recovered his self-control. Seeing the surprised chiefs watching, he looked determinately past a little imp, who was perched on one foot on the curving, high pommel, and laughed in a half-stupid, half-defiant way, as he said: "I'm mighty willin' to get a lift fur I'm tired o' walkin'; but, I must say, it's a damned unhansome bizness if you mean to turn me and Sultan loose without any pervishun train, in here behind them crawlin' Comanches, that's a-lyin' hid between us and the command; when I expected me and Oscar would see the baby. Why, so be an' I had to fight on it, I'm free to say, it ain't what I expected of real warriors."

And Bob skilfully counterfeited his late distressful cry, only he made it end in a defiant ring that seemed like the last notes of a prolonged war-whoop. As if to fit the gesture to the word, he threw his arms above his head, and then, bending forward in his saddle, with a succession of waving motions, he displaced the crowding spectres.

Any of my readers who have witnessed the terror and helplessness of a strong man, when beset by the phantoms of an imagination disordered by alcohol, will easily understand the wonderful effort made by Bob to fight his own deceptions, at the same time he deceived his enemy.

Lo-loch-to-hoo-la came close, and, throwing his arm over Sultan's neck, addressed Bob in the Comanche language. The poor fellow forced himself to listen understandingly, although the liliputian spectres were wildly rushing up the chief's arm to the very top of the waving feathers tied in his scalp-lock, from which, with the speed of thought, they sprang back to Sultan's head. The Pawnee commenced: "Say to the father of Ning-ah-shaw-na-qui-ta that Lo-loch-to-hoo-la will wait here in the mountains until the path through the forest is open to his friend. He will talk with the father of the child he found on the war-path; and the Great Spirit will say with whom she shall dwell. Lo-loch-to-hoo-la sends back the horse shod with lightning, that his friend may know the Pawnee will not forget."

Just then a knowing little imp, who had gravely stopped on the chief's ear to listen to the conversation, ran up on his scalp-lock, and, balancing for a second, bowed and winked to Bob with such an air of assenting wisdom that the trooper had much ado to restrain a ringing laugh. Before he recovered from the confusion of a half-grin and a desperate swallow, Coacoochee, affecting to think Lo-loch-to-hoo-la's last words meant dismissal, gave the cry: "To-ho-echee!"[1]

In an instant half a dozen young braves rode into the glen. A few minutes later Bob was in the centre of a party of horsemen, riding rapidly down the bed of the little creek he had ascended with Oscar and the Witchita. When they reached the point where the three branches united, they suddenly turned southward, in a direction that Bob knew would soon lead them into the trail from the Washita to the Comanche villages. It was evident to the scout that Coacoochee had deceived the Pawnee chief: that neither the horse Lo-loch-to-hoo-la wished to return, or its rider, were to go to the camp east of the Washita. This confirmation of his suspicions made him credit Coacoochee with the most sinister motives. In the highly-excited condition of his nerves and his imagination, to awaken distrust was to blind his judgment. The slightest evidence of bad faith was enough to change doubt to certainty. He now credited Coacoochee with treachery to Lo-loch-to-hoo-la, not only in the affair of the message to the father of the little captive, but also in his dealing with the child. Every change of expression in the look or manner of either of the young braves of his escort was another proof of their evil designs.

Added to all this was a startling change in Bob's illusions. He had seen the last phantom of the lost baby waving him adieu from Lo-loch-to-hoo-la's shoulder. At the edge of the wood, where he left the chiefs, a wild-cat sprang from the gnarled bough of an immense oak to his pommel.

Whenever he forced himself to look away from the apparition (that his superstition defined as the double of Coacoochee) a sort of weird fascination brought back his wandering gaze to the glittering eyes whose stare seemed to transfix him.

The night before the battle at the foot of the Peak,

[1] The gathering cry of the Seminoles.

Bob had gone to the surgeon for help in this derangement of the senses, that had then begun to fill space with delusions. Medical skill, at that date, could only give opiates. The drug gave him three hours heavy sleep before the battle, and helped to keep the nerves stimulated during the excitement of the forty-eight sleepless hours that had followed. In that night expedition through the Pawnee camp, he had lost the little box of opium that was to have lasted until the clear, sweet December air and healthy fatigue should work a cure. Knowing Bob's force, strength, and vitality, the surgeon had thought the remedy sufficient; he had not taken into his reckoning the chance of sudden deprivation of the potent drug. Add to this physical giving way, the drunkard's memory, that runs riot in recollection of indulgence, bringing to the palate the ghosts of taste, — more terrible in effect and persistence than the wandering spectres of vision, — and the reader will begin to understand the odds already against Bob, when this last imp sprang from the purgatory of unreal realities that surround the drunkard.

The poor fellow made as gallant a fight as ever did soldier on the tented field. Unselfish as brave, he kept constantly in his thoughts the little child, and the dangers that he now imagined surrounded her. For her sake he resisted his tormenter, and resolutely proved its unreality by touch. He hammered the pommel where his last and most formidable enemy perched, and, to give excuse for the blows, made them keep time to a melody he whistled gayly. Every time the hand passed through the shadowy foe was a second's respite from the chilling terror that, in spite of his almost superhuman effort, began to close about him in a sort of suppression that seemed to tighten and throttle the throbbing arteries that whizzed aloud with the rushes of the full pulse-tides. Suddenly the Seminoles with him uttered their war-cry, as they galloped into the broad Comanche trail, where, some twenty yards distant, a party of painted warriors were waiting. Bob's spectre sprang to the ground, rapidly increasing in size until it seemed to fill an immensity of space. The scout halted, horror-struck, as the terrible apparition rolled into his lap, the bleeding, decapitated head of Rue. With a choking cry, the poor fellow rose in his stirrups, threw up his hands in a last wild struggle, and fell to the ground in violent convulsions.

CHAPTER XXXII.

> And out and cam the thick, thick bluid,
> And out and cam the thin,
> And out and cam the bonny hert's bluid:
> Thair was nae life left in.
> > PERCY'S RELIQUES.

AT midnight the Osage Carson had sent through the Blue-River pass reached Camp Refuge. (It had been christened in a baptism of blood with the name Pike gave it in the clinching peroration of his first and last effort at oratory.) At the distant hail of the Indian the camp was aroused. Young Hancock, who was on watch, hastily called "Halt!" at the same time restraining the zeal of the guard, who had levelled their muskets at the moving figure dimly seen in the starlight.

Before the Osage reached the hillock, the officers, including the recently-elected captain of the teamsters, were grouped about the little howitzer, while every man of the small force was up and ready for action.

By the light of a couple of tallow-dips, that his aids assiduously sheltered from the breeze, Leszinksky read Colonel Kearny's dispatches and Carson's short note. The flickering little points of flame lit the face of the young commander, and the watchers who were crowded about read the evil tidings in his frowning brow and the lines of pain around the firmly-closed mouth. He handed the unfolded papers to Buford and Hancock, and, leaning upon the little gun, covered his face with his hands. A moment, and his thoughts were brought to the needs of the present by the question, "What shall we do, Lieutenant?"

Raising his face, without any effort at concealment, he wiped away the tears with which it was wet, and, in a voice that steadied as he ended the first sentence, he said, "We must instantly send messengers to all the forts." Then, turning to Pike and the crowd of expectant, anxious men, he continued, "They have had a battle with the Comanches near the Witchita Hills, and the regiment is hard hit. Captain Moore is killed."

A groan of grief and rage came from the little detachment of the dragoons who belonged to Moore's company; deep oaths and muttered curses from the infantrymen and teamsters, who were pressing close to hear the news.

The speaker, who it was evident was trying to master his grief, motioned for silence as he said, "Our comrades are over there, the other side of the Cross Timbers, with their wounded and dead, waiting for help. Step by step they have fought their way back. Embarrassed as they are they dare not risk the passage through the Cross Timbers until they are reinforced and the way is cleared —"

A voice interrupted: "We are ready, Lieutenant, to march this minute!" A chorus took up the cry: "Yes, we are ready!"

Again he quieted them with a gesture.

"We can best help the regiment by strict obedience to Colonel Kearny's orders. He commands me to hold this camp, and its supplies, now so needful, until reinforcements reach us. Then we are to advance to the ford above Wild Horse Creek, sending a detachment to clear the timbers, while we protect the crossing. I have no doubt that the Indians who attacked us are still watching this camp. For a messenger to pass their lines in safety will require prudence, as well as courage. It is a perilous path; every step of the way from here to Fort Washita is beset with danger. Yet it is the nearest point from which help can come. I want volunteers, — men who in the path of duty are not afraid of death."

From the young subalterns, from soldiers and teamsters, there were cries of acceptance. They were all by general acclaim volunteer messengers; each insisted, all claimed priority. Then individual fitness was urged. Resolute, modest men seemed braggarts in their insistance, in their discussion of qualities. Age sneered at youth, experience at speed; while all, according to their own showing, were gifted with strength and endurance. At last a compatriot of Pike, a wizen-faced, little atomy, a hanger-on of the camp, known in the regiment as "Little Misery," climbed on the giant's shoulder, and screamed out in a ridiculous little quavering treble his fitness: —

"I 'm the he what ought ter go. I on'y weigh ninety-eight poun'! I 've rid races in ole Missoury ever sinct I could stick on ter a hoss, an' I allus wun 'em. I 'm the buzzard as kin do it quick. I sails high in fa'r weather; but when I goes in fur meat, I kin lay low and fly. Who-o-p! I 'm the feller ter go. Don't listen at these bull-frogs a-braggin' how they 'll jump, but jes gim me that thoroughbred o' Leftenant Buford's, an' I 'll be at Fort Washita an' Towson an' back hyar before Pike gets it through his head that I 've gone."

He lifted the giant's hat, and pulled the yellow curls. There was a ripple of laughter as Pike caught the manikin between his thumb and forefinger, and held him at arm's length. Then, in half-shame at the untimely mirth, they noisily and with more warmth of temper resumed the discussion, looking askant at Little Misery, who, perched on the howitzer, fiercely shook his wiry knot of fingers at the stolid soldier who had placed him there.

For a few moments, Leszinksky tried in vain to make himself heard. Finally the contestants paused in a sort of half-hush for breath. With a grave smile he looked around the excited group as he said, "If left entirely alone here, I do not think I could make a successful defence of this camp; yet the supplies we are guarding are not only needful but invaluable to the wounded and suffering. The enemy attacked us because they knew the importance of the supplies here to the command they hoped to cut off. Now we can realize the value of our successful defence. If they had defeated us, had captured this camp, they would have been better armed for that battle at the Witchita Peak, and the retreat of the regiment would have ended in a general massacre before help could have reached them. We have here medicine, food, and ammunition. The reinforcements that come can come rapidly; they will need no supply train. But now I must call for volunteers to stay and help me guard this camp, which is truly a 'Camp of Refuge.'"

There were muttered words of assent, low-spoken doubts as to the right thing to do, and a few hastily-checked oaths. The men had begun to understand the character of their young commander; they had tested the fighting qualities of the soldier, and so they respected the Christian. The claims were not withdrawn, but the claimants were hushed; they began to think it might be as soldierly to stay as to go. The *morale* of the camp was coming to its best. Obedience would be rendered to command; but if choice were permitted, and the comparative risk could be estimated, each soldier would choose the path where Duty faced Danger.

After a short consultation, the announcement was made that Lieutenant Hancock and Little Misery were to go to Forts Washita and Towson. The young officer was to return with the first detachment of the reinforcement.

Pike's offer to go alone through the Cross Timbers, with news of the arrival of Carson's messenger and the successful defence of the camp and its supplies, was accepted. The giant was the first to leave the camp. Clad in a simple hunting-shirt and buckskin breeches, with Indian leggins and moccasins, his head thrust through a rough blanket, and covered with a wide-brimmed slouch hat; a heavy bowie-knife in his leathern belt, balanced by one of the recently-invented Colt's revolvers; a haversack, powder-horn, and bullet-pouch slung over his broad shoulders, and in his left hand a long-barrelled Mississippi rifle, he looked the colossal model of the frontier partisan, as he joined the little group of officers and men, who were in the corral made by the enclosing wagons, where Buford's thoroughbred was being saddled.

Perched on the backboard of a wagon, Little Misery, in all the pomp of a jockey who is about to ride the favorite to the running-post, was giving directions to the volunteer grooms who were rubbing the flanks of the splendid bay. Near by stood Leszinksky and Hancock in earnest talk, while Buford superintended the toilet of the steed whose speed was to bring safety to the comrades who were as dear to him as brothers, to the regiment in which centred his soldierly pride.

The manikin on his perch was the first to observe the approach of the giant; the broken treble in which he shouted: "Wh-o-o-p!" startled all the assistants. Tossing up and catching his ragged, brimless makeshift of a cap, he continued: "Hurray for ole Missoury! Her big bufferler 's a startin' on the war-path, an' her game buzzard 's a goin' ter fly. Hurray for the biggest Pike she ever riz! Now jes chaw yer tongue, ole feller, till it splits, so yer can fling yer jaw at 'em an' then sing out to them fightin' cocks, over yonder in that Injun pit, to bristle out their feathers, an' rip in with thar gaffs, fur the blue hen's chickens is boun' ter win. Tell 'em Little Misery an' Leftenant Hancock 's a comin' with a fresh main, an' by the time thar spurs strike, there won't be a skulkin' red rooster left to crow in the Comanche country. Wh-o-o-p!"

Pike laid his hand lightly on the manikin's shoulder, as he spoke to Leszinksky.

"I 'm ready to start, Lootinent. I 'm gwine to try it up the bed o' this little creek to the sand-hills; then I 'll cross to the Washiter. If the Injuns is a-watchin' the ford I may have a tussle with 'em. So be an' you hyar my gun you 'll know there ain't no lack o' the pesky varmints at the ford. But don't come or send any of the boys. I know they 'd be mighty willin' to come, but it would n't do no good, an' you 'ud be throwing away your chances. If thar ain't no savages about, I'll send you a sign. Thar's one thing I thought o' tellin' our ingineer"—and he smiled at Hancock. "If he and Little Misery will start with the Osage and go to the northeast about five miles, he can put 'em in a trail to Fort Washiter, that the Injuns won't be so apt to watch. I've been a talkin' to him, and he says it's a plain trail, and mostly open ground, so they'll have a fair track if they have to run fur it."

"We are well mounted and well armed, and can break through a small force."

The resolute look of the blue eyes, and the straight, elastic pose of the slight, boyish figure, said more than the words.

"Yes, sir. I know you're willin' to fight, an' you're steady and cool when you're in it. You fit like one o' our reg'*ment* might a-done, the other day,—steady and cool and no back down; that's the stuff to make soldiers. But you're young. Well, that ain't no harm." And again the giant smiled in a kindly way at the boy officer. "You'll come o' that, and you'll larn backwoods ingine*ering*; but we won't say no more o' that," he added, as he saw the flush in the young face. "I'm sure you'll fight like a brave man, without arthworks. On'y remember *this ain't no fightin' ride*. It's a hard thing fur a young man, and a plucky one at that, to do; but you'll have to give up your own feelins if you meet Injuns. *You* could risk the fight, I know, at heavy odds, but the reg'*ment* over yonder with the wounded and the dyin' can't take no risks. The bravest thing you can do now is to run from any Injun. It's hard; but if you'll think o' them over thar, you'll do it."

The young officer held out his hand, and as it vanished in Pike's broad palm, he said: "You are right, Pike, and I thank you for saying this so frankly. I see that our commander approves your advice. I shall remember that my courage must all gather into my horse's heels. It is not a fight, but a race to win; and the stakes are our comrades' lives.

Tell them over there that we are sure to get through, sure to bring them help."

"Yes!" screamed the manikin, who had wriggled from under Pike's restraining hand, and was now standing in an easy balance on the corner of the wagon, "You jes tell 'em the Hancock flyer is boun' tu win. He's got the wind and the bottom, an' he's a-goin' steady an' strong, and Little Misery's his running mate. Who-o-p! Cock-a-doodle-do!"

There was a kindly leave-taking with the men and officers, — warm grasps of the hand and heartfelt wishes for his safe arrival in the beleagured camp. Then Pike started on his perilous journey, accompanied for a short distance by Leszinksky, who had learned to value the sterling character of the usually taciturn soldier. For a few moments they walked in silence; then suddenly Pike stopped.

"Don't go any furder, Lootinent. It distarbs me, like. I'm a-thinkin' o' you, an' not watchin' my way. If thar's Injuns about, — and it's most like, — we must do our last talking hy-ar. I thought jes now I hy-ared a coyote up thar at that ridge; but it mought a-ben a Injun. Don't go any furder, sir; I've trouble in my mind."

"Very well; I will say good-by, here. You have my best wishes, Pike, for your own sake as well as for the sake of the regiment. You have been of great value here, as well as a great comfort to me. I have been attached to you heretofore by ties of grateful, affectionate regard; now you have taught me to esteem, to respect you. We are not only fellow-soldiers: we are children of the one Father. So, with prayers for your safety, I leave you in His keeping."

For a moment the giant held Leszinksky's hand, without a word. When he did speak, there were tears in the voice.

"You've done me a power o' good, sir. You're a blessin' to the reg'*ment*. I hadn't never quite forgot my mammy and her lovin' ways; but sometimes it 'pears like you and Mrs. Leszinsky have brung her rite from the grave to me. I allus tries now to do His will" (and he pointed heavenward). "I tries, but sometimes it's hard to beat out ole sins. I means to do right by man and beast, — by everything He made; and if I don't allus make it, why, He knows I tries. I'm more obleeged to you than I can say, sir, fur all you've done fur me, fust and last, — most of all, fur sayin' you'll pray for me. If I have to go 'through the deep waters,' I'll know you're a-prayin', and I'll know that our Father'll holp me."

Before Leszinksky could say another word, the brave, simple-minded fellow was gone.

Having finished their cavalry inspection, and selected as Hancock's mount a dark roan, wiry and strong, with a reputation for speed that ranked him in the regiment second to Buford's thoroughbred, the young officers ran up the little eminence to watch the starlit prairie until Leszinksky returned from his walk with Pike.

His selection as express-rider to Fort Towson had so inflamed the everbounding conceit of Little Misery that, with an air of taking place where he belonged, he followed the two young men, after giving the most pompously imperious directions to his former comrades of the stable.

"Now you kin stop a-rubbin' my hoss; he'll do at that. Gin him a mouthful o' that wet grass ter chaw on till we're off. It'll clean his gills, an' start him peert. Yer mought loosen the girths a notch or two, but don't forget to tighten 'em when yer bring him roun' to the start. An' that roan the leftenant's a-goin' ter ride, — jes' lead him up and down out thar till we're ready. He ain't game, like the thoroughbred; but he's a awful fast scrub when he's warmed. We mought need his best go right hy-ar at the start; so jes' walk him roun', an' limber him up."

The dragoons laughed good-naturedly, and the young officers could not restrain broad smiles at the manikin's assumption.

Leszinksky soon returned, and the most absolute silence was kept on the hill-top, where all were anxiously listening to every breath of the night that was likely to bring news from the daring yet modest soldier. In about fifteen minutes there came from the direction of the sand-hills the cry of a screech-owl. Leszinksky started, as the shrill voice of the manikin called from under the gun-carriage: —

"That's him, that's Pike! that's the kind o' a owl he is! I've hearn him do that a-fore. He kin go more liken a owl than a strange owl could, 'cep'en he war trained to it."

The young officers laughed; then, as King Stan raised his hand, all were silent. Again the cry, this time more distant; once again a far-off call; then, in the deep silence of the night, only the insect pulse-throbs of the prairie could be heard; and they knew that as yet the scout had found no foe.

The Osage was roused from his sleep; the horses were led around the little knoll to the wide-stretching prairie at the base of its eastern acclivity; and in a few moments the little party were vanishing in the distance, under the glimmering light of twinkling stars.

Leaving Pike to his solitary venture, we will follow the path to the northeast with the two horsemen and their Osage guide. As they left the camp, the wind from the north blew in gusts, and a low-lying bank of clouds came drifting southward.

The Osage ran in a loping gait by the horses, that were going in an easy gallop; from time to time he would lift his hand, and for a moment the horsemen would wait, motionless and silent, while he threw himself on the ground to listen, then springing to his feet, a quick exclamation of content was the signal for another dash.

Through the gathering darkness, and over a pathless prairie, the guide never once hesitated. The instinct of the savage leads through the trackless plains as unerringly as the compass of the mariner points the course through the trackless waters.

In a little over half an hour the party had reached the Blue River divide, and struck the open trail that led due south to the military road from Fort Towson to Fort Washita. Once started, the horses could be trusted to keep the trail, although every star was now blotted from the heavens, and a keen, biting "norther" was sweeping down from the plains.

The Osage went north to where Carson waited in the cottonwood grove.

Hancock and Little Misery rode southward under a beating rain, with the wind at their backs, the thoroughbred going in a steady, long-stretching trot along the rocky divide, until the trail led to the open prairie, then breaking into a sweeping gallop as he felt the springy turf, scarcely feeling the light weight of the little rider, whose firm, easy touch of the bridle, never fretting or vexing the splendid stallion, left him untired after miles of distance.

Little Misery's complimentary summing up of the roan that Hancock rode was well deserved. He *had* "limbered up," and he proved that a scrub may have grit and nerve as well as speed. Neck and neck he kept by the thoroughbred in that gallant ride through night and storm, though the odds of weight were against him.

At two o'clock they had left Camp Refuge. At seven, when the gray light had forced its way through the clouds and the rain, after a ride of fifty-five miles, they reached the military road where their paths separated. Hancock had only five miles more to go to Fort Washita: while Little Misery, on his untired steed, had before him a run of sixty miles to the post station, at the only settlement between Fort Towson and Washita not destroyed in the recent raid.

Little Misery stood up in his stirrups and shouted a parting "Hurray!" to Hancock as the young officer rode westward; the roan running at its best speed in this spurt that was to take him to the winning-post. Hancock gave a quick glance backward, as the little jockey waved his ragged cap and put spurs to the bay, to which he had given an instant's breathing-spell as he watched the roan's run. From a thicket of undergrowth, at the edge of the trail they had just left, there was a quick discharge of shot, a flight of whizzing arrows; and, as a party of Indian horsemen broke into the military road, at the point they had entered it from the trail, Hancock knew the foe they had evaded was close at their heels.

Urging his horse with voice and spurs to keep at his best, again the young officer looked back, and saw that he was free to ride his race with the enemy, without the sting of having to leave a comrade in extremity of peril; for Little Misery was just turning a distant bend in the road, leaving behind an already distanced foe.

In twenty minutes Hancock was at headquarters in Fort Washita with his dispatches. Two hours later he was on the road back to Camp Refuge with two companies of mounted infantry and two light field-pieces.

At the moment Little Misery put spurs to the bay, while still half-turned in his saddle to watch Hancock, the Indians appeared. In their anxiety to capture the famous thoroughbred unharmed, they would not risk an arrow that might glance in a sudden gust; but three of their best marksmen fired their rifles at the jockey. One ball took the cap he was waving at Hancock, a second cut through the heavy folds of the dragoon's cape a kind-hearted trooper had lent him; the third struck between the ribs just below the uplifted arm, and lodged in the chest.

The shot and the pressure of the spurs were simultaneous. The sudden spring of the stallion, by its reverse shock, prevented Little Misery from falling from the saddle. It threw him from his half-turned posture square into the seat, with his arms around the stallion's neck.

Four hours later the thoroughbred stopped at the stables at the post-station, where a party of dragoons had just halted. They unwound the bridle-reins from over the head and under the arms of the speechless, half-fainting rider, and unbuckled the suspenders with which he had fastened himself to the pommel of the cavalry-saddle. They found his dispatches in the breast-pocket of his ragged jacket, dyed with blood. The officer of the command hastily opened them, and sent them by an express-rider to the commanding officer at Fort Towson.

The beating rain and the chill of the "norther" had staunched the bleeding wound. Nature's styptics might have saved him. The kindly meant efforts at restoration destroyed Little Misery's last chance. They carried him into a warm room and gave him stimulants. As he recovered consciousness, the bleeding commenced afresh. There was no surgeon at the post or with the dragoons, so, with all the bandages they could invent, the hemorrhage continued. Between these efforts at help he told his story.

"When the damned redskin hit me I knowed I was done fur, but I jes' shut my teeth an' swore I'd come through an' holp git our fellers outen thar clutches. . . . The thoroughbred was a-goin' in a dead run, so it was most like a-layin' in a cradle. You see a saddle's about the on'y one ever I knowed —— Somehow I got off my gallusses, an' fastened my monkey to the pommel —— I swore a heap last night, 'bout ridin' such a big race with a cavalry-saddle; but the Judge who is up thar at the Grand Stand knowed what 'ud be most apt to bring me through, or he would n't a let me rid it with them big stakes up —— Tell the boys out thar in that devil's pit, that the game buzzard's had his last fly, but he brung 'em help —— I'm glad it's me was hit —— I ain't much 'count and the leftenant got off scot free —— Tell him good bye —— we had a bully race and we won what we was entered fur —— Hurray for old Missuory! *she* breeds the flyers.'' Then a few broken efforts at speech, a few tired sighs, and the brave little rider was at the Grand Stand.

His last sentences had come in broken gasps, but they were the epitome of his life, — rollicking, reckless, a rough, uncouth correlative of mirth and pluck. I give the words for what they are worth. They may teach the righteous to love a sinner and to believe in the breadth of God's mercy, the greatness of the Eternal

Economy that "gathereth the fragments that nothing may be lost."

His face was pallid and pinched. Life had dealt hardly with him; and death brought out the lines that poverty and ignorance and the crimes of his progenitors had traced. The evil that died with him was of the world's teaching. The good that was within him led him through the gate of death into the presence of the Teacher who said, "Greater love hath no man than this, that a man lay down his life for his friends."

CHAPTER XXXIII.

> OVER the mountains,
>   And over the waves;
> Under the fountains,
>   And under the graves,
>
> Under floods that are deepest,
>   Which Neptune obey,
> Over rocks that are steepest,
>   Love will find out the way.
>   OLD SONG.

TWO weeks later in our history Leszinksky and Carson, accompanied by Lo-loch-to-hoo-la and two Pawnee warriors, in the brightest of bright winter mornings, were climbing the winding path up the spur of the ridge that led around the cascade to the Valley of the Three Mountains. Leszinksky walked slowly beside the Pawnee chief, whose slight lameness seemed a greater disadvantage than it really was to the vigorous, agile Indian. As the subject of their conversation will come to our knowledge further down the current of this veritable history, we will borrow "Monsieur Balzac's cane," and invisibly keep step with Carson as with the two warriors he hastened up the mountain path through the rocky defile of the narrow cañon, beside the little river, that rushed down to its fall over the cascade from the high-lifted fairy valley.

His face glowing from the quick walk in the sharp, wintry air, and his heart equally aglow with hope and love, Carson sprang lightly up the gentle incline of the pebbly path, that suddenly ended in the rice-field from which the river flowed into the cañon.

For two reasons, Carson was a willing *avant courier*.

To do him full justice we place first his wish to save Margaret the shock of surprise at her husband's coming (even joy in her precarious health might be a danger); the after consideration, but one that *drew* as strongly, was his pardonable haste to see again the recently elected queen of his heart.

The young dragoon, who usually viewed hill and valley through the lens of practical use, as obstruction or advantage to progress, was, at the precise moment of his entrance into the valley, so enrapt with the mists of love's imaginings that he was for a moment caught by the charm of the picturesque and romantic landscape Nature had hidden high up in the bosom of the hills. But sympathy with the inanimate was too new and slight a sensation to hold Carson's thought, past that one second, from the longing desire to look upon a loveliness more attractive and more responsive to his admiration.

His first step out of the abstraction was into the positive. A little rill that ran into broken falls down a shelving ledge from the cleft corner of the cañon, from which spiral rings and shadowy puffs of vapor ascended, was a more curious attraction to the matter-of-fact soldier than mere beauty of scene. Ascending the easy steps of the shelving ledge, he reached a broad plateau of rock, where a tiny Indian child was busily gathering shiny bits of broken stone. At the sound of his step the child turned, and the golden curls of Baby Rue flashed in the sunlight. With a glad shout she sprang into his outstretched arms : —

"My Billy! My Billy Tarson!"

In a moment she remembered there was a person near by who was dear to her elfin Majesty; so she called, "Laha! Come, Laha, come!" Carson looked around. Standing near where the spring issued from a cleft in the rock was Alaha-chayna. The deep blush that dyed the half-averted face of the Indian maiden, the downcast eyes, and the slight trembling of the bending, willowy figure, would have betrayed her feelings to a more confident lover. The reader will remember that heretofore our blunt soldier had learned only Love's losses. In his ignorance, he thought these signal-flags of surrender meant repulse. But he had a stout heart; so, seeing no obstacle to *this* love in the prior right of a comrade, he determined to tempt fate to its utmost. He took into quick account auxiliaries and embarrassments: the last should be first, for they were worrying him in the shape of the two Pawnee warriors who were gravely regarding him from the foot of the ledge. Hoping they had not seen the maiden, in her sheltered place behind the jutting ledge, he called to them in the few words he knew of the Comanche tongue to go on up to the chief's lodge and announce the coming of Lo-loch-to-hoo-la and the white officers, adding with word and gesture that he would wait here with the child for her father.

The Indians gave mute responsive signs and walked on up the valley. It was well; for our imperious little princess had slipped from Carson's arms to enforce obedience to her command. Carson followed her across the wide plateau, giving one last backward look to assure himself of the fact that he was out of view of the warriors, who were rapidly crossing the rice-fields to the open path that led through the wood. As he reached Alaha-chayna and his baby ally there was a more alarming order: —

"Tiss my Billy, Laha! Tiss my Billy Tarson."

Seeing she was not obeyed to the letter, as the maiden hesitatingly lifted her drooping face and placed her little hand in Carson's expectant palm, the *enfant terrible* shouted in a shrill, insistent key, "Tiss him, I tell you: tiss him, Laha! Don't you hear me tell you?"

His embarrassment increasing with every syllable shrieked by the little tyrant, thinking to quiet her with a half obedience, Carson bent over the young girl's hand and pressed it to his lips. It is doubtful if Rue would have been content with the compromise had not her attention been suddenly attracted to a little bird, that lit on a jagged point of rock near her collected treasures.

Distrusting its intentions, she ran to guard her shining riches, and for a few brief moments was busy looking over the heap to see if she had been robbed. Possibly, if she had watched Carson she would have cared less for her property, in the content given by his perfect obedience.

Strange freak of human nature! Now that he could easily have commenced a decorous and eminently proper and edifying conversation, the young lover recklessly threw away the opportunity for mutual improvement given by Rue's last vagary and did the very thing the insistant child had urged. It was all wrong; but as a truthful historian I dare not withhold the fact. There is a strange temptation in scarlet lips when long, curling lashes droop over veiled eyes that dare not meet the bold glance of a wooer. And so, though her cheeks were aflame, he kissed her.

Poets and romancers linger over Love's first kiss,— and for that matter, so did Carson. But I, being only a relator of absolute history, am glad the telling of it is over. To my young readers it may seem an easy thing to do,— the mere relating of a trifling event in a simple narrative. Well, let any self-confident person put himself in my place, and he will find there are difficulties in the situation. An historian is not necessarily estopped from being a philosopher and a moralist. Facts are sometimes causes: a cause is "that which produces an effect." Now, this particular fact had a sequence or order of following. In truth, I might say it had a series. I like to be exact, so I will say at once, and have done with it, that it had a succession of sequences. Finding that, for some occult reason (the girl must have been bewitched), she did not or could not resist, or even raise those drooping eyelids, Carson kissed her again. Now, having accomplished my task not only as a truthful historian, but as philosopher, the moralist in me utterly refuses to go any further in this investigation the publicity of which can do no good in the way of warning. It is enough that he kissed her twice before I turned away,— refusing to see.

The process might have been repeated after this discreet historian turned his back, but for Baby Rue. Having driven away the predatory bird and reviewed her possessions, the young "voyvoda" bethought herself of her two slaves.

Then was demonstrated a remarkable problem, and one worthy of the study of a physicist, *i.e.* how instantaneous is the reaction of oscillatory bodies, if the circumference in which their attraction is perceptible is disturbed by the approach of any foreign agent. Leaving this for the investigation of the learned, the historian will resume his task, and go on with his register of events.

The moment the imperious baby claimed their attention, with a most wonderful unanimity, Carson and Alaha-chayna set themselves to instant obedience to her slightest behest, although her wishes were as changeful as a storm-tossed leaf.

Between the services called for, Carson *did* manage to make certain declarations and ask certain questions; and though the answers never seemed sufficiently explicit (to judge from the insistance with which the lover asked for minute repetitions), there were frequent seizures of a little hand in giving or taking some of the baby's treasures that emphasized his thanks for certain replies, that would have been inaudible to this historian had he even tried to listen. As all of this needed a management, a delicate diplomacy, heretofore untried by the blunt soldier, it required time. Yet the two principals in this little melodrama were so unconscious of the flight of minutes, that when they did take cognizance of the world beyond that little plateau, they were astonished to see within easy call two canoes, that must have crossed the little lake, and come the seven miles of length of the narrow river, since the arrival of the Pawnees at the settlement at the head of the valley. Margaret, Randall, and Coacoochee were in the first canoe; in the second were Bob Stearns and Oscar. The discovery of their approach was due to the roving eyes of little Rue. Carson had just told her of the speedy coming of her father; and it had immediately required all of his skill, assisted by the gentle persuasion of the Indian maiden, to keep her from a headlong race down the stretching shelves of the plateau. Her impatience was beginning to test the temper of the lover, whose constant attention she claimed, when he would so much rather have continued a conversation, for which she had hitherto been the convenient pretext. All of the loose treasures of Carson, all of the detachable ornaments of Alaha-chayna, had been offered in a vain effort to quiet the uneasy little despot. At the risk of his own eyes, and her fingers, Carson finally gave her his hunting-knife, which she had deigned to demand, hoping for one moment of freedom as she clashed it back and forth in the scabbard. Suddenly she threw aside the coveted plaything and with a quick spring escaped from Alaha-chayna's arms, and then rushed to the edge of the rock, where she woke the echoes of the cañon with the call:—

"Mamma! Mamma! Mamma!"

In an effort to escape Carson, who had hastily followed her, she ran across the plateau to where it gave a view of the entrance to the cañon; then, dancing about in an ecstasy of joy, she changed the shout to:—

"Papa! Papa!"

Carson caught her as she started down the shelving ledge to meet King Stan, who, with the Pawnee chief, was just crossing the steaming rill of the hot spring at the entrance into the valley.

A minute later Leszinksky clasped in his arms his wife, and the child of whose restoration he had at one time almost despaired.

After greetings had been exchanged, and broken bits of news told, the party separated into little groups according to the manner in which they were to go up the valley.

The first departure was a beautiful, fairy-like birchen canoe, that suddenly shot out of its hiding-place in the reeds; and with a few flashing strokes of the paddle Alaha-chayna was leading the little flotilla in the race up the river. As the graceful, erect figure vanished in a curve of the narrow stream, the two Indian chiefs were standing in the larger canoes, waiting for a distribution of the passengers.

Randall and Carson, after assisting Margaret to a seat in the canoe with Coacoochee, and waiting to see Leszinksky embarked with Rue and Lo-loch-to-hoo-la, walked on up the meadow-path, closely followed by Bob Stearns and Oscar, who were anxious to hear the news Carson had to tell.

The story was more uneventful than the listeners expected. The reinforcements had been gathered in so quickly and in such force that the Indians were over-awed. There had been only a slight skirmish at the ford of the Washita, and the crossing had been effected, after shelling the woods, without loss. In view of the immediate movement of at least half of the force on the Arkansas frontier to Texas, any further advance into the Comanche country had been thought unadvisable. Moreover, Lo-loch-to-hoo-la's voluntary offer to give up the child made further invasion needless, unless it was intended to punish the Comanches for the raid, in which it could not be proven that they had been active assistants.

Then Randall asked, "Where is the command?"

"The companies from the lower forts have gone back to their quarters. The volunteers are in a rage and likely to do mischief. The general feared they might, in their present temper, attack inoffensive hunting-parties, or even the Seminole villages, as they regard the Seminoles as allies of the Pawnees; and so, to prevent further difficulty, part of our regiment is temporarily encamped on the Canadian at the mouth of Little River; and our scouting parties are watching until the volunteers are disbanded."

"Where did you meet Lo-loch-to-hoo-la?"

"At the cottonwood grove. The morning I left there he told me how and where to leave signals if Leszinksky decided to come for Mrs. Leszinksky and Rue. I pledged my word to Coacoochee for Stan and myself, that we would never use or reveal, without his permission, the pass to the valley if we were brought here."

There was more talk of the meeting with Lo-loch-to-hoo-la, and then, as Bob and Oscar walked ahead, Randall said : —

"I don't wonder that *you* thought it needful to come for our party. We might have made the trip in safety under the guidance and guard of the Seminoles, as we did in coming. But possibly a certain lovely maiden would have remained in this vale of Eden."

Carson turned hastily. Seeing that Bob and Oscar had gone on to the lake and were out of hearing, he answered : —

"If Mrs. Leszinksky and Rue had been safe at Bouie's Hill, I would have come to see Coacoochee's daughter. This morning I asked her to be my wife, and she has promised her consent if I can win her father's. Now, Randall, you understand I want no more damned nonsense."

"Don't be a fool, Carson."

The young dragoon faced the doctor with such a red face and angry look that Randall laughed outright, but, seeing the rising temper he controlled himself, and added, —

"You would be a fool if you thought I did not thoroughly respect and esteem the lovely girl whose only weakness, as far as I can judge, is this promise to you. This is better luck than you deserve, youngster. But with all my heart I congratulate you, and if in any way I can aid you, count on my best. Does King Stan know of your success?"

"Yes. I told him of her, and how much I cared for her, before we came. As he started up the river just now, I told him it was all right."

Randall laughed pleasantly, and Carson, whose temper had vanished, looked delighted, until the doctor said : —

"But it is n't all right; and if you are not a more skilful diplomatist than most of our thick-headed dragoons, it will be all wrong. Coacoochee is sufficiently grateful to do you any ordinary kindness as between man and man; but his hatred to the whites is only glossed over with a few likings. I think he would as soon see his daughter dead as the wife of one of the race he has never forgiven for exiling him to these wilds."

Carson exclaimed in a resolute, angry tone, "If he refuses me, I will run away with his daughter."

"I do not believe you would, Carson. You are here as Coacoochee's trusted guest, — trusted with the secret of his last place of refuge. I do not think you would tarnish your own honor or tempt the woman you love to a disobedience that would come near breaking the heart of this grand savage."

"Damn his grandeur! I love his daughter better than he does."

"Then you will only try to win her as an honest man and a chivalrous soldier should. More than any one else, *you* are bound to respect her faith to her father."

"See here, Randall; I can stand that sort of thing from Stan, for his life is as pure as a saint's, and his religion goes into every act of his life; but, confound it, I won't stand schooling from a fellow who is n't a bit better than the rest of us sinners, — in fact, who has n't as good a chance hereafter; for you don't even believe in hell."

Randall's laugh was tantalizing as he answered: "That *is* a loss. But this happens not be a question of theology. It is simply a discussion of what a gentleman may do, if he would not soil his honor."

Here Carson's oaths came so much faster than his arguments that your historian prefers to skip the conversation and go on to where Bob and Oscar were waiting to ferry Carson and Randall over the lake to the little village that nestled close to the opposite shore, under the shelter of the shelving upland meadows, where were the comfortable log-houses of the chief and his family.

The ferryboat, made of untanned buffalo-skins, stretched over ribs of split oak-saplings, was light and strong. Bob and Oscar had unfastened it from its moorings, and, seated in it, were waiting the arrival of the two passengers, who were delayed by frequent pauses in their walk through the wood, when the interest or emphasis of the conversation required the aid of look and gesture.

The sight of Bob at his ease in the boat, and provided with a listener, assured your historian that the scout was talking long before sound could verify sight.

As this conversation (if monologue can be called conversation) fills a blank in our history, I will give it as I heard it: —

"Now, the more I think on it, the surer I am, Coacoochee meant to euchre the Big Chief in that matter of Sultan and me and you. He jest thought Louis Pacheco, who I'm free to say 's as much of a gentleman as a mulatto could be, would rope you into the traces with the black Injuns; and that the less chance I had to get back with Sultan to our leftenant, the better chance he had o' keeping the Pawnee chief from ever makin' friends for good with our folks. Now, when I could n't nohow make you understand, but you jest went and left me, and me bad with the manner-poker (*mania à potu*), why, I jest had to cave. I tell you that last sight I had o' that monstrous cat would a-fetched Julius Cæsar, and a-wilted him. I did n't know nuthin', so be and you don't count half-seein' things in a sort o' blind way, until I waked up the next mornin' in that Comanche lodge, tied fast. It mought a-been, like they said arterwards, to keep me from a-gettin' hurt; but it looked mighty like I was a prisoner, though I'm free to say the black drink that old squaw brung me did me a power o' good. It cl'ared my head and let me sleep in a way no reg'lar surgeon ever did. I wish Doctor Randall knowed what that physic was made on; it's time some o' the reg'lars had l'arnt somethin' 'bout curin' the grip whiskey gets of a poor devil who's a tryin' to stop and can't. Why, you see, if I got a pull at a bottle now, I could n't nohow let it go by me, now my promise is up and the little cap'n res-*cu-ed*."

"Don't, Marse Bob; don't try that no mo'; 't allus gets you down, sir."

"How the devil am I to try it withouten any liquor?"

Just then Randall and Carson reached the lake, and the question remained forever unanswered.

The Seminoles had profited by their residence in the Cherokee country. The dinner, given to our party of friends in the comfortable log-house that had been Margaret's since her arrival in the valley, was as perfect in the manner of service, as excellent in quality and variety of fish, game, fruit, and vegetables, as, at that time, could have been expected in the home of the wealthiest settler.

Alaha-chayna had been constantly with Margaret and Baby Rue; but with instinctive courtesy the Indians now left the so recently reunited family to the freedom of unrestrained conversation with their friends. After dinner the elfin princess, missing some of her customary courtiers, imperiously demanded to be taken to Alaha-chayna. Notwithstanding a glance from Randall, that dyed his face several shades deeper than his tawny locks, Carson immediately rose to accompany the wilful child.

In the quiet of Rue's absence, Randall and Leszinksky discussed the chances for King Stan's success in the mission entrusted to him by General Arbuckle.

Once more the tribes were to be invited to a council. The inducement held out to the Seminole chief was the final settlement of the rights of the so-called Black Indians, while the alternative of peace or war was to be offered to the Pawnees.

Then Leszinksky told the story of Lo-loch-to-hoo-la. It was only another black page in the record of Indian agents. A tribe cheated and despoiled; families gathered into a reservation far from the hunting-grounds, and then left to starve, while pale vampires grew rich on the very life-blood of Indian women and children. Back of all this was a more terrible shadow, — a broken and landless nation, defrauded through the treaties that had been forced upon a helpless people or signed by confiding, unlettered chiefs, calling in vain to the government that had robbed its tribes of their lands for the miserable pittance that had been promised for their bare sustenance.

Just here, that the feeling of an honest soldier may reach the people, who should (and I trust yet will) sweep this iniquity from the land, I give the last of the story in Leszinksky's words.

"When, at the close of the simple record of his wrongs, the landless chief and childless father looked into my eyes, and asked, 'My brother, is this just? Is the white man the owner of the earth? I loved the land upon which I was born; my body is made of its sands. The Great Spirit gave me eyes to see it. The sun shines to warm it, the rain falls to fertilize it, the moon brings back to it the spirits of our people. Yet I cannot live upon it because the great chief of the whites has seen that it was good, and has taken it for his children.' I was speechless through shame. Every word was true. Every word cut through the sophisms of the spoilers. Unless we change our entire Indian policy we will, as we deserve, stand before the world dishonored through the acts of dishonest agents and by the evidence of broken treaties."

As Leszinksky ceased speaking, Randall walked about uneasily. Margaret's eyes flashed through tears. At last Randall said:—

"Then you can do nothing with Lo-loch-to-hoo-la. The Pawnee will not go to the council?"

"Yes; he has promised for my sake, and for Rue's sake, and because of the kindness you and Margaret showed his wife, that he will be friends with the people that left him nothing."

There was a tenderness in the tone, a simple lovingness, that went from the speaker's heart to the hearts of his listeners. Randall pulled his hat over his eyes, and walked out in the meadow. Margaret, weeping on her husband's breast, sobbed out a request that ruled the current of her child's life.

"*We* will love him, Stan; he shall find a home with

us. Promise me that if I should not live, — I am not strong as I was in the old days, and I may not stay with you long, — so you will promise me that this brave, simple Indian, who loves our child as his own, shall be always sure of a place by your hearth, and a welcome from the little child he saved and gave back to me. You must never send Rue away where he cannot see her."

Struck to the heart by the shadow of this possible loss, King Stan promised.

. . . .

The next morning there was a slight fall of snow, and, as the clouds continued to gather, the departure of the visitors was delayed. In fact, all were willing to prolong their stay. Leszinksky was anxious to shield his wife from exposure to the threatening storm, and was glad of an opportunity to know more intimately the Seminole chief. Moreover, all of the party considered Carson, as all were desirous his wooing should be successful. The young cavalryman was in high spirits. Having won where he most feared repulse, he never seemed to think of the serious obstacles yet to be overcome. His hopefulness infected the others; even the gentle Alaha-chayna smiled gayly at his boyish romps with Rue, for whom his affection overflowed, for to her capture he owed his present happiness. Besides he had good reason for hopefulness, for he knew his interests were in able hands.

Randall had won a firm place in the chief's regard from the first moment of their meeting; and now was added the quality of thankfulness. The week before Leszinksky's and Carson's arrival, Coacoochee's first son was born, and Randall's skill had saved the child's life, the Indian women (the only accoucheurs of the tribe) having hopelessly given up all effort to resuscitate the apparently lifeless infant. After saving the child, his services had been of great benefit to the mother. Here, too, Margaret would be an efficient ally, as the warmest friendship already existed between Rue's mother and the kind-hearted, loving daughter of Osceola, who had cared for our little princess when ill with the slight malarial fever that had followed her night's exposure upon the Canadian River.

The day after Carson's arrival, Margaret spent the morning with Che-cho-ter[1]; and, between minute inspections of the little, mummy-like baby wrapped in swaddling clothes, the love-tale was told, — a tale to which few women are insensible; but one especially interesting to two young mothers who were happily wedded. Che-cho-ter's influence in favor of the lover of her step-daughter was promised, and none could be greater with Coacoochee. For to his affection for his wife add his almost passionate regard for the memory of the high-souled warrior, her father, and you will see that the partisan Margaret had won in the chief's household was the most valuable ally Carson could count.

The third night, when the storm had passed, leaving the valley shrouded in snow, beside the fire, where the yellow glow of burning pine reflected its rich light and diffused its pleasant resinous odour, a happy, hopeful party talked over Carson's chances. Even Randall, who had at first been doubtful of success, seemed confident of the chief's final surrender.

There was a heavy knock on the door, and into this pleasant gathering, this joyful reunion of intimate friends, came the two Indian chiefs. Lo-loch-to-hoo-la walked to where Margaret sat beside her husband, in whose arms Rue had fallen asleep, while Coacoochee stood in the centre of the room, looking frowningly around the little circle. Carson and Randall both arose as the door opened. Surprise reached its height as Bob and Oscar hurriedly entered.

Coacoochee said, "Thieving Creeks and white slave-hunters have been to the Seminole villages on the Canadian. They have taken away in chains twenty of the black warriors who fought with Coacoochee in Florida. They fired upon unarmed Seminoles within the lodges, and they have killed the sister of Coacoochee. If the news reaches the people in the village" — and he

[1] Morning Dew.

pointed to the little settlement — "your lives are endangered. You have come here as my guests, trusting to the protection of the Seminoles. We are here to take you through to your people. There is no time to lose, for fugitives who have escaped the slaughter may come, and I will not be able to appease with words the avengers of blood. The Pawnee chief has a score of men who are faithful and can be trusted; they are already down the valley with the horses. The boats are waiting below the village. Bring the child and her mother, and come." The manner of the chief was abrupt and imperious.

Leszinksky commenced: "Chief—" when Coacoochee stopped him.

"It is useless to talk. Tell your general he has sent you to the Seminoles upon a fruitless errand. We cannot live in peace in the Creek country. It is full of white slave-stealers and murderers. They shoot us, and chain our allies, and drag them away captives. But the red man's heart is free: he will not desert the blacks, who were his neighbors in the land of his birth; neither will he let those who came with peace in their hands be harmed."

Again the door opened: this time, a fairer vision, — Alaha-chayna, who, with tears falling down her sweet face, began to prepare Margaret and Rue for the journey. Carson took her hand and led her to Coacoochee.

"Chief, I love your daughter. I cannot leave her without telling you the truth. She is willing to marry me; and to-morrow I intended to ask you to trust me with her happiness. Now, I ask you to keep her for me, until a white man can prove to you that he is honest and loyal. You will wrong her if you refuse me the time and the trial I ask."

As the audacious declaration was made, Randall and Leszinksky looked at each other in alarm; all closed about the group in the centre of the room, as if to shield Carson from the chief's displeasure.

For a moment Coacoochee's eyes flashed into the blue eyes of the young dragoon. The angry glance met the steady light of truth. Intense feeling had given Carson unwonted dignity, while the occasion called out a splendid exhibition of the highest courage. The chief now turned to his daughter; there were quick, short questions and low replies in the Seminole tongue. Bravely, through it all, the young maiden left her hand in Carson's as she answered her father, her voice growing fuller and steadier as the questioning went on. There was a moment of breathless silence. Coacoochee again seemed to read with a look the very soul of the young soldier; then he addressed Randall: "I have said that the heart of an Indian is free. I trust in your care the daughter of a chief. Take her with you to the house of your friends," — he waved his hand at Leszinksky and Margaret, — "and see that she goes with honor and a pure name to the home of her husband."

Then they saw him, as a shadowy figure, who led the way in silence to the boats below the village. After they were embarked, they again saw him, a solitary figure, in the swift canoe that preceded them down the river. Below the shelving ledge of the hot spring were two ponies, that were to take Margaret and Alahachayna to the little glen where the few faithful followers of Lo-loch-to-hoo-la waited with the horses. Coacoochee lifted his daughter to her seat in the fanciful Mexican saddle, and, after a murmur of sweet Indian words, kissed her, and with a quick clasp of Carson's hand placed it in the hand of his child, and he went up the valley as the moon came out of the clouds, and a burst of silvery light lit its bridal-robe of snow.

APPENDIX.

THE LESZINKSKYS.

THE HISTORY OF A FAMILY THROUGH THE MIDDLE AGES.

> THE old order changeth, yielding place to new,
> And God fulfils himself in many ways.
> TENNYSON.

APPENDIX.

THE LESZINKSKYS.

THE HISTORY OF A FAMILY THROUGH THE MIDDLE AGES.

A PSYCHOLOGICAL AND GENEALOGICAL STUDY OF THE LESZINKSKI. — The personal history of the Leszinkskys, one of the proudest of the princely houses of Warsaw, is a summary of the history of Poland. The early chroniclers pretend to carry back their annals to the remotest periods; going so far as to trace descent from Lech, a great-grandson of Noah. This superstructure of ancestry is derived from a fanciful affinity to the name of Lech, one of the monarchs who figure in their ancient and fabulous legends, and which is also found in the genealogy of the patriarchs.

Ground for this traditionary pretension of the Leszinkskys is given in the changes of the family patronymic. From the Lechzinczski of the voyvodes, through the Leszczynski of the palatines, to the Leszinkskys of the French and American Revolutions, there is an unbroken chain of descent, easily traced, even through the dim and clouded history of the Middle Ages, by the splendor of their martial achievements.

The first of the Lechzinczski voyvodes had fought the Seljukian Turks, as allies of the Greek Emperors of Constantinople, when the Ottoman Turks or Osmanlis were yet a wandering tribe from Khorassan. It was one of their proudest boasts that for two centuries the banner of the Lechzinczski was the oriflamme of victory wherever Christian and Moslem met; it had never in all that time retreated before the Crescent. On two stricken fields, where the standards of the Greek emperor were surrendered, the Polish voyvodes refused quarter and perished with their contingent. Out of these disasters grew a hereditary enmity that took the

Lechzinczski colors into the van of every battle where shone the silver Crescent of the Turk.

When pagans, and later in their history when devout though fierce Catholics, they were true and unfaltering allies of the Greeks.

In 1355 a cadet of the family married the heiress of Kabilovitsch, one of the most powerful of the Servian nobles. The young Lechzinczski took the arms and name of his wife's family, who were closely related to the King of Servia.

In 1376, immediately before the fall of Nissa, the Castle of Kabilovitsch was captured by the Turks. The old Kabilovitsch and his son-in-law died in defence of their stronghold; the garrison was put to the sword, and the wife, two sons and three daughters of Lechzinczski-Kabilovitsch were carried captives to Adrianople, the newly-acquired capital of the Ottomans in Europe.

Amurath the First accepted ransom from the King of Servia for the mother and her youngest child, a daughter, but refused to liberate the others. His favorite wife adopted the two older daughters. The sons were to be forced recruits in the famous corps of Janissaries, which was then composed of the flower of captured Christian youth, who, cut off from all ties of country and kindred, trained to renounce the faith in which they were born, carefully educated for the profession of arms, and tempted with liberal rewards and honors, constituted a military brotherhood that grew to be the most powerful instrument of imperial ambition ever devised by subtle statecraft.

The elder brother, Stanislaus, then nineteen years of age, resisted all threats, all seduction. Milosch, the younger, yielded to persuasion and flattery, and assumed the uniform. The brothers had been constantly separated; but Milosch seemed to be so content with his position and so pleased with his comrades, that he was permitted to see his brother, his captors believing that his representation of the service and its rewards would have sure effect upon the mind of a youth broken by solitude and harsh treatment.

Stanislaus was unbound and brought to the tent of the Aga of Janissaries. Milosch sprang to meet and embrace him; but Stanislaus plucked from his brother's belt a jewelled dagger and plunged it to the hilt into the breast of the Aga, saying, "This for the dishonor you have forced upon my father's son!" Then he turned upon the guard, and fell, pierced by a dozen sword-thrusts. The lesson of courage and constancy was not lost. Milosch tore off the now abhorred uniform, repressing his sobs to declare his hatred of his brother's murderers. He would undoubtedly have been the victim of the sultan's anger but for the interference of the Prince of Caramania, a newly reconciled ally, to whom Amurath had just given in marriage his adopted daughter, the twin-sister of Milosch, having betrothed the younger daughter to his own son, Prince Saoudji. Milosch was taken by the prince to Caramania, and treated with the greatest kindness and indulgence; but although he became much attached to his brother-in-law, he sullenly resented his sister's desertion of the Christian faith.

The prince, sympathizing with the boy's conflict of feeling, sent him, accompanied by a princely escort and laden with rich presents, to the Greek Emperor Palæologous, the hereditary friend of his father's race.

The young voyvode, strikingly handsome and recklessly brave, in a few years became the favorite of the court. He was the acknowledged leader of the young nobility, distinguishing himself in every conflict of arms where the now enfeebled Greeks made attempt to resist the constantly encroaching power of the Ottoman Turks in Europe. When at length Palæologous, disheartened by his losses and the immense military superiority of Amurath, decided to treat with the Turks for an offensive and defensive alliance, Milosch openly expressed his contempt for the prudential considerations of the emperor, and haughtily took leave of the court, going direct to Caramania, trusting to engage his brother-in-law, the prince, with whom he had kept up kindly relations, to oppose the Turkish power in Asia, whilst a coalition of the Bosnians, Servians, and other Sclavonic tribes should attack Amurath's European provinces. Having succeeded in his self-appointed mission, he returned to Constantinople, on his route to Servia, to receive intelligence which utterly wrecked his most cherished personal hopes. A stronger feeling than hatred to the Turks had led the young voyvode where, through dangers met and conquered, ambition pointed the path of success. He had loved, with all the intensity and daring of youth, a Byzantine princess, the niece of the emperor. During his absence she had been given in marriage to the sultan, as the seal of the new alliance of Greek and Moslem. Notwithstanding the difference of faith and the little estimate in which women were held by the Mahometans, such marriages were not uncommon in the history of the Greek emperors. These alliances were propitiatory offerings to stop conquest, offerings accepted by the wily Turks as reason for the future acquisition of new territory.

APPENDIX.

The young Lechzinczski-Kabilovitsch sought his sister, the wife of Prince Saoudji, and forced her to arrange an interview, in which he intended to overwhelm with scorn and reproach the woman who had bartered his love for a crown. He found only a pale, heart-broken victim of kingly craft, whom he forgave whilst swearing to avenge her wrongs and his own. In this mood he arrived at the court of the King of Servia and found the country ripe for revolt against the Turks, who, since the fall of Nissa, had exacted from the Servians a yearly tribute of one thousand pounds of silver and one thousand horse-soldiers. The tax of silver alone was for that age heavy; but the yearly burthen of furnishing and equipping a thousand horsemen was still more grievous to a prince already crippled by the loss of the most important city in his kingdom.

The history of the Middle Ages furnishes the record of no more daring adventurer, no diplomat more skilled in intrigue, than the young Milosch Kabilovitsch. Energetic and resolute, the very rashness of his courage was an element of success, giving him a marked ascendency over the turbulent and restless Sclavonians of Bosnia, Servia, and Poland. To the fierce and intractable will of the Polish voyvode, born the ruler of life and death of the serfs on his immense estates, he added the passive and stolid power of resistance to obstacle he had learned from the Turks, joined to the *finesse* and politic statecraft of the Greek court, then, it is true, in its decadence, but which, despoiled by military power, was the centre of every political coalition of Eastern Europe. Such a character could not fail of leadership in the complications which at that time puzzled the wisest and most experienced statesmen.

The Ottoman power was steadily moving to its zenith. Orchan, the predecessor of Amurath the First, in a reign of thirty-three years had not only conquered, but had almost completed the work of making a homogeneous country of the fairest provinces of Western Asia. Gaining a foothold on the European continent, he established his growing power by a marriage with the emperor's daughter and an alliance with the Greeks. The first essay of his successor had been to extend the conquests of Orchan in Europe.

Ever after the capture of Adrianople the Greek emperor had cringed to the sultan; but treaties and alliances were only the flimsy coverings of hate and fear. The Greek court was the hidden focus of every intrigue that had for its object the humiliation or downfall of the Turks.

Through the efforts of Milosch-Kabilovitsch, a close and

secret alliance had been formed by his brothers-in-law, Prince Saoudji and the Prince of Caramania, with Andronicus, son of the Emperor Palæologous. The Prince of Caramania took the initiative, surprised and defeated Ali Pasha, and then threatened Brusa, thus drawing Amurath with the larger portion of his army to Asia. Prince Saoudji, who had been left in command at Adrianople, immediately united his forces with the young Greek nobility and their followers under Andronicus, and in open revolt established their camp near Constantinople.

Amurath hurried back across the Straits, leaving Prince Bajazet to hold the Caramanians in check. He summoned the Greek emperor to his presence to answer for the conduct of Andronicus. Palæologous denied all participation in the rebellion; and to allay the suspicion of Amurath, agreed to join in the attack upon their sons.

The return of Amurath disconcerted the plans of the princes, rendering the diversion of the Prince of Caramania useless, and forestalling the arrival of Milosch-Kabilovitsch with their Servian and Polish allies. They retreated to the town of Didymotichi, where they were besieged into surrender. Prince Saoudji was beheaded in his father's presence. The adherents of the princes were put to the sword, and the Princess Saoudji saved herself and her young children by a rapid flight into Bosnia.

Notwithstanding these disasters, the resolution of Milosch Kabilovitsch never faltered. He had been met on his return from Poland with the news of the utter defeat of the princes, the execution of Prince Saoudji, and the condition of his fugitive sister.

At the head of the Poles and Hungarians he hastened to Bosnia to her relief. There, joined by the Servian and Bulgarian force already in the field, he made a sudden and impetuous attack upon the advancing Ottomans, whom he completely routed and destroyed.

Unfortunately for the coalition, Milosch was severely wounded in the engagement. He was carried to the Castle of Kabilovitsch, which he had retaken from the Turks and which was now the asylum of the widow of Prince Saoudji and her children. During a previous visit to Poland he had taken with him his mother and younger sister, who had until then resided at the court of their kinsman the King of Servia. By this sister's marriage with the Lechzinczski voyvode, the acknowledged head of the family, he had strengthened his cause with the Poles, but his enforced absence from the allied army at this time lost them the fruits of the victory he had gained. Jealousies and dissensions, the vacillations and delays which usually attend a confederacy composed of rival powers, kept the forces of the allies inactive at the very moment when vigorous action was most needed.

The Turks under Ali Pasha, who burned with a desire to wipe out the record of his late defeat in Asia, marched northward in heavy force across that mountain-chain of the Balkan which by the recent treaty of Berlin has been assigned to them as their natural barrier against invasion. Schumla surrendered; Tirnova and Pravadi were stormed and captured; Bulgaria was completely overrun; the king surrendered at discretion, and the kingdom was annexed to the Ottoman Empire, which thus advanced its northern frontier to the Danube.

The Servians, alarmed at the utter destruction of their confederate, now earnestly sought to collect the remaining forces of the anti-Turkish league, and instantly prepared for a desperate resistance. Servia, Bosnia, Poland, all of Sclavonic blood, except Russsia (which at that time was held in wretched slavery by the Mongols), united in this conflict of races. Besides these Sclavonic nations, the Skijeetars of Albania, the semi-Roman people of Wallachia, and the Magyars of Hungary, — who, like their kinsmen, the Ottoman Turks, had won by force a settlement in Europe, but, unlike the Turks, adopted the creed and civilization of Christendom, — now joined in one great effort against the invading Moslem. No further aid was obtainable. The ruling kingdoms of Western Europe heard with indifference of the perils to which Eastern Europe was exposed by the encroachments of this new Mahometan power. The weak Richard the Second ruled in England. The almost imbecile Charles the Sixth was king of France. The German Empire, under the worthless Wenceslaus, was in a wretched condition. War was raging between the Robber Knights and the burghers of the free cities from the Rhine to the Danube. The schism in the papacy divided the Catholic power, and the two popes — one at Avignon and one at Rome — hurled anathemas at each other and at the heretic Greeks. The old crusading spirit had died out, and the rising of the Crescent in the eastern horizon of Europe only served to light the path of the turbulent and powerful nobles who contended for supremacy in the West.

There are times in the history of nations when one man is of more worth than an army. The great need of the allies was a leader. They outnumbered the Turks nearly two to one. Unhappily, they also outnumbered them in commanders. Amurath had taken the field in person. Under him was marshalled a well-disciplined and thoroughly trained soldiery, led by the most famous officers of the time: Ali Pasha, Prince Bajazet — surnamed "Yilderim" or the "Lightning" for the terrible rapidity of his charge, — Timourtash, Yoldan Bey and Prince Yacoub. Either of these leaders was the superior, in military chieftainship and strategetical skill, of the princes of the confederation; but, able as they were, they were only the lieutenants of a general who had proved himself matchless in the hardest fought fields of Asia and Europe. Amurath was there in person to hold the van with his Janissaries; and when on the 27th of August, 1389, the sun arose over the plains of Kassova, it was the sun of victory to the Turkish sultan. The night before, the conference of the confederate princes had broken up in stormy disputes. Ill-digested plans had been discussed and thrown aside. The hour had struck, but the *man* was wanting.

Milosch Kabilovitsch, the soul of the coalition, barely recovered from his wound, had risen from his bed at the earnest entreaty of the King of Servia; but with all the haste he could make in his enfeebled state, he was still a day's journey away. Courier after courier met him with entreaty, that grew to prayer. The Poles and Hungarians refused to go into action until he should arrive, and obstinately stayed with the rear-guard. The Servians hesitated until their sovereign, King Lazarus, shamed them into following his banner.

There were quarrels for place and command that threw the troops into confusion until the fierce charge of Prince Bajazet forced them to make common cause against the Turks. Vuk Brankowich at the head of the Servian and Albanian force on the right wing, fought desperately until the Bosnians on the left gave way, and Prince Bajazet was at liberty to lead his command, flushed with success, against the already hard-pressed Christian right. At the same instant, the Janissaries under Amurath advanced against the centre, which was held by King Lazarus, following a charge of the Akindji and Azabs, and the field was virtually won by the Turks.

Charged furiously in every quarter, obliged to fight in confusion and disorder, their own strength and that of their horses exhausted, Vuk Brankowich and his command died gloriously, around their standards.

At this crisis of disaster, the Poles and Hungarians, moved by some new and sudden impulse, advanced with a wild cry, and rode down the Turkish irregulars like reeds; and then, with levelled spears, they charged the advanced division of the Janissaries. They broke through the ranks of that famous corps, and sent the Spahis flying, like leaves in the wind.

But the day was lost before this glorious charge was made.

The Janissaries rallied and re-formed in the rear of the Polish and Hungarian squadron, cutting off all chance of retreat; whilst in front a steady forest of hostile spears began to extend and wheel their inclosing lines around the doomed band. At this moment their ranks opened, and a man rode toward the standard of the sultan, throwing away his spear, making no effort to do aught but parry attack. Supposing him a deserter, he was dismounted and brought into the presence of Amurath. Pretending he had important secrets to reveal, he was admitted to approach the sultan, whom he stabbed with a sudden and mortal stroke of his dagger. Quickly turning on the guard, Milosch Kabilovitsch — for it was he — although still suffering from his wounds, thrice cleared himself from the press of vengeful foes and fought his way to his horse, as the Poles once again broke through the Janissaries and surrounded him. Whether it was then, or afterwards, he received his death-blow, was never known; for one by one man and horse went down, until the ground where the greatest of the voyvodes perished was piled with the dying and dead.

It is interesting to a student of psychology to trace family characteristics through the changes of centuries, as they are intensified or modified by new infusions and the culture that results from grafting.

There are no more well-defined or salient figures in history than are to be found in different groups of the Sclavic race; and in no group of that race are more marked types than in this of the Lechzinczski.

In all families there are certain individuals who seem to gather into their own personality the very essence of race, thus becoming its interpreters and representatives. The history of the Lechzinczski-Kabilovitsch furnishes the key to the understanding of character, as well as to that of the alliances of the family in the Orient. Inflexible will and unyielding adhesion to a faith that grew dearer from persecution, joined to a high and noble regard for the untarnished honor of his house, placed the name of the young Stanislaus Lechzinczski-Kabilovitsch on the first and most glorious page of the family archives. Milosch was a variety of the same type; but the mixed Turkish and Greek training had its effect upon the impressionable Sclav. His courage was aggressive as well as resolute. Intellectually he was the giant of his race. The central and governing figure in every political and military coalition of Eastern Europe and Western Asia, he despotically ruled the councils of the Confederation until the end of his short but brilliant career upon the field of Kossova.

The three sisters of Stanislaus and Milosch were no less remarkable. Distinguished for their wonderful beauty, known in every court of Europe and Western Asia as the "three lilies of Kabilovitsch," they impressed themselves upon their time and were efficient allies of Milosch. Imperious, ambitious, loyal always to the traditions of their house, clinging together through all changes of fortune, self-poised at the summit of success, unfaltering in purpose, unshaken in resolution in the midst of disaster, they seemed to make good the claims of the Sclavi to descent from the Amazons. Entering princely houses, they ruled the alliances of those houses, and to their influence can be traced points of departure in polity which in after years marked the beginning of new dynasties.

The Princess Nifisay, the eldest, had always great influence with her adopted father, Amurath. Even after the battle of Iconium, she succeeded in disarming his rage against her husband, and won honorable terms for the revolted Caramanians. Her only son married his cousin, the daughter of the Polish Lechzinczski.

The Princess Saoudji was the centre and moving spirit of the revolt of Adrianople. After her escape to Bosnia she was queen absolute in the camp of the allies. Left by Milosch chatelaine of the Castle of Kabilovitsch, she defended it with a small force of Poles and Albanians against a three days' assault of the vanguard of the Turks, when the arrival of Bajazet himself, with overwhelming numbers, forced its surrender; but even then she made terms for the safety of the garrison. Distrusting her brother-in-law, Prince Bajazet, who had signalized his accession to the throne by the murder of Prince Yacoub, the next in succession, she confided her only son, Prince Osman, to the care of a faithful Albanian. He, finding escape into Poland or Hungary impossible, adopted the bold and, as it proved, successful expedient of crossing into Asia, where he found shelter and protection for the young prince at the court of the Emir of Nedjid. The Princess Saoudji, with her daughter, was released by Prince Bajazet and permitted to go to her sister in Poland, where she hoped to find her son arrived. When the young Prince of Caramania came for his promised bride, the daughter of Elizabeth, the youngest of the "lilies," she learned from him of the safe arrival of her son in Derayeh, the capital of Nedjid. She prepared to rejoin him, but an alliance proposed for her daughter with Gedymin, Grand Duke of Lithuania, who afterwards wrested the Ukraine from Russia, detained her until its completion. This delay and another at the court of Caramania, prevented her arrival in Nedjid until after her son's accession to the throne, he having been adopted by the late emir, whose daughter he had married. Later in history, at the time of the Mahometan reformation, we find the Emir Saoud, son of Osman, military leader of the Wahabees.

The marriage of Elizabeth, the youngest of the sisters of Milosch, with the Lechzinczski voyvode, was the epoch from which dated the rapid advancement to power of the family in Poland. Her grandson, the first palatine, — who ranks third in the great names of the Leszinkskys, — was the conqueror of the Teutonic knights, who until then had been the terror of the Poles as well as of the free cities of the Rhine. The Zolkiewskis, the Sobieskis, the Czartoryskis, proudly trace their descent from the youngest and fairest of the "lilies of Kabilovitsch"; and there are characteristics, personal and mental, in these families which show a marked resemblance of race. The great Zriny, the defender of Szigeth, — not unworthily named the Leonidas of Hungary, — was a grandson of Elizabeth.

With the name of John Sobieski in the family annals is joined that of Palatine Raphael Leszczynski (the change of patronymic came with the palatinate), the fourth star of the first magnitude in our record. Educated at the court of Louis the Fourteenth of France, skilled in all martial and knightly accomplishments, the personal friend and companion in his wanderings from court to court of King Charles the Second of England, the entire resources of his estate in Poland were used in his friend's service, and his life freely adventured in frequent and hazardous journeys to England and Scotland, whenever the need of the king required there a devoted and trusty friend. After the Restoration, finding the debts owing him *had escaped the king's memory*, and scorning to recall his services, the palatine visited his relatives in Hungary. True to the hereditary enmity of his house, he sought service with Monticuculi, general of the Austrian and Hungarian army, in the war against the Sultan Mahomet the Fourth.

At the battle of St. Gothard, the palatine, at the head of the imperial cavalry, repeatedly charged the ranks of the Janissaries. Repulsed time after time, with thinned ranks, the Christian cavalry wavered, when Leszczynski passed the word along the line that they "must break the Turks or perish." Riding in front of his men bareheaded, the palatine halted, and, holding his hand toward heaven, made the prayer so famous in history, "*O mighty Generalissimo who art on high! if thou wilt not this day help thy children, the Christians, at least do not help these dogs, the Turks; and thou shalt soon see something that will please thee.*" Either the prayer was heard or else the spirit of the mighty palatine had found an answering chord in the hearts of his men; for in this charge the famous infantry was not only broken, but literally trampled to death beneath the hoofs of his cohorts.

In defence of Candia against the Turks some years later, the palatine was again a volunteer. After the fall of Candia he came back to Poland in time to aid Sobieski and some few of the great nobles to break the humiliating treaty made with the Turks by the King of Poland. At Lemberg he was the right arm of Sobieski, who there gained the most brilliant victory of the age. At the liberation of Vienna the palatine again led the charge against the Janissaries, but he fell, mortally wounded, in the moment of victory. He was succeeded in the palatinate by his son Stanislaus, afterwards King of Poland.

Again we have a Leszczynski so prominent in history that we have only to name him the fifth in our constellation. The character of King Stanislaus, his uprightness, courage, equanimity, and patience, prove the effect of civilization, the culture of time, and the modification of grafts, upon the untamed fiery spirit of his ancestor, the great voyvode.

"Stanislaus Leszczynski," said one of his contemporaries, "has a happy facility of manners that makes him win his way to all hearts. Courageous and at the same time mild in disposition, he is also prepossessing in appearance." At the time of the disputes in the Polish Succession, after the death of Sobieski, Charles the Twelfth of Sweden declared he had "never seen a man so fit to conciliate all parties." The changes of fortune which met King Stanislaus; his abdication to give peace to Poland; his recall to the kingdom; the marriage of his daughter Marie to Louis the Fifteenth of France; the treachery which led to the surrender of Dantzig, the only city of Poland that could stand a siege; the second abdication of royalty; the peerless integrity which decided his rival to trust to the care of the ex-king his children, whom the fortunes of war had left homeless; the words with which the warm-hearted and forgiving philosopher received them, — " Heaven no doubt drove me from my country that I might be able to afford you an asylum in your misfortune,"— all the events of his life, and its numberless romantic incidents, brighten and adorn the page of the earlier part of the eighteenth century. With only one episode we have to do. During a visit of King Stanislaus to the Pasha of Moldavia, at the time of his escape after the surrender of Dantzig, pleased with the charming face and manner of a boy offered for sale in the market-place, he bought the child and brought him to Lorraine, and afterwards took him to Paris. It then transpired that the boy was the son of the Emir of Nedjid, consequently a descendant of Princess Saoudji. The family of the emir had been captured at their summer home in the mountains.

The two daughters, twins, had been destined for the sultan's harem at Constantinople, but were lost by their captors, the ship being taken by an Algerine pirate. The boy had been sold to a slave-merchant from Moldavia, and happily rescued by King Stanislaus, who was now about to entrust him to the French envoy to Arabia to be restored to his father, when the child asked that he might first visit a cousin of his father, a baron of Brittany, himself a descendant of the Moors of Grenada.

King Stanislaus accompanied the boy to Brittany, where, to their joy, they found the twin-sisters, whose ransom had been effected by the son of this relative who was in the port of Tripoli at the time of the pirate's return. He had brought the girls to Brittany, the Ottoman wars in the East having made their return to Arabia for the time impossible.

The beauty and intelligence of one of the sisters captivated the still romantic and impressionable old monarch; his kindness to her brother commanded her gratitude, and a private marriage was quickly arranged.

The marriage of the Catholic king to his Mahometan bride, who refused to give up her faith, was celebrated by a Huguenot preacher; consequently it was not legal in that country or time. But the king chivalrously kept his plighted faith, and when, the following year, his young wife died in Paris in child-bed, he openly acknowledged the marriage and his son.

The ex-king died in Paris in 1766. The young Count de Deux Ponts, then fifteen years of age, bore his barren title only by courtesy of the royal family of France.

Poland had now another sovereign, and the Duchies of Bar and Lorraine, by the treaty signed at Vienna in 1735, were, upon the death of King Stanislaus, to devolve to the crown of France. In addition, the council declared the French king heir of the Duchy of Deux Ponts. The sale of some valuable jewels sent to his mother by the Emir of Nedjid, immediately after her marriage, sufficed for the boy's education and keep.

The hauteur and coldness of his royal relatives in France had disgusted young Stanislaus with kings and courtiers, and when, in 1777, his comrade and friend, the young Marquis de la Fayette, proposed to him to form one of his company of volunteers to America, the offer was instantly accepted.

So the sixth star of the Leszinksky rose in the Western horizon, brightening steadily from the moment the young Count de Deux Ponts landed at Georgetown, — his sole inheritance his father's sword and his mother's wedding-ring with the simple inscription, "*Stanislaus à Ruchiel.*"

The 25th of April, 1777, the Marquis de la Fayette, the Barons Kosciusko, Pulaski, and de Kalb, the Count de Deux Ponts and six French gentlemen, having landed the day before at Georgetown, entered the city of Charleston, South Carolina. They were received in the most hospitable manner by the Whigs. In fact, their arrival could not have been better timed had they especially desired to secure an enthusiastic and cordial welcome. It was the most distressing period in the history of the colonial struggle. The slender resources of the revolutionists were beginning to give way. There had been a rapid inflation in the prices of the actual necessaries of life, whilst luxuries were already far beyond the means of the less wealthy planters of the South, and the small farmers of the North.

The first successes of the Continentals had led to overconfidence; the reaction caused undue depression. Arnold had retreated from Canada, which was now in the unmolested possession of the British troops. Washington had given up Long Island, after the capture of two of his generals and a heavy proportion of his small force. The reverses in the field had such an effect upon the undisciplined troops that notwithstanding the consistent force of character of the commander-in-chief, he had half-despairingly exclaimed, "Are these the men I am to defend America with?" The patient endurance and resolute courage of "the gentleman from Virginia" were sorely tried by the insubordination of the men and the incompetence of the commissariat.

The Southern colonies had not yet felt the full force of the war; but the fierce partisanship of the Tories taught them what they might expect from domestic foes if once supported by British regulars. The leading clansmen among the Scotch Highlanders settled in North and South Carolina were now loyal supporters of the government to which they had surrendered upon the field of Culloden. That tried adherent of the Stuarts, Donald Macdonald of Keppoch, was now in

Carolina, as faithful to the house of Hanover as he had been in Scotland to the Young Pretender. Even McLeod, forgetting the butcheries of the Duke of Cumberland, accepted a command in the Household Troops. These Highland gentlemen were monarchists *purs et simples;* single-thoughted and devout in their beliefs, they were still Royalists, though the " Young Chevalier " had died in exile, and the crown was the inheritance of the family that had supplanted him.

Until 1777 the contest in the Carolinas had been altogether one of opinion. The two leading clansmen, Macdonald and McLeod, had been in constant communication with the Royalists of the North and the generals of the regular army; but their absence from home had not as yet been signalized by any interruption of neighborly intercourse between the two factions. The most noted Whig gentlemen were with the Continentals in Virginia, and the Carolinians at home had come to regard the war more as an occasion for the expression of sympathy, than as an actuality in which they had personal interest. Still *sympathy* was intense, and *partisanship* was growing daily more bitter, more separating in its social effect.

In this state of affairs the landing of these foreign allies, though few in number and officially unauthorized by the French Government, was more significant than would first appear at this distant date. It was to the downcast Whigs the harbinger of a new epoch, the earnest of future help. The immediate effect was electric: the patriots grew bolder in act as well as expression. Men were ashamed not to be in arms for a cause they had declared to be just and righteous, when foreigners had come to offer help.

The progress of these gentlemen through the country was an ovation. They lit the torches of war that Sumpter and Marion kept alive. It was not alone the tried and untried swords of Lafayette and his friends that were offered to the Continental cause that summer in Philadelphia, but the faith and hope of the South, that brightened at their approach, and that burned steadily through all subsequent trial and disaster.

But we have only to do with what befell the sixth hero in our line. Stanislaus Leszinksky, Count de Deux Ponts, served as a volunteer *aide* with Washington until after the battle of Brandywine, when, in token of its appreciation of his brilliant service and gallant behavior, Congress offered him the command of a regiment. This he declined, preferring to serve on the staff of Pulaski, the son of his father's most devoted adherent in Poland and his own personal friend.

Five months afterward, when Pulaski resigned his independent command to join Washington at Valley Forge, he was accompanied by Major Leszinksky. Again, when the famous Pulaski Legion was formed, Leszinksky was one of its officers.

From March of 1779 until the following autumn the Legion was in constant, active service in the Carolinas; and there grew an enthusiastic and lifelong friendship between the young officer and the great partisan generals, Sumpter, Marion, and Pickens. At the siege of Savannah, where Pulaski was killed, Major Leszinksky lost an arm. Before he was entirely recovered, he started North to join Von Steuben's division in Virginia. In North Carolina he was captured by Fanning, the brutal Tory leader, and condemned to be hung, in retaliation for the recent execution of a noted Tory horse-thief. The fortunate arrival in Fanning's camp of General Macdonald saved Leszinksky.

Macdonald's good offices did not stop there. Finding the young Pole suffering from his inflamed wound and distrusting Fanning's good faith, he insisted on Major Leszinksky's being paroled, and offered him the hospitality of his home in Warrington, where his family then were, until he should be perfectly recovered. The offer was thankfully accepted.

The Macdonald afterwards may have thought this soldierly kindness ill repaid. For when Marion at length arranged Leszinksky's exchange for a tardy British gallant he had picked up in the swamp, Major Leszinksky's leave-taking was so sudden that he did not say adieu to his host, although he carried away with him the Macdonald's young cousin, the fair Janet, — daughter of "Stern Angus of the Isles," — who was on a visit to her cousins.

Janet Macdonald was married to her Polish Lochinvar in Richmond. But from that instant her name was a forbidden word in her father's house. The unforgiving old Highlander carried his wrath so far that he quarrelled with General Macdonald, who had introduced "sic a godless papisher to the feckless fule wha had rin wi' him to the deil."

At the end of the war "Macdonald of the Isles" went back to Scotland, where he had fallen heir to a large landed estate, and Janet Leszinksky was never again counted even as "a far-away Macdonald." But her fair face and gentle manners had won her favor among her husband's friends and comrades. During her husband's absence with his command, she was always a welcome guest at Monticello. The young pair were favorites of Mr. Jefferson and his daughter.

The republicanism of the great Democrat so infected the

Polish descendant of kings that after the surrender of Yorktown we hear no more of the title of the Count de Deux Ponts; but General Leszinksky, the retired Continental officer, ended his life in Charlottesville, where he had been ever since the close of the war, Professor of Modern Languages in the University of Virginia.

Her father's curse had clung to poor Janet. Three sons had been still-born; for the life of the fourth she paid her own. At her request the son she left bore the name of her brother Donald. On the death of General Leszinksky, a few years later, Mr. Jefferson wrote to "Macdonald of the Isles" in his grandson's behalf. The letter was never answered, and Mr. Jefferson was appointed the boy's guardian.

High-tempered and quarrelsome, come of a race of soldiers, Donald Leszinksky was entered in the army at sixteen years of age. He fought under Jackson in the War of 1812; was dismissed the service for insubordination in 1814, and re-instated at the earnest entreaty of his father's old comrades. He married the only daughter of Judge Mason of Albemarle, in 1817, and was killed in a duel in 1818, two months before the birth of his son Stanislaus.

Messrs. Roberts Brothers' Publications.

THE NO NAME (SECOND) SERIES.

SIGNOR MONALDINI'S NIECE.

Extracts from some Opinions by well-known Authors.

"We have read 'Signor Monaldini's Niece' with intensest interest and delight. The style is finished and elegant, the atmosphere of the book is enchanting. We seem to have lived in Italy while we were reading it. The author has delineated with a hand as steady as it is powerful and skilful some phases of human life and experience that authors rarely dare attempt, and with marvellous success. We think this volume by far the finest of the No Name Series."

"It is a delicious story. I feel as if I had been to Italy and knew all the people. . . . Miss Conroy is a strong character, and her tragedy is a fine background for the brightness of the other and higher natures. It is all so dramatic and full of color it goes on like a lovely play and leaves one out of breath when the curtain falls."

"I have re-read it with great interest, and think as highly of it as ever. . . . The characterization in it is capital, and the talk wonderfully well done from first to last."

"The new No Name is enchanting. It transcends the ordinary novel just as much as a true poem by a true poet transcends the thousand and one imitations. . . . It is the episode, however, of Miss Conroy and Mrs. Brandon that is really of most importance in this book. . . . I hope every woman who reads this will be tempted to read the book, and that she will in her turn bring it to the reading of other women, especially if she can find any Mrs. Brandon in her circle."

In one volume, 16mo, bound in green cloth, black and gilt lettered. Price $1.00.

Our publications are to be had of all Booksellers. When not to be found, send directly to

ROBERTS BROTHERS, Boston.

Messrs. Roberts Brothers' Publications.

THE "NO NAME" (SECOND) SERIES.

HIS MAJESTY, MYSELF.

"The last 'No Name' novel cannot long remain anonymous. 'His Majesty, Myself' is so remarkable a piece of work that its author must be known. The title-page is concise and brilliant, the opening chapters are concise and brilliant; powerfully drawn characters come and go in the story; brilliancy gives place to pathos, pathos deepens into tragedy, tragedy is relieved by wit, wit softened by tenderness. Scenes of the homeliest simplicity alternate with those of the most intense emotion and terrible anguish. Characters are dissected, are analyzed with consummate skill; events told with masterly dramatic power; shams are riddled with arrows of scorn; the hidden things in human hearts are set in the light, and readers are forced to judge themselves in this powerful revelation of human nature." — *Boston Daily Advertiser.*

"The last novel of the 'No Name Series' has made a decided sensation. It gives the most graphic and scathing description of the result of sensational preaching — of the preaching of the gospel of Christ with Christ left out. It is a thoroughly manly and healthy book to read. Joseph Cook, at a late Boston Conference, spoke of it thus: 'I have just read "His Majesty, Myself." It is a powerful and manly book from beginning to end. It is full of bright, keen Orthodoxy.' This is high praise, but none too high. The author, whoever he be, is an Orthodox evangelical Christian, who has iron in his blood and brain, and who writes with a gold pen, diamond-tipt. Old Princetonians will find among its characters some acquaintances and friends, professors and students." — *The Presbyterian.*

"This is one of the strongest novels the present year has produced. The course of a sensational clergyman who gives his flock truth garnered from the newspapers instead of from the Bible, and proclaims himself far more than his Lord, is thinkingly depicted. The whole book is one of the keenest descriptions of the terrible nature of selfishness we have ever read, and if it is not marked instantly as one of the most powerful of the most remarkable series to which it belongs, we shall be greatly surprised." — *Christian Intelligencer.*

"No one will take exception to the statement that 'His Majesty, Myself,' the latest 'No Name' novel, is a powerful book. It is a work which is as marked in vigor as it is in originality. No one but a man of genius could have written it. No person can read it without receiving a marked impression. It is one of those stories which *must* remain in the memory, and this long after tales which have more of unity and are much more." — *Saturday Evening Gazette.*

"As an exhibit of sound religious thinking and pure religious feeling, as far removed from 'loose notions' and weak sentiment on the one side as from dead formalism and cold cant on the other, it has few equals. He has written a Fifth Gospel, and we reckon him a true evangelist," says a retired clergyman.

In one volume, 16mo. Green cloth. Price $1.00.

Our publications are to be had of all Booksellers. When not to be found, send directly to the Publishers,

ROBERTS BROTHERS, Boston.